# Interservice Rivalry

## and

## Airpower in the Vietnam War

Dr. Ian Horwood

D0556251

Combat Studies Institute Press
Fort Leavenworth, Kansas

Library of Congress Cataloging-in-Publication Data

Horwood, Ian, 1957-
 Interservice rivalry and airpower in the Vietnam War / Ian Horwood.
  p. cm.
 1. Vietnam War, 1961-1975--Aerial operations, American. 2. Interservice
rivalry (Armed Forces)--United States. I. Title.

 DS558.8.H67 2006
 959.704'348--dc22

                                    2006031966

Cover design by Michael G. Brooks.


CSI Press publications cover a variety of military history topics. The
views expressed in this CSI Press publication are those of the author and
not necessarily those of the Department of the Army, or the Department
of Defense.

A full list of CSI Press publications, many of them available for down-
loading, can be found at http://www.cgsc.army.mil/carl/resources/csi/csi.
asp.

For sale by the Superintendent of Documents, U.S. Government Printing Office
Internet: bookstore.gpo.gov  Phone: toll free (866) 512-1800;  DC area (202) 512-1800
Fax: (202) 512-2250 Mail: Stop IDCC, Washington, DC 20402-0001

ISBN 0-16-077276-1

# Foreword

The Combat Studies Institute is pleased to publish this special study, Interservice Rivalry and Airpower in the Vietnam War, by Dr. Ian Horwood. Dr. Horwood, a British historian, has explored the rivalry between the armed services of the United States relating to the employment of tactical airpower during the Vietnam War. Not being an American, he is able to put a fresh perspective on this complex issue.

This study focuses on tactical airpower in South Vietnam between 1961 and 1968. Dr. Horwood avoids a lengthy discussion of the air war over North Vietnam, focusing instead on the combat operations in the South. Interservice Rivalry and Airpower in the Vietnam War examines a number of issues which are relevant to the use of airpower in irregular warfare. Among them are command and control of airpower, the use of airpower at the tactical and the operational-strategic level of war, the role of helicopters, and different service understandings of the proper role of airpower in a counterinsurgency.

The Army is, of course, keenly interested in the air-ground integration as it performs its role in achieving military success on the ground. Always contentious since its invention a century ago, the proper role for airpower in war is even more complex in the irregular wars which the US has faced since the end of the Cold War, and which it faces today in the Long War. We at CSI believe this study will provide useful insights for military professionals. CSI- The Past is Prologue!

Timothy R. Reese
Colonel, Armor
Director, Combat Studies Institute

# About the Author

Dr Ian Horwood was born in Luton in Bedfordshire, England. He holds a BA in politics and modern history from the University of Manchester, an MA in history from the University of Missouri-Columbia; and a PhD in history from the University of Leeds. He has taught history and American studies at York St John University since 1994 where he is Senior Lecturer and Head of the Contemporary History Program. He lives in York with his wife and two children.

# Contents

Foreword .......................................................................... iii

About the Author ................................................................ v

Introduction ...................................................................... 1

Chapter 1. The Doctrinal Background .................................... 4

Chapter 2. Competing Visions of Airmobility:
The Howze and Disosway Reports of 1962 ............................ 37

Chapter 3. Command and Control ........................................ 63

Chapter 4. Tactical Airlift in Vietnam .................................. 101

Chapter 5. Close Air Support in Vietnam .............................. 119

Chapter 6. Khe Sanh: Interservice Rivalry or

Interservice Cooperation? .................................................. 139

Conclusion ...................................................................... 175

Bibliography .................................................................... 191

# INTRODUCTION

*There was undoubtedly enthusiasm among some professionals as well as the Administration and the public about what airpower might accomplish. Americans like to think in terms of an immaculate war in the wild blue yonder and some Air Force publicists have encouraged this Madison Avenue fantasy. The Air Force is a young service led by enthusiasts who had to fight hard to establish its validity against military traditionalists and from time to time it has oversold its capabilities.* *

The primary objectives of this study are to establish the nature and levels of rivalry and dispute between the United States armed services over matters relating to the military application of airpower during the Vietnam period, and to assess the extent to which such rivalry may have distorted US operational policy in Southeast Asia. It is probably a truism to suggest that interservice rivalry has always been endemic among military establishments in the modern age, yet there are few monographs that deal specifically with the subject. Presumably, interservice rivalry is so commonplace that it excites little comment among military historians and analysts, except in passing. However, if interservice rivalry is so typical of military organisms then it constitutes one of their defining characteristics and is worthy of study for this reason alone. Furthermore, it is also worthy of study by virtue of the fact that it may be an influential factor in the making of military decisions by which wars are fought, won and lost. Clearly, this suggests that interservice rivalry may be significant from both a purely historical point of view and also in terms of its contribution to the military capabilities and effectiveness of different military establishments.

The historical development of airpower suggests that interservice rivalry is especially prevalent in this particular area of military activity. From the very beginnings of military aviation, armies and navies have argued as to how the new assets should be used, how they should be developed and which service should control them. This was certainly the case in the United States.

The problem has been compounded, rather than resolved, by the development of independent air forces.

*Hanson W. Baldwin, Introduction to Jack Broughton, *Thud Ridge* (New York, 1985) xii-xiii.

These entities were founded on the basis of the strategic air warfare philosophy originally put forward by the classical airpower theorists like the Italian Giulio Douhet, the British Hugh Trenchard or the American Billy Mitchell, often at the expense of the more tactical supporting roles preferred by the surface forces. Here, again, the United States is a good example with the emergence of an independent US Air Force dominated by advocates of strategic warfare from an Army whose ground forces demanded tactical air support as the primary responsibility of the new air arm.

In the US case, interservice rivalry over issues connected with the military application of airpower may be especially acute because of the enormous resources at stake in the competition between the armed forces over budgets and responsibilities, and the existence of the US Marine Corps as virtually a fourth armed service complete with its own organic "air force" including state-of-the-art helicopters and fixed-wing aircraft.

Interservice rivalry seems to be a constant fact of military life in peace time. Indeed, armed services may sometimes even measure their relative success in terms of the accumulation of resources and authority at the expense of their sister services, regardless of the extent to which this detracts from their peace time preparations for the pursuit of national objectives in time of war. The achievement of those objectives becomes more significant—though not necessarily paramount—in wartime.

The differing service requirements in times of peace and war may perhaps be illustrated by the issue of the close air support of US ground forces in both the Second World War and the Korean War. In both cases, the services were obliged to revisit close air support arrangements established in peace time because they were so clearly failing the test of combat. At the end of both conflicts, however, detailed arrangements for the close air support of ground forces that had seemed so absolutely vital in wartime were abandoned under the new conditions of the peace.

The issue of close air support, along with several other long-standing interservice airpower disputes concerning theater-level command arrangements and tactical airlift re-emerged in the Vietnam War. Here, they were further complicated by the US Army's employment of helicopters, en masse for the first time, as the primary method of maneuver, supplanting foot or road vehicle mobility for large combined arms formations up to divisional size: a technique known as "airmobility." The development of this concept, along with its concomitant requirement for a vastly increased US Army aviation establishment, including armed, fixed- and rotary-wing aircraft was bound to call into question the exact nature of the relationship between the US Army and the US Air Force.

This study concentrates on tactical airpower in South Vietnam and deals with the air war over North Vietnam only insofar as it influenced interservice issues in the South. In order to fully understand the interservice airpower issues that emerged during the Vietnam War, it is first necessary to look back at the pre-Vietnam doctrinal background that preceded them. In regard to the Vietnam War itself, the study's starting point is the arrival of the first US combat aircraft in South Vietnam in 1961, and concludes with the pivotal year of 1968. The latter date is of necessity somewhat fluid, but it forms a rough stopping point because rivalry over airpower issues between the US armed forces seems to have been in decline after this date, or at least it seems to have been subject to attenuation by compromise agreements which were in force until the end of United States involvement in Southeast Asia. Expressions of these compromises are to be found in post-1968 documents, but these reflect pre-1968 experience.

# CHAPTER 1

## THE DOCTRINAL BACKGROUND

**Doctrine**: The fundamental principles by which the military forces or elements thereof guide their actions in support of national objectives.[1]

During their participation in the war in South Vietnam, the armed forces of the United States were afflicted by serious interservice disputes over airpower issues. Broadly, the main areas of disagreement concerned the command and control of airpower assets, close air support of ground forces and the application of the new concept of air mobility to military operations. As the origins of these disputes predated the Vietnam War, it is necessary to understand something of their historical development prior to United States involvement in Southeast Asia before one can fully appreciate them in their Vietnam context.

The American military establishment that went to war in Vietnam still bore the indelible imprint of the Second World War. The last great global conflict constituted a watershed in the development of United States military doctrine. Those systems and techniques developed for the command and utilization of the nation's armed forces during the Second World War —and which had brought it such stunning victories—set the standard by which the United States expected to wage war in the foreseeable future.

### COMMAND AND CONTROL

Drawing on the successful experience of the Second World War, the administration of President Harry Truman attempted to formalize what it perceived to be the war's lessons for military command and control. The resulting 1947 National Security Act did not, however, resolve some outstanding command and control issues that had manifested themselves during the war, and it created some new ones, which became apparent only in the crucible of Korea. Still unresolved, these difficulties remained latent, ready to re-emerge in the 1960s, this time exacerbated by the peculiar circumstances of war in Southeast Asia.

During the Second World War, the first of the great combined operations conducted by the Allied coalition took place in late 1942 with the amphibious landings in French North Africa codenamed Operation TORCH. Traditional methods for coalition warfare called for the employment of separate, co-equal, operational commands for each nation's forces, with attached liaison missions from their opposite numbers. However, it soon became obvious that this would not suffice for an international amphibious operation of the scope and complexity envisaged. Clearly an unprecedented level of international command integration was called for and the arrangements adopted for North Africa were to set the pattern for the Allied theater commands—subsequently designated "supreme headquarters"—throughout the remainder of the war.

Circumstances dictated that the commander in chief of the Allied Expeditionary Force for TORCH must be an American officer. At the Arcadia conference in Washington, in December 1941, Prime Minister Winston Churchill and President Franklin D. Roosevelt had agreed on a policy of prioritizing the defeat of Germany over that of Japan, but it was a Japanese attack in the Pacific that had brought the United States into the war. It was, therefore, vital to focus the American public's attention on the war with Germany as soon as possible. An invasion of French North Africa by predominantly American forces seemed to offer a relatively low-risk way of achieving this objective.

While the French still bore the British considerable ill will for their attacks on French forces earlier in the war at Mers El Kebir and Dakar, the Vichy French authorities in North Africa might be reasonably amenable to an explicitly American landing; perhaps they would even allow it to proceed unopposed? As most of the personnel involved in TORCH would be from the United States Army, it seemed logical that the commander in chief should be an American Army officer, and the Allied leaders' choice was General Dwight D. Eisenhower. This established a pattern in which the Combined Chiefs of Staff allotted theater commands to officers of the numerically preponderant nationality and service. Given the peculiar political circumstances of TORCH, the Combined Chiefs also chose an American as Deputy Commander in Chief of the Allied Expeditionary Force: Major General Mark W. Clark, a practice which was not sustained in subsequent Allied theater command arrangements.

In a relatively uncontroversial decision—since the British provided the bulk of the forces involved—the Allied naval forces committed to TORCH were centralized under the command of British Admiral Sir Andrew Cunningham, who was directly answerable to Eisenhower. Matters were more complicated in the air, however, where both Britain and the United States provided sizable forces. Consequently, control of the air forces committed to TORCH was divided between a United States command under Brigadier General James H. Doolittle and a British command under Air Marshal Sir William Welsh. As neither of these officers was directly responsible to TORCH's commander, Eisenhower retained two air advisers on his own staff —one from each nationality—to assist him. Thus, airpower for the TORCH landings was not centralized under the theater commander's direct control.

The command arrangements for air assets and existing United States Army tactical air support doctrine were soon found wanting in North West

Africa. During the early days of the campaign, the Army Air Force's tactical assets were, according to existing doctrine as established in War Department Field Manual FM 31-35, *Aviation in support of Ground Forces* (1942), parcelled out to individual ground formations which exercised operational command over their attached supporting aircraft.[2] These arrangements resulted in piecemeal defensive operations while the numerically inferior German air force was left free to seize the initiative by concentrating against individual Allied units. The British tactical air forces allocated to TORCH did little better, despite the fact that the Royal Air Force's Western Desert Air Force had built up a sophisticated body of tactical air support doctrine that did emphasize the centralized control of air power. This was to form the basis for a revision of Army Air Force tactical air support doctrine when, after several defeats, the Combined Chiefs centralized the total air strength committed to North Africa under Eisenhower's direct control.

Following the Casablanca Conference in January 1943, the responsibilities of Eisenhower's Headquarters Allied Forces were broadened to those of a "theater" command encompassing all Allied forces operating in North Africa or those that could have a direct influence on the campaign there. Thus, General Bernard Montgomery's British Eighth Army came under Eisenhower's command. The Combined Chiefs also created an integrated Mediterranean Air Command composed of both British and American air assets, under Air Chief Marshal Sir Arthur Tedder, which was directly answerable to Eisenhower's headquarters on matters relating to North Africa.[3] Under the new command arrangements, Mediterranean Air Command had equal status with the ground forces operating in North Africa. This made Eisenhower's Headquarters Allied Forces, effectively, what in modern parlance would be called a "unified" command where all the services had theoretically equal status. This can be contrasted with the concept of a "specified" command in which one service is given exclusive authority for the conduct of a campaign, while the others adopt only subordinate roles. In practice, the service "equality" of Eisenhower's command was attenuated somewhat by the fact that while Tedder was responsible for air power within the command, Eisenhower himself served as his own army component commander, giving the land forces a measure of priority; this was a practice that Eisenhower was to continue as Supreme Commander in Europe.

Mediterranean Air Command included the Northwest African Air Forces under General Carl A. Spaatz that integrated both British and American air assets. Spaatz was theater air component commander both in name, and in fact, in that, despite some opposition from Cunningham, he had responsibility for all air power within North West Africa.[4] Spaatz, in turn, controlled an integrated Northwest African Tactical Air Force, again including both British and American forces, under Air Vice-Marshal Sir Arthur Coningham.

6

Drawing on his previous experience as commander of the Western Desert Air Force, Coningham insisted that in order to realize the potential flexibility of air power, and facilitate its concentration at decisive points, the ultimate authority for the deployment of his air resources must be removed from the ground commanders and placed in the hands of air force officers who would then cooperate with the ground forces subject to the doctrinal precept that the first priority for air power must be air superiority, not close air support. Eisenhower endorsed this as the basis of air power doctrine in North Africa.[5]

These revised arrangements proved successful with Eisenhower declaring that:

> Perhaps the greatest advantage of our new organization was its flexibility. Aircraft of the different combat formations could be fused in a single mission as the need arose and as a result the local commander had for direct support the combined weight of the strategic and tactical forces when he needed it.[6]

One of the factors stimulating the overhaul of command relationships regarding air power in North Africa had been the American defeat at Kasserine Pass in February of 1943. The details of the revised air command system were delivered to a board investigating Kasserine by the Deputy Commander of the Northwest African Tactical Air Force, Brigadier General Laurence Kuter, and, as a consequence, were adopted as official United States service doctrine in War Department *Field Manual 100-20: Command and Employment of Air Power* on 21 July 1943.

The authors of FM 100-20 insisted that a single theater commander should be responsible for both air and ground forces. They declared that air and ground forces were coequal, that tactical airpower must be placed under centralized command and that a tactical air commander must be able to mass his aircraft when decisive targets presented themselves.[7]

With his success in North Africa and his proven diplomatic skills in fostering the smooth cooperation of Allied forces, Eisenhower was the obvious choice for the command of the Supreme Headquarters Allied Expeditionary Force (SHAEF) tasked with the liberation of Western Europe. Given his own role in the North African campaign, Tedder was also a logical choice as Eisenhower's Deputy Supreme Commander. His appointment reflected the importance of British forces and airpower in the coming campaign, which would open with the amphibious assault on the Normandy coast, code named Operation OVERLORD.

Drawing on the experience of North Africa, the Combined Chiefs of Staff established SHAEF as an integrated, unified theater command which included a centralized air component in the shape of the integrated Allied Expeditionary Air Force (AEAF) whose commander, Air Chief Marshal Sir Trafford Leigh-Mallory, would report directly to Eisenhower. The AEAF was, however, only a temporary expedient for the period of the invasion and its subsequent build up. After its disbandment in October 1944, SHAEF's air forces were only centralized on a national basis with the RAF supporting British forces and the USAAF supporting the US Army Ground Forces.[8]

In any case, Leigh-Mallory did not control all the air forces committed to OVERLORD. The invasion's planners hoped to use the Allied strategic air forces—RAF Bomber Command and the USAAF's Eighth Air Force—in the run-up to, and in immediate support of, the invasion itself. However, their commanders were adherents of classical airpower theory. They believed that airpower could win the war independent of a ground campaign and they did not wish to see the strategic air war interrupted by "tactical" operations in Western Europe. Only reluctantly did they accede to the use of their aircraft in support of the Normandy invasion, and they succeeded in keeping them outside the AEAF command structure. It was left to Tedder to liaise between the AEAF and the strategic air forces during the air operations associated with the invasion, a role for which Eisenhower believed him well suited:

> Otherwise a commander is forever fighting with those airmen who, regardless of the ground situation, want to send big bombers on missions that have nothing to do with the critical effort.[9]

The command and control lessons arising from the United States' experience in the Second World War seemed to be that coalition forces should be commanded by an officer of the most heavily represented nationality and service; that such forces, especially when engaged in complex amphibious operations, should be closely integrated; that the importance of naval and air forces in modern warfare dictated a unified command structure for combined operations in which all the services were coequal and that all airpower assets should be centralized under the authority of the theater commander.

The success of arrangements like those in North Africa and Europe, and a quest for greater efficiency, were factors behind the movement for service unification after the Second World War. Such a development found special favor with USAAF officers who, paradoxically, hoped to achieve independent status within a unified military establishment, and while the Army Ground Forces had protested the adoption of coequal status by the USAAF during the war, they raised no special objections to service unification after it. Only Navy officers were opposed to unification on the grounds that they believed it would make the armed forces less, rather than more efficient, but their objections were overruled by President Truman. Consequently, the 1947 National Security Act unified the services under the administration of a single National Military Establishment—later the Department of Defense—led by a civilian secretary. The act established an independent United States Air Force and a unified Joint Chiefs of Staff on which all the services had equal representation.[10]

With the outbreak of the Korean War, the Joint Chiefs of Staff established a unified Far East Command (FECOM) under General Douglas MacArthur who was also commander in chief of the United Nations Command. As a unified theater commander, MacArthur might have been expected to have remained independent from his three-service component commands, but like Eisenhower before him, MacArthur chose to act as his own Army component commander, employing his Far East Command Staff—composed primarily of Army personnel—in the additional role of a theater-level Army headquarters staff.[11]

During the early days of the war, the naval component of FECOM, Naval Forces Far East (NAVFE), was answerable directly to MacArthur for all its operations, including those conducted by its aircraft that flew from the carriers of Task Force-77 (TF-77) off the coast. Clearly, this ran counter to the Air Force's belief in the essential requirement for the centralization of air resources under a single air commander answerable to the theater commander. Furthermore, NAVFE pressed for the allocation of a dedicated Naval area of air operations over Korea for which TF-77 would have exclusive responsibility. This, too, was inconsistent with the Air Force's requirement that an air component commander should be able to apply any and all air assets at any point of his choosing.

Far East Air Force (FEAF) commander Lieutenant General George E. Stratemeyer requested that he be given operational control of all aircraft operating over Korea, regardless of their service of origin. MacArthur agreed and, by mid-1952, after some debate as to what actually constituted operational control, NAVFE complied under protest.[12] The situation was further complicated by the addition of Marine aircraft in Korea. Stratemeyer insisted that these aircraft should also come under his control, but the Marines put up a fierce resistance. They envisaged their air assets as supplemental firepower for their lightly armed ground formations in their primary role of amphibious assault. Thus, Marine Corps pilots were ground support specialists and their commanders insisted they should remain outside any centralized Air Force system at the exclusive disposal of Marine ground forces. Ultimately, a compromise was reached. Marine aircraft did come under the control of FEAF, but any sorties surplus to FEAF requirements remained at the disposal of the Marines.[13]

Following the Second World War, the USAAF, and later the USAF, set about codifying its basic doctrine in the light of its experience during that conflict. The Air University at Maxwell Air Force Base, Alabama, became the service's doctrinal development center. Long in gestating, the first fruits of its labor finally emerged after the Korean War as AFM1-2 *United States Air Force Basic Doctrine* (1953). The drafters of this document insisted that air power must be centrally controlled at the highest level of command, a principle that remained fundamentally unchanged through three revisions of AFM1-2.[14] Thus, according to AFM1-2 (1959), exploitation of the inherent flexibility of air power, required that air forces must be responsive at all levels of operation to employment as a single aggregate instrument,' but the very flexibility of this instrument inevitably leads to competing demands upon its services which might result in it being frittered away in piecemeal effort. Consequently, "Command arrangements at all levels must be adequate to preclude such wastage, which could be disastrous. In all aerospace efforts—regardless of their nature or scope—segmentation must be avoided by centralizing control of the aerospace forces that are allocated and employed."[15] Implicit within these statements are the notions that the single aggregate instrument that is air power includes not only the "aerospace forces of the Air Force—the fundamental aerospace forces of the nation," but also the air forces operated by the other services, and that as the air power specialists, such centralized control should be exercised by Air Force officers.[16]

Success during the Second World War recommended the efficiency of the unified supreme headquarters model where the commander in chief was responsible for all military forces—regardless of their service of origin—committed to a single theater of operations and in which all services have equal status. The proclivity towards unified command structures was reinforced by the 1947 National Security Act's establishment of the Joint Chiefs of Staff, itself a unified body. While the supreme headquarters of the Second World War were technically unified bodies, practice dictated that theater commanders should be drawn from the numerically preponderant service involved in any campaign. This tended to mean army officers and, more specifically in the United States' case, Army Ground Forces officers, though there were exceptions in which Supreme Commanders were Navy officers. Under no circumstances were Supreme Commands allotted to Army Air Force officers, though they did fill the role of deputy supreme commanders.

The experience of coalition warfare in the Second World War suggested that theater command arrangements should be as closely integrated as national sensibilities would permit, while still leaving the United States ultimate freedom of action. This had worked well between two technologically sophisticated and culturally similar countries like Great Britain and the United States. Part of the reason for this success was the fact that Britain and the United States' contributions to the war against Germany might be said to have been very roughly equal, with Britain providing the bulk of the resources at first while the United States built-up its war effort. Eventually, the United States assumed the role of senior partner, but by this time the integrated command arrangements were well established, and while there clearly were serious problems between the western Allies at times, they must be said to represent an outstanding example of international military cooperation.[17]

In the Pacific, the United States so clearly bore the brunt of the war against Japan that her preeminence was never in dispute, though the British did bear primary responsibility for the South East Asia Command. In practice, because the balance of forces was usually in the United States' favor, American officers enjoyed a monopoly of the decisive theater commands during the Second World War.

In regard to airpower, the centralization of air assets under the direct control of the theater commander, exercised through his air component commander, was a fundamental principle arising from Second World War experience. In practice, this meant a USAAF officer; and after the creation of the independent air force, a USAF officer. This lesson was employed in Korea where all air assets were eventually brought under the operational control of an Air Force officer. This incurred resistance from both the Navy and the Marine Corps. They had not built up their own air assets only to see their operational control pass to another service. Centralization under Air Force control was particularly offensive to the Marines whose airpower doctrine stressed the organic nature of their own air assets. Having lost a measure of operational control over their own airpower in Korea, the Marines were determined that this should not happen again in Vietnam.

Another historical factor acting upon the command and control arrangements for the Vietnam War relates to MacArthur's performance as head of Far East Command during the Korean War. MacArthur became so powerful that he dared to challenge Truman's direction of the war. While the general's insubordination eventually resulted in his dismissal, the affair contributed, in no small part, to the Democrats' defeat in the 1952 presidential election. Subsequent to Korea, it has been politically incumbent on any president to ensure that no military commander can become so powerful as to believe that they can dictate policy in their own right.

Designed to render the services more efficient and less parochial, the unification authorized in the 1947 National Security Act, in some respects, had the opposite effect. The individual service chiefs were to serve their parent services for most of their careers before joining the Joint Chiefs. Loyalty to the parent service was to prove, therefore, a difficult habit to break. Indeed, there was little incentive to do so. The Chairman of the Joint Chiefs did not have the authority to promote or demote members of the Joint Staff who, on completion of their short tours, returned to their parent services. These factors tended to perpetuate individual service parochialism in the Joint Chiefs, preventing it from functioning as a military executive in the manner of a general staff. Only the mediocrity of bureaucratic compromise moderated this tendency.[18]

The process of unification also engendered an enduring sensitivity among the services about responsibility for roles and missions. In Vietnam, this sensitivity manifested itself in a series of demarcation disputes—in particular those between the Army and the Air Force over responsibility for the close air support mission and air mobility.

## CLOSE AIR SUPPORT

According to an agreement between Secretary of Defense James F. Forrestal and the Joint Chiefs of Staff, reached at Key West, Florida, in March 1948, close air support was defined as, "the attack by aircraft of hostile ground or naval targets which are so close to friendly forces as to require detailed integration of each air mission with the fire and movement of those forces."[19] This definition was to remain valid up to, and during, the Vietnam War.

From its inception with the formation of the Aeronautical Division of the United States Army Signal Corps on 1 August 1907, the primary function of US military aviation had been the support of land forces, originally by the provision of intelligence data from airborne reconnaissance missions and then, increasingly, by the provision of close air support by armed aircraft. Suitably expanded, such tactical air support had been the primary function of the Army Air Service of the American Expeditionary Force during United States participation in the First World War in Europe, and it remained so for the Army Air Corps between the World Wars. Of all the aspects of the new field of military aviation, tactical air support was, not surprisingly, that which most interested the Army General Staff and, prior to the Second World War, it was they who dictated official doctrine to the Army's air arm. Thus, the Army Field Service Regulations of 1923 emphasized close support of the land forces as the Air Corps' primary mission.

However, despite the tactical nature of official Army air doctrine many, indeed most, Air Corps officers came to hold conflicting views of the best manner in which to employ the service's airpower. Their vision was shaped by the ideas of the classical airpower theorists like the Italian Giulio Douhet, the First Commander of the British Royal Air Force, Hugh Trenchard, and the United States' own Billy Mitchell. These theorists all believed that the airplane's greatest military potential lay in its use as a weapon of strategic bombardment. This view of airpower as an offensive weapon, best used independently of the land forces, became firmly established within the Air Corps Tactical School from the early 1930s onwards.[20]

As part of the expansion of the United States military establishment that preceded entry in to the Second World War, Army Chief of Staff, George C. Marshall, established the Army Air Forces on 20 June 1941. The new force included an Air War Plans Division tasked with producing a plan for the employment of United States airpower in the European war. The Air War Plans Division was primarily composed of strategic airpower enthusiasts who had been instructors at the Air Corps Tactical School. Thus, the core of their master war plan, completed in July 1941 and known as AWPD-1, was a strategic bomber offensive which, the planners hoped, would bring Germany to her knees without a land campaign. In the event that this proved insufficient, the planners did also prepare for the air support of a ground war in Europe.[21]

Thus, the United States entered the Second World War with an airpower doctrine containing two conflicting strands. On the one hand, the Army Air Forces possessed a body of tactical air support doctrine largely dictated by the Army's ground commanders. In this tactical doctrine, air power assets were to be divided between ground units and subject to their operational control.[22] On the other hand, Army aviators themselves no longer considered tactical air support as the service's primary function. Their views were reflected in the new strategic emphasis of AWPD-1.

While the actual detail of AWPD-1 was somewhat overtaken by events, strategic bombing campaigns lay at the heart of Army Air Forces efforts during the Second World War. Nevertheless, it remained necessary for the service to provide air support to the ground forces throughout the war. However, as we have seen, existing tactical air support doctrine proved unsuccessful during the early days of the Army Air Forces first tactical campaign in North Africa. As a result, Eisenhower transformed the air support system by placing the entire Army Air Forces' strength under his own, centralized, control. The revised arrangements proved successful and established the centralization of air assets as a key principle of airpower doctrine.[23]

FM 100-20 made clear that there was more to tactical air operations than the close air support that was the primary focus of the Army Ground Forces. In order to wrest the initiative from the Luftwaffe in North Africa, the Army Air Forces had found it necessary to attack the German air force itself prior to conducting other operations more directly in support of the troops on the ground. Thus, air superiority over the battlefield had become the primary tactical air mission. This was reflected in FM 100-20 with close air support coming only third in the Army Air Forces' list of priorities.[24] Furthermore, the manual hinted at the extent of the Army Air Forces ambitions. The classical airpower theorists believed that airpower was the decisive weapon, capable of winning wars independently of the other arms and therefore superior to them. The logic of this thinking suggested that airpower should be exercised by an independent air force. No such suggestion was made in FM 100-20, but the manual did declare that the Army Air Forces and the Army Ground Forces were now possessed of equal status, a claim that the latter arm found difficult to accept.[25]

Despite their greater interest in strategic air warfare, the Army Air Forces were pledged to provide support to the Army Ground Forces. Their North African close air support system was successfully continued and refined in Italy, and then Western Europe after the Normandy landings. Different close air support systems were, however, applied to suit local conditions in the Pacific theaters.

In the South and Central Pacific theater, the United States pursued a campaign characterized by a series of amphibious operations against Japanese fortified islands that resembled nothing less than siege warfare. In the interwar years, the US Marine Corps had carved out an amphibious warfare role for itself, which it was to retain after the Second World War. Consequently, the Marines developed their tactical air doctrine with amphibious operations in mind. They came to envisage their integral air arm as flying artillery in support of their lightly armed ground formations. Thus, the Marines required relatively lavish amounts of air support compared to their Army cousins who could usually rely on greater artillery support—standard Marine procedure called for the support of each Marine division in the field by a Marine air wing.

In order to fulfill this artillery substitution role, Marine aircraft had to be available to the ground commanders within five or ten minutes. Therefore, the Marines adopted the standard procedure of allotting aircraft to ground formations on an "air alert" basis in which "cab ranks" of fighter-bombers would orbit the combat zone awaiting strike requests from Marine forward air observers who accompanied the ground forces into combat at the battalion level.

By contrast, the Air Force tactical air doctrine, developed during the Second World War, assumed the Army would normally use its own artillery for the support of its troops in immediate contact with the enemy, reserving the use of airpower for deeper targets. As these would not come into contact with the ground troops for some time, the Air Force considered that requests for air support could most efficiently be handled by Air Force aircraft scrambling from ground bases rather than orbiting overhead.[26] This would, of course, take much more time from request for support by the ground commander to aircraft over target, than the five to ten minutes required by the Marines. Indeed, it might even be argued that Air Force tactical air doctrine included little provision for close air support at all, since the service deemed this more properly an Army artillery mission than an air one.

Following the Second World War, Army Air Forces Commander, General Carl A. Spaatz, promised Army Chief of Staff, General Eisenhower, continued support in the form of a dedicated Tactical Air Command (TAC). This command was established in March 1946. The following year, the Army Air Forces achieved its objective of independence when it split away from the Army Ground Forces to form the United States Air Force. Paradoxically, this was a consequence of an act designed to unify the services under the administration of a single National Military Establishment led by a civilian Secretary of Defense. Under the provisions of the act, both the Navy and the Marine Corps were permitted to retain their aviation assets while the Army was permitted to retain, "such aviation . . . as may be organic therein."[27] Consequently, the various branches of the Army retained their organic aviation.

Simultaneously, with the National Security Act, the President endorsed the supplemental Executive Order 9877 designed to specify the different functions of each of the armed forces. The order specified exclusive Air Force responsibility for "air transport of the armed forces, except as provided by the Navy . . . for essential internal administration and for air transport over routes of sole interest to naval forces where the requirement cannot be met by normal air transport facilities," strategic air warfare, air superiority operations, air lift and support for airborne operations, air support to the land forces and "coordination of air defense among all the services."[28] This did not prevent the emergence of friction between the services over responsibility for roles and missions. The main areas of dispute at this time were between the Navy and the Air Force over the provision of air transport and responsibility for strategic air warfare, an area in which the Navy was eager to carve out a role for its carrier air power. A lesser dispute developed between the Army and the Air Force over responsibility for air defense.

Concerned to resolve these differences between the Air Force and the Navy, Secretary of Defense, James Forrestal, called the March 1948 Key West conference. The resulting agreement, signed by the President on 21 April 1948, was intended to provide a definitive, comprehensive statement of the "functions of the armed forces and the Joint Chiefs of Staff" which would replace that contained in Executive Order 9877. Regarding air support for the land forces, the new agreement provided a more detailed breakdown of the actual missions involved than Executive Order 9877 had done. Under the agreement, close combat and logistical air support to the Army was to include air lift, support and re-supply of airborne operations, aerial photography, tactical reconnaissance, and interdiction of enemy land power and communications. As such, the Key West agreement extended the definition of air support to include not only reconnaissance, close air support and air superiority, but also logistical air support, support of airborne operations, and interdiction of enemy land power and communications. All of these missions were, according to the agreement, the exclusive responsibility of the Air Force.[29]

However, expansion of the Army's organic aviation and the Army's increasing use of the helicopter were to engender friction with the newly created Air Force and encounter obstructions from conservatives within the Army itself.[30] A key problem was that neither Executive Order 9877 nor the Key West Agreement had actually defined what constituted "organic" Army aviation.

Air Force concern over this issue led to discussions between the two services' chiefs of staff, with the objective of more precisely defining the roles of Army aviation. The resulting Bradley-Vandenberg Agreement of 20 May 1949 established the principle Army aviation functions as various surveillance missions in the immediate combat zone, emergency medical evacuation and limited aerial re-supply. The agreement also defined certain aviation functions for the support of the Army which were to be conducted by the Air Force. While these differed in some detail from the Army aviation roles, they were broadly similar in many respects and included medical evacuation, aerial supply and aerial photography.[31]

Also in the late 1940s, the Air Force and the Army held talks on the establishment of a system for the coordination of joint operations. These talks foundered because the Army insisted on a measure of operational control of its supporting air assets. This demand was especially unpalatable to the Air Force because it contravened the principle of the centralization of airpower assets along with the Air Force's insistence that all such assets should be under Air Force control.

Army Chief of Staff, General J. Lawton Collins, reiterated his service's view early in the Korean War when he protested the coequal status of the Air Force and Army in close air support operations and called for the subordination of Air Force aircraft performing such operations to the army and corps commanders. Furthermore, he suggested that the Air Force should provide each Army division serving overseas with its own dedicated fighter-bomber group.[32]

In Korea itself, in 1950, the Army got to experience the apparent benefits of Marine tactical air doctrine at first hand when Marine aircraft provided dedicated support to Army units during the defense of the Pusan perimeter and the Inchon landings, and Army officers liked what they saw. Drawing on this experience, General Edward M. Almond, commanding the Army's X Corps, recommended in December of 1950 and again in July of the following year, that a group of fighter-bombers be allotted to the operational control of each Army division. However, in August 1952, Army General Mark Clark forbade further Army requests for changes in the existing Air Force system on the grounds that it and the Marine systems were designed for different circumstances and that adoption of the latter by the Army would be prohibitively expensive for any more than a handful of divisions in the field.[33]

Collins had even suggested that Army preferences should be taken into account in the development of future aircraft for the close air support role. This reflected another fundamental difference of opinion between the Army and the Air Force: this time over the nature of tactical aircraft. As we have seen, the Air Force held a broad definition of tactical air war which included air superiority and interdiction in addition to close air support. In order to retain the flexibility offered by centralization and also for budgetary considerations, the Air Force's preference throughout the 1950s and 1960s was to develop multirole, high-performance aircraft that could seize air superiority and then be shifted between the different tactical air support missions. This inevitably meant jets, as they offered the additional benefit of increased survivability in the ground attack role as a direct result of their high speed.

However, the acquisition by the Air Force of such jet multirole fighter-bombers also resulted in some problematic concomitant developments with regard to the Army's immediate aviation concern of close air support. The high speed of jet aircraft, which contributed to their survivability during a ground attack pass, also reduced the time available for the pilot to visually acquire the target, leading to a decline in the accuracy of the attack. Even if the pilot wished to fly slower, the relatively high stalling speed of such aircraft limited his ability to do so. Jet aircraft also tended to fly higher than the old piston-engine fighter-bombers in the interests of fuel economy. This also led to poorer target acquisition and, thus, lower accuracy. Fuel economy considerations also militated against the use of jet attack aircraft to perform standing patrols over the battlefield. It was much more fuel-efficient to hold such aircraft on runway alert from which they could be scrambled quickly at the request of the ground troops, and this, of course, was the way in which the Air Force had operated its close air support system since the Second World War. Jet bases, however, had to be relatively distant from the battlefield because of the increasing length of the concrete runways required by the high-performance aircraft of the time. Unfortunately this also reduced reaction time and, according to the Army, was detrimental to the morale of ground troops who would not have the comfort of knowing that their air support was orbiting overhead. Finally, jet, multirole aircraft were expensive, leading to a reduction in the overall number of aircraft available for tactical air support duties.

Consequently, the Army wanted the Air Force to develop specialized aircraft optimized for the close air support role. These dedicated "CAS" aircraft would have quite different attributes to those required for the air superiority and interdiction missions. They would be cheaper and they might not even be jets at all. Dedicated CAS aircraft would be slower and fly lower than their multirole cousins for better target acquisition and bombing accuracy. They would have good, short take off and landing performance to enable them to operate from rough strips close to the front-line. This would produce good reaction times, but the lower overall performance of the aircraft would also result in greater fuel efficiency that would enable them to loiter over the battlefield for long periods, if necessary.[34]

All versions of AFM1-2 established the principle of the centralization of airpower assets at the highest possible level. Never wholeheartedly endorsed by the Army, such an arrangement was, however, increasingly unattractive to a service which increasingly came to believe it had been abandoned by the Air Force.

There was considerable justification in this claim. As we have seen, until the eve of the United States' entry into the Second World War, the principal function of the Army Air Corps had always been the tactical support of the Army's land forces. This was, however, a doctrine forced upon Air Corps officers by the Army's leadership. When, during the Second World War, the aviators themselves gained responsibility for generating Army Air Forces doctrine then the service's emphasis had shifted to the strategic air warfare favored by the classical airpower theorists. It is, perhaps, no surprise then, that it was a widely held belief within the Army Air Forces that its nuclear attacks on Japan represented the ultimate vindication of the view of the classical airpower theorists that airpower alone could win wars. While the case was less conclusive in Europe, most Army Air Forces officers believed that the strategic bombing campaign against Germany had also been one of the most significant factors in the defeat of the Nazis.

After the Korean War, many Air Force officers felt instinctively that attacks by the service's heavy bombers had been the key factor in forcing the Chinese to agree to a truce and that, if suitably unfettered by the politicians, strategic airpower might have produced a decisive victory over the communists independently of the stalemate on the ground. Furthermore, the nuclear emphasis of the New Look defense review of the Eisenhower administration actively encouraged Air Force concentration on strategic nuclear delivery at the expense of tactical air support. This emphasis on strategic bombing in general, and nuclear attack in particular, is reflected in all four versions of AFM1-2 published throughout the 1950s.[35]

Even in the specific area of tactical air support, the Army Air Forces' priorities, as reflected in FM 100-20 had moved from close air support to air superiority and interdiction, and there were those in the Army who were critical of the Air Force's close air support performance in both the Second World War and Korea.[36] Furthermore, in the atmosphere of tight budgets and strategic priorities existing after the Second World War, Tactical Air Command had always taken second place to the nuclear-armed Strategic Air Command—only two years after its creation, TAC had lost its independent status and come under the auspices of Continental Air Command.

Eventually, even those Air Force officers who were supposedly tactical air support specialists—the TAC pilots themselves—seemed to abandon the Army. In 1950, TAC began to adapt its fighter-bombers for the carriage of small nuclear weapons, a process that received further stimulus from the Eisenhower administration's New Look defense policy. After 1954, the command committed itself to the theater nuclear attack mission.[37] Even if the Korean War did seem, in some ways, to reaffirm the importance of tactical aviation, Secretary of the Air Force Thomas K. Finletter announced in 1955 that "the Korean War was a special case and airpower can learn little there about its future role in United States foreign policy in the East." Thus TAC developed into what Alain C. Enthoven and Wayne K. Smith have described as a sort of "junior Strategic Air Command," a development that was dictated more by intraservice political considerations than by the perceived nature of any potential military threat.[38]

Air Force General Gabriel P. Disosway has subsequently said of the period, "nuclear was the popular thing at the time and if TAC was going to get anything they had to do it by nuclear, but they went completely overboard." Disosway, later a stern critic of Army air mobility and armed Army aircraft accepts that the Air Force neglected the Army after the Second World War when it put all its resources into Strategic Air Command at the expense of TAC and that, having rebuilt its tactical air support capability in Korea, repeated the error after that war.[39] By the late 1950s, Air Force fighter-bomber pilots were required to qualify in nuclear bombing techniques, but not in conventional bombing, strafing or rocket firing.[40] Whatever the reasons for this, the effect was to increase Army interest in establishing its own tactical air capabilities.

This process had been under way since the late 1940s with the bulk of the Army's effort going into the logistics and troop lift support that was to metamorphose into the modern concept of air mobility. Some Army aviation enthusiasts, however, also favored the adoption by the Army of its own close air support capability. There had been a number of instances during the Second World War in which Army light aircraft had been armed with rifles and bazookas, and at least one Army pilot had fired his .45 caliber pistol from his aircraft in anger, but extension and formalization of these ad hoc capabilities was not covered by existing official Army doctrine.[41] While the delineation of responsibility between the services for air mobility overlapped or was unclear, close air support was, unequivocally, an exclusive Air Force mission, a point that Secretary of Defense Charles E. Wilson reiterated in a 1956 memorandum.[42]

The Army was, therefore, initially cautious about the adoption of organic close air support.[43] Nevertheless, unofficial theoretical studies and field tests of armed Army aircraft proceeded at both the Army Infantry School at Fort

Benning, Georgia and at its Aviation School at Fort Rucker, Alabama. These experiments involved both armed helicopters and armed light aircraft, and two Army exercises: ABLE BUSTER and BAKER BUSTER, held in the mid-1950s, were designed, in part, to test armed light aircraft in the antitank role.[44]

Until the early days of US involvement in the Second World War, the primary role of the Army Air Forces had been the provision of close air support to the Army Ground Forces, but wartime experience had downgraded tactical air support in favor of strategic air warfare and even within the realm of tactical airpower close air support had slipped to third in a list of priorities which placed air superiority and interdiction as more important. The close air support system which the Air Force developed as part of its Second World War experience differed from that of the US Marine Corps, in that it placed the ultimate responsibility for the deployment of air resources in the hands of the Air Force while the Marine system assumed that response to the requests for close air support of the ground commanders was the primary responsibility of air power.

During the 1950s, the Air Force codified a body of basic doctrine based on its Second World War experience. This doctrine contributed to an increasing disenchantment within the Army regarding the support it received from the Air Force. Increasingly, Army commanders called for a restoration of the pre-eminence in the air support relationship with the Air Force that they had enjoyed at the beginning of US involvement in the Second World War, and for the allocation of dedicated close air support aircraft to Army formations.

The Air Force continued to deemphasize tactical air support in the 1950s. For a time, the Korean War seemed to reassert the importance of close air support for the Army, but adoption of the theater nuclear attack mission by the Air Force's Tactical Air Command in the mid-1950s showed that the Air Force regarded its Korean experience as anomalous, and stimulated demands within the Army for the appropriation of its own armed aircraft. Experiments along these lines led to Air Force claims that the Army was attempting to take-over legitimate Air Force roles. A clash was, therefore, inevitable when, in Vietnam, the Air Force sought to get back into the tactical airpower business.

## AIRMOBILITY

One of the principal doctrinal developments of the Vietnam War, perhaps *the* principal doctrinal development of the war, was the United States Army's employment, for the first time in history, of helicopters as the primary method of maneuver, supplanting foot or road-vehicle mobility, for large combined-arms formations, a technique known as airmobility.

Only slowly had the combination of the words "air" and "mobility" acquired this meaning. Back in the 1940s and 1950s, the term "air mobility" had simply meant the air transport of troops and supplies into the combat zone from some point outside it. Dramatic enough in its day, this air mobility was not to be confused with the deeper penetration operational maneuvers performed by airborne parachute and glider forces. It did not, originally, imply dedicated airmobile units, or organic fire support and, despite the increasingly frequent use of the term: "air assault" neither did it imply opposed landings by airmobile troops.[45]

The particular form air mobility was to take in the US armed forces involved the employment by the Army of its own "organic" aviation assets, rather than those of its sister service: the Air Force. A perpetuation of developments which had occurred relatively early in the United States' participation in the Second World War, this arrangement was to be marked by associated interservice dispute.

The Air Force did not, of course, exist as a separate service during the war. At the beginning of the United States' participation in the conflict, military aviation tasks were conducted by a branch of the Army: the Army Air Corps which, as a result of wartime expansion became the Army Air Forces. However, on 6 June 1942, the War Department approved the provision of organic aviation for the Army's field artillery branch in order to carry out observation tasks for the guns. Despite Army Air Forces opposition to this development, other branches of the Army Ground Forces were also to receive their own organic aircraft during the war.

While the 1947 National Security Act created an independent United States Air Force, this did not halt the expansion of Army organic aviation, or the Army's increasing use of the helicopter.[46] Also, as we have seen, despite Air Force hopes, the Bradley-Vandenberg Agreement of 20 May 1949 did not result in the loss of Army aviation roles to the Air Force; rather it resulted in the formalization of a duplication of roles between the two services, which was likely to remain a source of friction for the future.

In order to prevent the Army from acquiring more capable aircraft which might encroach on roles which the Air Force reserved for itself, the Air Force sought, and received, the Army's acceptance, in the Bradley-Vandenberg Agreement, of weight limitations on Army aircraft. Army fixed-wing aircraft were not to exceed 2,500 pounds empty weight while Army helicopters were to be restricted to no more than 4,000 pounds empty weight.[47]

Despite the limitations imposed on its aviation assets by the Bradley-Vandenberg Agreement, the Korean War stimulated the Army's use of the helicopter as a means of overcoming some of the difficulties raised by the country's rugged terrain and poor infrastructure. In fact, the Army might have preferred to employ something in between the helicopter and the fixed-wing aircraft if a sufficiently developed machine had been available. In the early 1950s, such "convertiplanes" appeared to offer more potential for Army surveillance and air mobility tasks than helicopters.

Early US Army helicopters suffered from such serious vibration that it was difficult to use field glasses from them and the Army, therefore, preferred to use fixed-wing aircraft for observation duties.[48] Consequently, the April 1950 Army Airborne Panel enthusiastically endorsed the development of both the heavy-lift helicopter and the convertiplane.

The heavy-lift helicopter offered the prospect of short-range passage of troops and equipment over terrain obstacles, but the convertiplane offered to revolutionize airborne warfare. Its Vertical Take-Off and Landing (VTOL) performance and high forward speed would free airborne operations from their dependency on runways and eliminate the problem of "scatter" associated with conventional airborne operations.[49] Army-funded research of this type of aircraft led to the experimental Bell XV-3 tilt rotor which was flown successfully from 1953. However, at the time of the Korean War, the helicopter was the only practical VTOL aircraft.

The war stimulated the expansion of Army aviation with the service requesting both increased numbers of aircraft and aircraft of greater capability which invariably meant heavier aircraft. More capable Army aircraft presented a threat to the Air Force because they would have the potential to perform a greater variety of tasks. This might result in a natural expansion of Army aviation roles and missions which could only come at the expense of the Air Force. Was the Army trying to usurp legitimate Air Force roles? In order to resolve Air Force fears on this issue, talks took place between the service secretaries' staffs leading to the signing of a memorandum of understanding between Air Force Secretary Thomas K. Finletter and Army Secretary Frank Pace in October 1951. On the surface, this agreement appeared to be something of a compromise. It satisfied the Army to the extent that it ended weight restrictions on the service's aircraft, but it also seemed to satisfy the Air Force by providing a definition of Army aviation roles which appeared quite restrictive. The agreement limited Army aviation to the provision of assistance in ground combat and logistics within the combat zone which it defined as "normally not" in excess of fifty to seventy miles deep, and it insisted that the Army not duplicate existing Air Force capabilities in reconnaissance, interdiction, close air support and troop airlift, including "assault transport."[50]

Korea, however, continued to provide the Army with plenty of opportunities for the provision of organic air assistance in ground combat within the combat zone and Army aviation continued to grow. Between 1951 and 1952 the number of Army aircraft rose from 1,721 to 2,392. Within these totals, Army helicopter numbers increased from 122 to 284 with larger, heavier, more capable models entering the Army's inventory, as sanctioned by the October agreement.[51]

Further Air Force complaints to the Joint Chiefs of Staff led to another round of inter-service discussions resulting in another agreement between Pace and Finletter on 4 November 1952. Though this new agreement did re-impose a weight limit for fixed-wing Army aircraft, it raised this to 5,000 pounds, and it left the door open for the further development of Army aircraft by including the proviso that the service secretaries could request a review of the restrictions in order to keep this limitation realistic in the light of technical developments . . . The technical development of Army helicopters, however, remained completely unhindered by weight limits. The November 1952 agreement also expanded the Army's area of air operations to a combat zone "normally understood" to be fifty to a hundred miles in depth. Furthermore, the provisions of the agreement expressly excluded "convertiplane-type aircraft" which the Army could continue to develop.[52] The second Pace-Finletter Agreement, then, effectively sanctioned further incremental expansion of Army aviation both in terms of raw aircraft numbers and roles and missions.

One specific area in which the Army and Air Force clashed over the demarcation of roles between the services was that of air mobility. Noting the Army's increasing interest in this role, the Air Force's Tactical Air Command called, in 1949, for the development of Air Force troop carrying helicopter units, but Air Staff interest was low and funds were limited. Consequently, little progress was made until the Korean War rekindled Air Force interest in the project.[53] The Air Force then set about forming such units and, in order to do so, it obstructed Army transport helicopter orders for which it bore responsibility under existing interservice arrangements. The Air Force refused to fulfill the Army orders until it had purchased like numbers of aircraft with which to equip its own assault helicopter squadrons. Therefore, these units competed directly with organic Army aviation in terms of both mission and equipment. The Army fought back by turning to the Navy and Marine Corps as alternative sources for the transport helicopters held up by the Air Force.[54]

The controversy continued into the mid-1950s with the Air Force Chief of Staff insisting that the helicopter was "just another aircraft' and that the Air Force had every right, therefore, to operate assault aircraft squadrons while similar Army units should be disbanded. The Army, however, held the Air Force strictly to the letter of the 1952 Pace-Finletter Agreement. This specified that Army aircraft could transport "Army supplies, equipment, and small units within the combat zone' while Air Force troop carrier aircraft were limited to the "airlift of Army supplies, equipment, personnel, and units from exterior points to points within the combat zone.'[55] The Army insisted, therefore, that it had no use for Air Force assault helicopter squadrons within the combat zone. In 1956, the Air Force conceded the argument and transferred its assault helicopter squadrons to the logistic support of other Air Force units.[56]

In retrospect, the Air Force's acceptance of the second Pace-Finletter Agreement, and its abandonment of the assault helicopter squadrons may appear surprising. However, contributory factors must surely have been the service's fixation on strategic bombing and its contemporary desire to secure a nuclear role for its tactical aircraft.[57] In 1946, the Air Force's Commanding General, Carl Spaatz, said that long-range bombers and their escorts were the "backbone' of the service, relegating the Tactical Air Command to a secondary role.[58] We already know that the Air Force's senior leadership had never been particularly enthusiastic about the assault helicopter squadrons with their slow ungainly machines. In any case, if the Pace-Finletter Agreements upheld the existence of an Army airmobile capability—which they did—then the Army could refuse to use the equivalent Air Force squadrons—which it did—leaving them with no practical role.

Aside from its existing philosophical inclination toward strategic air warfare, the policy of massive retaliation demanded that the Air Force place nuclear delivery at center stage. Consequently, TAC's leaders came to realize that if the command were to survive, it, too must adopt a nuclear role.[59] Limited expansion of Army responsibilities in the immediate combat area, including helicopter "air assault' may have seemed a small price to pay in exchange for a nuclear Tactical Air Command whose missions would, in any case, necessarily have less to do with the immediate battlefield than those of its conventionally armed forerunner.

Despite Air Force objections, Army aviation did greatly expand during the Korean War, but its proponents also faced different types of opposition from within their own service. Against the background of the rundown of conventional forces caused by the New Look, Army conservatives objected to the deflection of funds, which might have been spent on armored forces, to what they regarded as an ineffective technological toy.

In addition, there were also those Army officers who, in their anxiety to preserve the gains made by Army aviation thus far, were reluctant to continue its development beyond certain limits, at least in the short term, lest this provoke the Air Force into a response which might threaten the entire Army aviation program. This sensitivity was particularly acute regarding the thorny issue of armed helicopters which, in Army hands, might be seen to contravene the second Pace-Finletter Agreement's restriction on Army duplication of Air Force close air support capabilities.[60] Such a development was sure to provoke an angry response from the Air Force. Shortly after the Korean War, Colonel Edward L. Rowny, an instructor in infantry tactics at the Army Infantry School in Fort Benning, Georgia, conducted a series of theory sessions involving the use of armed helicopters. Soon after, Rowny was summoned to Washington where he was admonished for exacerbating interservice rivalries and ordered to cease the sessions, even though he had been careful to run them on a voluntary, off-duty basis only.[61]

While Army aviation had been growing since before the end of the Second World War, it was the Marine Corps which first produced systematic doctrine for the employment of the new rotary-wing technology. The Corps began to study the use of helicopters in response to its observations of the CROSSROADS nuclear tests at Bikini Atoll in the Marshall Islands in 1946. These indicated that naval forces would be very vulnerable to nuclear attack unless widely dispersed, but such dispersal would preclude the Marines' primary mission—amphibious assault—at least by conventional means. The Marines set out to resolve this problem, lest they be left without a *raison d'etre*, and found their answer in the speed and range of the helicopter. Marine Commandant, General Alexander A. Vandegrift, therefore, ordered the Marine Corps School (MCS) to begin work on establishing doctrine for the use of helicopters in amphibious operations.[62]

Led by Colonel Robert E. Hogaboom, the School's "Helicopter Board' defined the Marines' assault helicopter as a vehicle capable of lifting 15 to 20 fully armed marines and, in 1948, prepared a plan for a Marine helicopter wing with 240 such aircraft capable of transporting a Marine regimental combat team in a single lift. The Marine Corps also established an experimental helicopter squadron, designated HMX-1, to develop helicopter assault doctrine in amphibious operations in parallel with the work of the MCS Helicopter Board.

Unfortunately, no such machine as that envisaged by the Helicopter Board existed and HMX-1 at first had to make do with the HO3S-1 which could lift no more than two fully equipped Marines, in addition to its pilot. In May 1948, HMX-1 participated in Exercise PACKARD II when its five HO3S-1s simulated the landing of one regimental combat team from the decks of the USS *Palau*, an operation which involved the transport of sixty-six men and their equipment in thirty-five flights. Thus, Marine airmobility doctrine outran the technology required for its fulfillment. This situation was to reoccur in the Army, and though helicopter performance rose steadily throughout the 1950s, it was not to be fully resolved until the development of the turbine powered helicopter represented by the UH-1 Iroquois ("Huey') series.

Revised in the light of PACKARD II and the availability of the new Marine HRP-1 helicopter, which was capable of lifting ten passengers, MCS published its helicopter doctrine manual in November 1948 as *Amphibious Operations-Employment of Helicopters (Tentative)* or amphibious operations manual Phib-31. This remained the standard Marine doctrinal publication for the tactical use of helicopters throughout the Korean War.[63]

Phib-31 was to form the basis for the Marines' "vertical envelopment' concept, adopted in February 1951, by which initial Marine assaults are "all helicopter' affairs with the Marines landing to the rear and on the flanks of the enemy. The beach is then cleared from the rear and only when it is secured do reinforcements and supplies come in by boat "over the beach.'

During the Korean War, the Marine Corps quickly established the use of the helicopter for observation, liaison and medical evacuation purposes and they, again, preceded their Army cousins in making the first tentative steps toward combat air mobility. On 13 September 1951, aircraft of Marine helicopter squadron HMR-161 carried out the first Marine mass helicopter re-supply mission near the Soyang River. In twenty-eight flights, HMR-161 carried 18,848 pounds of supplies and seventy-four Marines over a distance of seven miles. In April 1951, HMR-161 conducted the first helicopter lift of a combat unit in history when it transported 224 marines to the front line.[64]

The Marines also began the process of experimenting with armed helicopters as early as 1950, but these arrangements remained informal until the Vietnam War. Until then, the Corps' priority was the use of the helicopter for airlift of troops and supplies.[65]

In April 1954, General James Gavin published an influential popular article on air mobility, based (as far as security permitted) on a series of studies conducted under Gavin's authority while he was responsible for Army planning and operations as Assistant Chief of Staff.[66] Here, he suggested that troops mounted in helicopters and assault transports—"sky cavalry'—could perform the traditional cavalry roles and provide a flexible reserve of firepower. This combat air mobility differed from the mere transportation role by which the term had previously been defined.

An embryonic "Sky Cav' organization composed of both ground and airmobile elements and derived from these studies, was included in Exercise SAGE BRUSH at Gavin's urging in 1955. On that occasion, the exercise evaluators were so critical of the scheme that it was abandoned.[67] Thereafter, tests of airmobility and armed helicopters proceeded on a limited, unofficial basis within the Army.[68] Much of this ad hoc experimentation took place at Fort Rucker, Alabama which the Army, on 1 February 1955, had established as its Aviation Center under Brigadier General Carl Hutton.[69] From 1956, continuing Aviation Center experiments with Sky Cav turned to formations which were completely air mounted and which included armed helicopters.

Whereas the reality of unsophisticated conventional war in Korea had stimulated the expansion of Army aviation and its use of the helicopter, it was the threat of the nuclear warfare which stimulated airmobility thinking within the Army in the later 1950s. Army planning for the nuclear battlefield was itself stimulated by the "New Look' defense policy ushered in by the incoming Eisenhower administration. This stressed the theoretical deterrent value of "massive retaliation' and the substitution of nuclear weapons for conventional forces as a means of reducing defense expenditure. Thus, if the Army was to retain a role and, therefore, a slice of future defense budgets, it must demonstrate an ability to operate on a battlefield in which both it, and its enemies, employed tactical nuclear weapons.

Consequently, in 1956, the Army instituted its "Pentomic" (for pentagonal-atomic) reorganization by which its divisions were divided into five task forces, supposedly able to operate independently when dispersed due to the threat of nuclear attack against concentrated targets. Army aviation proponents were quick to conclude that the helicopter provided considerable potential for rapid dispersal when faced with such a threat and also the capability for rapid concentration to exploit the effects of the US Army's own nuclear firepower.

The budgetary squeeze of the New Look, the ongoing expansion of Army aviation and the development of new weapons continued to create friction within the Joint Chiefs of Staff and the Department of Defense over service roles and missions. This prompted Secretary of Defense, Charles E. Wilson, on 26 November 1956, to issue a memorandum on the "Clarification of Roles and Missions to Improve the Effectiveness of Operation of the Department of Defense.' In this memorandum, Wilson limited Army aviation to four roles: observation, airlift, medical evacuation and liaison. The memorandum specifically forbade Army aircraft from providing close air support and specifically limited the Army's airlift role to application "only to small combat units and limited quantities of material to improve local mobility, and not to the provision of an airlift capability sufficient for the large-scale movement of sizable Army combat units which would infringe on the mission of the Air Force.'[70]

The Secretary re-imposed an empty weight restriction on Army helicopters at a maximum of 20,000 pounds and reiterated the 5,000 pounds weight limit for fixed-wing aircraft, a category in which he now included convertiplanes and VSTOL types. As usual, the Secretary saw fit to redefine the parameters of the combat zone as extending one hundred miles forward and one hundred miles to the rear of the front line, and he also resolved an ongoing dispute between the Army and the Air Force over intermediate range ballistic missiles by assigning their operational employment to the latter service and to the Navy for ship-based variants.[71]

The limitations imposed on the Army by the 1956 Wilson memorandum were later to be criticized by the then Army Chief of Staff, General Maxwell Taylor, who blamed the Air Force for recruiting the Secretary in its "resistance' to legitimate Army efforts to escape from its "dependence' on the former service.[72] Testifying before Congress in 1958, General Gavin argued also that strict interpretation of the Wilson memorandum would be both inefficient and distort the manner in which the Army carried out its aviation roles. According to Gavin, even the limited airlift mission permitted the Army could not effectively be fulfilled with fixed-wing aircraft of less than 5,000 pounds empty weight. Therefore, these tasks would have to be performed by helicopters which were more complex and expensive than equivalent fixed-wing aircraft.[73]

This was probably correct, as far as it went; however, the 1956 memorandum, or at least its outcomes, may have proved more accommodating to the Army than Gavin thought. In the first place, the secretary had doubled the area for which the Army might justifiably claim primary authority. Evidence that the Army would actually be permitted to exercise this authority was provided elsewhere in the memorandum where Wilson granted the Army exclusive responsibility for the development of tactical surface-to-surface missiles whose range did not exceed the depth of the combat zone—that is two hundred miles.

Furthermore, while a weight limitation was re-imposed on Army helicopters, placing a theoretical cap on their capabilities, the new authorized maximum weight was five times that established by the Bradley-Vandenberg Agreement of May 1949. Given that the Air Force was less enthusiastic about helicopters than fixed-wing aircraft, this part of the agreement might be seen as a classic compromise, permitting Army aviation development where it would least upset the Air Force, while placing severe limitations on Army fixed-wing aircraft, about which the Air Force was more concerned. This may not have been the perfect arrangement for the Army, but it did leave the way clear for further Army aviation development, and something like this formula would re-emerge in the 1966 McConnel-Johnson Agreement during the Vietnam War. In any case, the weight limitations in the 1956 Wilson memorandum were not always strictly applied.

Even the loss of the IRBM may have been, in one respect a gain for Army airmobility. Experience with airborne forces in the Second World War alerted the Army to the vulnerability of its all-wooden gliders. The Army, therefore, developed the XCG-20 all metal glider. This metamorphosed into the C-122 powered "assault transport' which had the advantage of not requiring a tug aircraft to tow it, and its payload, into battle.[74] Further refinements led to the C-123 Provider. However, as part of the agreement creating the independent Air Force, the Army had to buy its aircraft through the former service. General Gavin has claimed that the Air Force, having no requirement of its own for an assault transport, over-developed the C-123 into a replacement for its C-119 Flying Boxcar, considerably increasing its weight in the process.[75] The resulting aircraft was unsuitable for the small, minimally prepared air strips from which the Army intended it to operate. According to the Air Force, however, the C-123s were transferred to logistic roles in support of Air Force strike aircraft because, in joint exercises, they were found to be too vulnerable in combat.[76] The Army decided, therefore, to purchase the already developed DHC-4 Caribou STOL transport aircraft from De Havilland Aircraft of Canada.

As a sweetener for his controversial IRBM decision, Secretary Wilson acceded to a request by the Army Chief of Staff for Army procurement of the DHC-4 which, at approximately 17,000 pounds empty weight, far exceeded Wilson's own limit for Army fixed-wing aircraft. However, in his 1956 Roles and Missions memorandum, the Secretary specifically reserved for himself the right to make such exemptions and mentioned the DHC-4 as an example.[77] Army operation of the DHC-4-which it re-designated CV-2-was to prove as controversial in the 1960s as had the IRBM issue in the 1950s. The dispute between the Army and the Air Force over the former service's operation of the CV-2 in Vietnam was to result in the 1966 decision by which the Army renounced its CV-2s to the Air Force (where they were again re-designated as C-7s) in return for the Army's retention of the Armed helicopter.

Following his resignation in 1958 over what he believed to be the Army's lack of preparedness for limited war, General Gavin gave his thoughts a further public airing in his book, *War and Peace in the Space Age*. Here he explained that the Army had learned precisely the opposite lessons from the Second World War to those absorbed by the Air Force. According to Gavin, the war's strategic bombing campaigns had shown the classical airpower theorists like Giulio Douhet and Billy Mitchell to be in error. Airpower, said Gavin, was not the ultimate weapon. Its real importance lay in the mobility and firepower it offered to the Army.

The Air Force, however, remained obsessed with strategic bombing, particularly the delivery of nuclear weapons. For Gavin, the very creation of an independent air force—one of the classical airpower theorists' central themes—was perhaps an error in itself. If the Second World War showed the importance of army-air cooperation, then had not the services separated "at the very time when they should have been becoming more closely associated?" Gavin also pointed out that the Marine Corps had held on to its own aircraft.[78]

Another of the principal figures in the development of Army airmobility was Colonel—later General—Robert R. Williams. As Chief of the Air Mobility Division of the Army's Office of the Chief of Research and Development between 1959 and 1961, Williams recommended that the Army establish a systematic plan for its future aircraft requirements.[79] Army Chief of Staff General Lyman Lemnitzer approved and instituted an Army Aircraft Requirements Review Board under Lieutenant General Gordon Rogers which convened in April 1960. One of the Board's members was General Hamilton H. Howze.

Late in 1954, General Gavin had appointed Howze as Head of the Army's Aviation Office in the Department of Defense. This title was later changed to Director of Army Aviation. In this role, Howze presided over the development of the UH-1 helicopter which was to provide the backbone of Army airmobility assets in the 1960s. Developed on the behalf of the Army by the Air Force, the UH-1 program only narrowly escaped cancellation by the latter service when technical problems with the rotor blades emerged. After Army protests, the Air Force agreed to persevere with the project and the technical difficulties were resolved.[80]

In 1957, towards the end of his tour at the Pentagon, Howze conducted a series of studies based on map exercises drawn from the Command and General Staff College at Fort Leavenworth and the Infantry School at Fort Benning. Varying the forces of one side with the addition of organic aircraft, Howze proved, to his own satisfaction, that in a lot of the exercises "airmobile infantry with small air cavalry attachments could . . . [get] the job done with smaller forces, at less cost and . . . more quickly . . . "[81] Howze presented his findings to Army Chief of Staff, General Taylor; Secretary of Defense Wilson and the Secretary of the Army, arguing that the addition of airmobile forces to the Army "would provide new and exceptionally valuable capabilities,' though he was careful not to claim that non-airmobile forces would become obsolete as a consequence.[82]

As a member of the Rogers Board, Howze continued his proselytizing with the insertion into the Board's report of an addendum entitled "The Requirement for Air Fighting Units.' Here, he called for the creation of "air fighting units . . . which may be called air cavalry,' as opposed to the simple augmentation of ground formations with more aircraft for the purpose of increasing their mobility. Such units would employ their own aircraft in the direct fire support role and would "find particular applicability in any battle area in which the threat of area weapons forces wide dispersion . . . as well as in "brush fire" actions against relatively unsophisticated opponents.'[83]

Whereas, during much of the 1950s, Army aviation enthusiasts had regarded airmobility as a panacea for the nuclear battlefield, Howze's reference to "brush fire' wars reflected an increasing interest among them in the application of the concept to low-intensity conflict. This was to be endorsed and fostered by the Kennedy administration with the greater emphasis on conventional forces and counterinsurgency contained within its "flexible response' policy.

Army aviation proponents surmised that airmobility would be particularly applicable to counterinsurgency operations. It would restore mobility to the security forces in the kind of rough terrain in which insurgencies thrived; it would enable them to patrol large areas and, having found the enemy, it would facilitate the rapid concentration of forces required for local superiority. As such, it would serve as a force-multiplier, perhaps reducing the theoretical ten-to-one ratio of security forces to insurgents dictated by traditional counterinsurgency practice.

The Kennedy defense review led to the so-called ROAD (Reorganization Objectives Army Division) reorganization of the Army's Divisions which took place between January 1961 and July 1962. ROAD divisions abandoned the pentomic structure in favor of a more traditional three brigade task forces formation. As part of the reorganization, drawing on the Army Aviation Center's airmobility experiments, Army Chief of Staff, General George Decker, took the opportunity to include Sky Cav, now renamed "Air Cavalry' troops in the Armoured Cavalry Squadrons of each ROAD division. These units included armed helicopters and were the first airmobile units in the Army's order of battle, but while they did have a real combat role, these limited reconnaissance and screening forces did not constitute fully fledged airmobility in the sense that we now understand it.

The development of airmobility up to 1962 was beset by a rivalry between the Air Force and the Army, the origins of which, predated the 1947 National Security Act. That act invited further interservice dispute because its definitions of the individual services' aviation roles and missions were inadequate. Successive efforts to specify, definitively, service aviation roles and missions never adequately resolved the areas of disagreement and, in some cases, may actually have exacerbated them. Most importantly, they never did eliminate the main irritant to the Air Force —the continued and seemingly remorseless expansion of Army aviation.

The weight limitations placed on Army aircraft within the service agreements were certainly arbitrary, but contrary to Gavin's opinion, they do not seem to have greatly distorted the form of Army airmobility in that they were, in the main, subject to possible exemptions of which the Army did take advantage. In addition to his waiver of the weight restrictions on the CV-2, Secretary Wilson also acceded to a request by General Howze, when he was Director of Aviation, to procure the OV-1 Mohawk which weighed in at 12,000 pounds gross.[84] The OV-1 was originally developed for the Marines Corps. In the late 1950s, the Army was able to convince Wilson that if the Marines, despite their having jets, required a STOL, turboprop, surveillance aircraft then the Army probably needed one, too.[85] The development of VSTOL technology—particularly that of the helicopter—offered great opportunities to the services, but because of its novelty and the inadequacy of the interservice agreements it also offered fertile ground for further interservice dispute.

The original pioneers of airmobility were the Marines, but airmobility doctrine was perfected by the Army. Some conservatives within the Army leadership opposed airmobility, but it did have a number of friends in high places who were able to use their offices to foster its development. Significantly, the most important among these general officers like Gavin, Taylor and Howze all had pedigrees within the Army's airborne arm. Under their sponsorship, a considerable body of airmobile doctrine was added to that generated within the Marine Corps, and the concept received positive stimulus from Korea, the nuclear battlefield and developing Army interest in counterinsurgency.

Both Army and Marine airmobile doctrine outran the technical means to realize its full potential, and the technology can not really be said to have caught-up with the doctrine until the development of the turbine-powered helicopter. The ripening of this technology roughly coincided with the Army's adoption of air cavalry and the beginning of its efforts to explore the possibility of large, combined arms, dedicated, airmobile formations. The first such unit formed was the 11th Air Assault Division (provisional) which, as the 1st Cavalry Division (Airmobile) was the first Army combat unit to deploy to South Vietnam in 1965. The 11th Air Assault Division (Provisional) was an experimental division designed to test the airmobile procedures developed by the 1962 Army Tactical Mobility Requirements Board, more commonly known as the "Howze Board.' The Howze Board generated a comprehensive vision of airmobility that the US Army was to implement for the first time in South Vietnam. This vision was so extensive that it represented a direct threat to formally established US Air Force roles and missions. It is to the origins of the Board, and its deliberations that we now turn.

# Notes

1.  Department of Defense Dictionary of Military and Associated Terms (2003), www.dtic.mil/doctrine/jel/doddict/, 21 August 2003.
2.  William W. Momyer, Airpower in Three Wars (New York, 1980), 40.
3.  Ibid., p. 41.
4.  Ibid., p. 44.
5.  David Syrette, The Tunisian Campaign, 1942-1943, Benjamin F. Cooling (ed.), Case Studies in the Development of Close Air Support (Washington, DC: Office of Air Force History), 172-174.
6.  David P. Handel, "The Evolution of United States Air Force Basic Doctrine." Unpublished Research Study (Maxwell AFB, AL: Air University, 1978), 34.
7.  Richard G. Davis, The 31 Initiatives: A Study in Air Force—Army Co-operation (Washington, DC: Office of Air Force History, 1987), 8. Kurt A. Chichowski, "Doctrine Matures Through a Storm: An Analysis of the New Air Force Manual 1-1" thesis (School of Advanced Airpower Studies, Air University, Maxwell AFB, AL, 1993), 8 & Syrette, op cit., pp. 184-5.
8.  Momyer, op cit., 50.
9.  Forest C. Pogue, The Supreme Command, United States Army in World War II, The European Theater of Operations (Washington, DC: Office of the Chief of Military History, 1954), 62, 123 & 396.
10.  National Security Act, 26 July 1947, Richard I Wolf, The United States Air Force, Basic Documents on Roles and Missions (Washington, DC: Office of Air Force History, 1987), 61-83.
11.  Robert F. Futrell, The United States Air Force in Korea, 1950-1953 (New York, 1961), 43-4.
12.  Momyer, op cit., 57-59.
13.  Ibid., 59-62.
14.  Handel, op cit., 37-40.
15.  United States Air Force Basic Doctrine, (Washington, DC, 1 December 1959) (Hereinafter cited as AFM1-2, 1959), 7.
16.  Ibid., 6-7.
17.  This follows an argument in the British official history. Michael Howard, History of the Second World War, Grand Strategy, Vol. IV, August 1942-September 1943 (London, 1972).
18.  Edward Luttwak, The Pentagon and the Art of War (New York, 1985), 24-27, 43, 86 & 272.
19.  James Forrestal, "Functions of the Armed Forces and the Joint Chiefs of Staff" [The Key West Agreement]), (21 April 1948), Wolf, op cit., 154-166.
20.  James L. Cate, "Development of United States Air Doctrine, 1917-1941," Eugene M. Emme (ed.), The Impact of Air Power, National Security and World Politics (Princeton, 1959), 187-189.

21. Ibid., 190.

22. Handel, op cit., 52-53.

23. Special Subcommittee on Close Air Support of the Preparedness Investigating Subcommittee of the Committee on Armed Services, United States Senate, "Report on Close Air Support' (Washington, DC, 1972), 15.

24. Handel, op cit., 34-35.

25. Davis, op cit., 8.

26. Futrell, op cit., 659-60.

27. National Security Act, 1947, Wolf, op cit., 63-83.

28. Executive Order 9877, "Functions of the Armed Force" (26 July 1947), Wolf, op cit. 87-90.

29. "The Key West Agreement," Wolf, op cit., 154-166.

30. James M. Gavin, War and Peace in the Space Age (New York, 1958), 109.

31. Christopher C.S. Cheng, Air Mobility: The Development of a Doctrine (Westport, CT., 1994), 19-20.

32. Davis, op cit., 10-11.

33. Futrell, op cit., 660-1.

34. J. Hunter Reinburg, "Close Air Support," Congressional Record (17 May 1962), A3712-3713.

35. Ibid., 16-19; Handel, op cit., 37-40; AFM1-2 (1959), 7-8 & 13 & see also Chichowski, op cit.

36. Edwin L. Powell, BG., Interview, Senior Officer Oral History Program, US Army Military History Institute (hereinafter referred to as MHI), Carlisle Barracks, PA. (1978), tape 1, transcript 50.

37. Ibid., tape 1, transcript, 32.

38. Harold K. Johnson, Gen, Interview, Senior Officer Oral History Program, MHI, 1972-3, Vol. II, tape 8, interview 8, transcript, 36; Earl H. Tilford, Setup: What the Air Force Did in Vietnam and Why (Maxwell AFB, AL, 1991), 32-33 & Alain C. Enthoven & Wayne K. Smith, How Much is Enough? Shaping the Defense Program, 1961-1969 (New York, 1972), 9.

39. Gabriel P. Disosway, Gen, USAF, Interview, US Air Force Oral History Program, Air Force Historical Research Agency, Maxwell AFB, AL, 1977, pp. 196-197 & Caroline F. Ziemke, "In the Shadow of the Giant: USAF Tactical Air Command in the Era of Strategic Bombing, 1945-1955," Unpublished PhD. thesis (The Ohio State University, 1989), 302.

40. Disosway, op cit., 246-247 & Tilford, op cit., 36.

41. Delbert Bristol, Col, Interview, Senior Officer Oral History Program, MHI, Carlisle, PA, 1978, tape 1, transcript, 12-13.

42. Memorandum by the Secretary of Defense for the Members of the Armed Forces Policy Council, Subject: "Clarification of Roles and Missions to Improve the Effectiveness of Operation of the Department of Defense," 26 November 1956, Wolf, op cit., 293-301.

43. Edward L. Rowny, It Takes One to Tango (Washington, DC, 1992), 15-16.

44. Davis, op cit., 13.

45. In fact the term "air assault' is still customary for airmobile operations,

whether opposed or not.

46. Gavin, War and Peace in the Space Age, 109.

47. Cheng, op cit., 19-20 & Wolf, op cit., 237.

48. Bristol, op cit., tape 1, transcript, 14.

49. Cheng, op cit., 33-34.

50. Memorandum of Understanding between the Secretary of the Army and the Secretary of the Air Force, 2 October 1951, Wolf, op cit., 237-240.

51. Davis, op cit., 23.

52. Memorandum of Understanding Relating to Army Organic Aviation between Secretary of the Army Frank Pace Jr. & Secretary of the Air Force Thomas K. Finletter (hereafter cited as "Pace-Finletter Agreement," 4 November 1952, Wolf, op cit., 243-245.

53. Ray L. Bowers, The United States Air Force in Southeast Asia, Tactical Airlift (Washington, DC: Office of Air Force History, 1983), 29.

54. Bristol, op cit., tape 1, transcript 22-23.

55. Pace-Finletter Agreement, 4 November 1952, Wolf, op cit., 243-244.

56. Bowers, op cit., 30.

57. Wolf, op cit., 241.

58. Tilford, op cit, 8-9

59. Ziemke, op cit., 302.

60. Pace-Finletter Agreement, 4 November 1952, Wolf, op cit., 243.

61. Ironically, Rowny's extracurricular activities were brought to the attention of the Army Chief of Staff by Army reserve Captain, Congressman Henry Jackson (WA) who, having attended one of the sessions, was so impressed that he wanted Rowny's ideas established as Army doctrine. Rowny, op cit., 15-16.

62. Kenneth J. Clifford, Progress and Purpose: A Developmental History of the United States Marine Corps, 1900-1970 (Washington, DC, History and Museums Division, Head Quarters United States Marine Corps, 1973), 71-72.

63. Ibid., 73-7 & 84.

64. Ibid., 82-83.

65. Ibid., 104.

66. John J. Tolson, Vietnam Studies, Airmobility (Washington DC, Department of the Army, 1973), 4.

67. Vincent Demma, "War Gaming and Simulation in the Development of the 11th Air Assault Division" (Washington DC, US Army Center of Military History [hereinafter referred to as CMH] Information Paper, 1992), 4.

68. Frederic A. Bergerson, The Army Gets an Air Force: Tactics of Insurgent Bureaucratic Politics (Baltimore, 1980), 72-78.

69. Hamilton H. Howze, The Howze Board, Army (February 1974), 12.

70. Clarification of Roles and Missions, 26 November 1956, Wolf, op cit., 296-297.

71. Ibid., pp. 295-300. Doubt was cast on the Air Force's exclusive responsibility for the delivery of United States' strategic nuclear weapons by the development of ballistic missile technology. For a time, both the Army and the Air Force worked on their own strategic missile systems until the Wilson memo served

notice on the Army team, led by Wernher Von Braun, at Huntsville, Alabama. Von Braun's team remained intact and became the research organisation which developed the boosters for the American Apollo moon shot program of the 1960s and 1970s.

72. Cheng, op cit., 106.

73. Ibid., 107.

74. Ibid., 142, n. 87.

75. Gavin, 109-111.

76. Bowers, op cit., 29.

77. Clarification of Roles and Missions to Improve the Effectiveness of Operation of the Department of Defense, 26 November 1956, Wolf, op cit., 295-296.

78. Gavin wrote a still earlier article entitled "The Future of Armor" (1947) in which he argued that armour must be lightened to permit its transportation into battle by air. James M. Gavin, "Cavalry and I Don't Mean Horses," Harpers (April 1954), 54-60 & War and Peace in the Space Age, 100.

79. Bristol, op cit., tape 1, transcript, 49.

80. Hamilton H. Howze, A Cavalryman's Story: Memoirs of a Twentieth Century Army General (Washington, DC, 1996), 192-193.

81. Howze, "The Howze Board," 13.

82. Howze, A Cavalryman's Story, 185-186.

83. Howze, "The Howze Board," 14.

84. Howze, A Cavalryman's Story, 185.

85. Howze, "The Howze Board," 12.

# CHAPTER 2

## COMPETING VISIONS OF AIRMOBILITY:
## THE HOWZE AND DISOSWAY REPORTS OF 1962

*The Army should proceed vigorously and at once in
the development of fighting units (which may be called
air cavalry) whose mode of tactical employment will
take maximum advantage of the unique mobility and
flexibility of light aircraft—aircraft which will be
employed to provide, for the execution of the missions
assigned these units, not only mobility for the relatively
few riflemen and machine gunners, but also direct fire
support, artillery and missile fire adjustment, command,
communications, security, reconnaissance, and supply.*[1]

As we saw in the previous chapter, a number of aviation enthusiasts
within the United States Army were able to build up a considerable body of
airmobile doctrine during the 1950s, despite the lack of commitment of many
of their service colleagues, and the existence of an associated interservice
dispute with the Air Force. In the early 1960s, some of these same Army
officers found the opportunity both to promote and perfect a vision of
airmobility to the point where it was ready for battlefield application. Field
tests, war games and operational studies of an Army airmobility concept
suggested that the new techniques had application across much of the
spectrum of military activity in which the service might become involved,
but airmobility seemed to offer particular advantages on the low-intensity,
counterinsurgency battlefield with which the Army might have to contend
in Vietnam or Laos. Army airmobility proponents were not slow to exploit
this counterinsurgency connection as a means of securing the support of the
Kennedy administration for their own plans.

Always the subject of hostility from the Air Force, the crystallization
of the Army's thoughts on airmobility forced the Air Force to respond with
its own alternative airmobility concept. Ultimately, the Army's version
won through over that of the Air Force, but the realization of the full Army
airmobility vision, as foreseen by its advocates within the service, proved
too rich for Secretary of Defense Robert S. McNamara's blood and only a
limited "immobilization" of the service's table of organization took place.
Nevertheless, airmobility was to have a dramatic effect on the manner of the
US Army's prosecution of its war in Southeast Asia, where it continued to be
a source of dispute with the Air Force.

## THE HOWZE BOARD

In 1960, the Army Aircraft Requirements Review—or Rogers—Board called for a considerable increase in Army airlift capability to supplement ground transportation, but it did not recommend the Army's wholesale adoption of airmobility as we now understand the concept. Indeed, this would have been beyond the board's purview, but its report did include Lieutenant General Hamilton H. Howze's memorandum on "The Requirement for Air Fighting Units," and it did recommend the preparation of an associated study on the practicality of such units and whether an experimental unit should be established to test the concept.[2]

The following year, as part of a general survey of military spending, McNamara's Department of Defense instituted a review of the Army's aviation plans.[3] As part of this process, the Army submitted studies of its entire aviation program and its specific plans for the Fiscal Year 1963 budget to the Office of the Secretary of Defense.[4] The Office of the Secretary of Defense ordered Colonel Robert R. Williams, then a staff officer in the Office of the Assistant Director (Tactical Weapons), Office of the Director of Defense Research and Engineering, US Army Element of the Office of the Secretary of Defense, to prepare a response from the Secretary to the Army's studies.[5] The reader will recall that Williams's previous assignment had been as Chief of the Air Mobility Division of the Army's Office of the Chief of Research and Development and that Williams himself had initiated the establishment of the Rogers Board on which he served as secretary. An Army pilot, Colonel Williams had also been the first President of the Army Aviation Board between 1955 and 1958.

Williams concluded that the service had not established a "coherent" rationale behind its aircraft procurement plans; therefore, these plans were not based on the Army's real needs since the Army did not actually know what these were. In the process of preparing his response to the Army's studies, Williams consulted with "certain people" on the Army General Staff, including Lieutenant General Arthur G. Trudeau who, as Army Chief of Research and Development, had previously been Williams's boss. At the conclusion of his tour at the Pentagon, Williams passed on to his replacement in the Office of the Secretary of Defense, Colonel Edwin L. Powell, the task of completing the draft response to the Army's studies. On his departure from the Pentagon for the US Army Aviation Center at Fort Rucker, Alabama, Williams insisted to Colonel Powell that the form finally selected by the Secretary of Defense be the "right thing," that is one that would encourage the development of Army airmobility.[6]

The approval of these "certain" senior Army officers should not be construed as evidence of a commitment at the highest levels to airmobility. Most of the Army was, in fact, opposed to its development on the grounds that precious resources were more urgently needed elsewhere, and there was considerable skepticism in the Army as to whether airmobility—dependent as it was on the fragile helicopter—could work in practice.[7] Williams and Powell were Army aviation proponents. As such, they were members of an insignificant minority within an Army whose leadership was dedicated to the kind of mechanized warfare that had brought it so much glory in the European theater at the end of the Second World War. In 1962, they found themselves in uniquely influential positions where they were able to realize their own minority views through the medium of the Secretary of Defense himself.

Williams and Powell prepared two memoranda from Secretary McNamara to Secretary of the Army Elvis J. Stahr Jr., one formal and the other a more "personal" note. In these two "airmobility memoranda," Williams and Powell proposed the establishment of another Army board to assess the potential of aviation for the service and identify any new formations and aircraft required for the realization of airmobility in the light of the new opportunities offered by advances in aircraft technology. In particular, they suggested that aircraft offered the Army considerable increases in tactical mobility, but, significantly, they also referred to the use of aircraft as "weapons platforms." Williams and Powell asked whether new vertical take-off and landing (V/TOL) or short take-off and landing (STOL) fixed-wing aircraft designs might constitute cheaper alternatives to helicopters and they also suggested that, "Consideration should be given to completely air-mobile infantry, antitank, reconnaissance, and artillery units." As a starting point, the Army should use existing unimplemented studies of airmobile divisions and their subordinate units including "aerial artillery," but this time "bold new ideas . . . [must] be protected from veto or dilution by conservative staff review."[8] Aware that costs were never far from McNamara's mind, Williams and Powell also asserted that the Army's adoption of airmobility would go hand-in-hand with a reduction in less efficient ground transport resulting in no net increase in expenditure. They even went so far as to recommend to the Secretary specific officers and civilians to sit on the proposed board, to be led by General Howze, then commanding the XVIII Airborne Corps at Fort Bragg, North Carolina. Another Army pilot, Howze was, as we have seen, also a long-time Army aviation enthusiast. He had been Director of Army Aviation between 1954 and 1957 and he had also been a member of the Rogers Board. On 19 April 1962, under his own signature, McNamara passed the two airmobility memoranda, as prepared by Williams and Powell, to Secretary of the Army Elvis J. Stahr Jr.

That McNamara did not originate the memoranda that stimulated the formal introduction of airmobility into the US Army, and which bear his name, should not surprise us. It is, of course, perfectly natural that in a complex bureaucracy like the Department of Defense, the Secretary should delegate authority to members of his staff. It is equally understandable that one of the roles of the Office of the Secretary of Defense should be to formulate policy options for acceptance or rejection by the Secretary, and that this responsibility should extend to the actual drafting of policy initiative memoranda. The significance of these particular policy proposals lay in the fact that they represented the views of the members of one particularly zealous faction within just one of the armed services.

Williams and Powell were part of an Army aviation brotherhood whose views were not necessarily shared by the Army's more conservative leaders. They put forward proposals that conformed to their own special project for Army aviation and those proposals obviously found favor with the Secretary of Defense himself. They appealed to McNamara because they offered the prospect of increased efficiency in terms of a more mobile Army with only a slight increase, or perhaps even no increase, in overall costs. This was attractive in terms of both the conventional, and the nuclear battlefield where increased Army mobility offered the prospect of easy dispersal from the threat of enemy nuclear firepower. McNamara, therefore, adhered to the airmobility memoranda format put forward by Williams and Powell, one that was designed to override any conservative inertia within the Army's senior leadership.

Indeed, the results of the proposed Army study were presupposed by the final paragraph of McNamara's "personal memo" to Secretary Stahr: "I should be disappointed if the Army's re-examination merely produces logistics-oriented recommendations to procure more of the same, rather than a plan for implementing fresh and perhaps unorthodox concepts which will give us a significant increase in mobility." The Army must produce a more radical vision based on airmobility and, at the urging of Williams and Powell, McNamara pressed an airmobility board membership on the Army composed largely of Army aviation or airborne officers predisposed to finding in favor of the airmobility concept.[9]

The Army rose to the occasion by establishing a Tactical Mobility Requirements Board, under Howze's chairmanship, to explore the new opportunities offered to the Army by aircraft. On 20 August 1962, the Howze Board submitted a report that fully lived up to the expectations implied by McNamara's memos.

Until the time of McNamara's memoranda airmobility doctrine in the Army had outrun the technology required to realize it, but by 1962, airmobility was an idea whose technological time had come with the introduction of the turbine powered UH-1 (Huey) series helicopter into the Army inventory; new technologies like vectored thrust and tilting rotors offered even greater possibilities for the future. It might be said, therefore, that technology was driving the development of airmobility. However, there seems no doubt that airmobility's proponents within the Army sincerely believed that the concept would generate great improvements in military efficiency. The development of airmobility cannot, therefore, be said to be the application of technology for technology's sake.

In order to produce its report, the Howze Board conducted a series of field tests and war games comparing formations equipped with organic aircraft against conventional infantry and mechanized divisions in counterinsurgency operations in Southeast Asia, unsophisticated conventional warfare in the Middle East and Southeast Asia, and sophisticated non-nuclear war in Europe and Korea. Approximately forty tests took place over an eleven-week period at Fort Bragg, for which 150 Army aircraft were assembled plus, for one week, sixteen Air Force C-130 Hercules transports. Elements of the 82nd Airborne Division provided the necessary ground troops.

Largest of the field tests were three exercises in which Army aircraft were substituted for ground vehicles. These emphasized warfare in East Asia and in particular low-intensity warfare in Southeast Asia. The first of these exercises, STEW-62, re-enacted a situation from the First Indochina War with the movement of an airmobile task force two hundred miles from Fort Bragg to the swamps of Georgia. This utilized Air Force aircraft to place the Army units in a position from which they could mount an "airmobile assault" against an irregular enemy. KILL QUICK-62 took place in the Appalachian Mountains and simulated counterinsurgency operations in Laos. PUSAN-62 re-enacted some regiment-size operations from the 1950 defense of the Pusan perimeter during the Korean War.[10]

The Board employed eight different war games, set in Western Europe, Southeast Asia, the Middle East and North East Asia, first simulating conventional organizations and then repeating the exercises with airmobile units. The Board did not, however, consider the gaming definitive and believed that they should continue after the preparation of the Board's report.[11]

In addition to the tests and war games conducted in the United States, a team of representatives from the Howze Board visited Vietnam between 30 June and 7 July. The team came to believe that airmobility offered solutions to a number of the tactical and logistical difficulties presented by the war in Vietnam and recommended the employment of three air assault divisions there.[12]

According to the Board's analysis, airmobile units would enjoy considerable advantages over conventional units on account of their maneuverability and firepower, with the greatest advantages accruing in the unsophisticated conventional environment, followed by the counterinsurgency environment. The new formations were likely to perform at their worst in sophisticated conventional warfare.[13]

Given the Kennedy administration's interest in low-intensity warfare, and against the background of the struggle in Vietnam, it was no accident that the Howze Board emphasized this type of conflict in its deliberations. The counterinsurgency potential of airmobility was particularly significant: airmobile forces promised the ability to patrol large areas of difficult third-world terrain and, having found the enemy, fix him in place while rapidly concentrating the firepower to eliminate him before he melted back into the countryside. This would free the Army from the theoretical ideal ratio of ten security troops to every one insurgent. Thus, airmobility represented a potential force multiplier on the low-intensity battlefield. To this extent, the real battlefield requirements of Vietnam drove the development of airmobility. It is no surprise, therefore, that an airmobile unit—the 1st Air Cavalry Division (Airmobile)—was the first US Army combat unit ordered to Vietnam by President Lyndon Johnson in 1965.

In the Howze concept, Army airmobile forces would be reliant on the Air Force and the Navy for air and sea lift to the theater of operations and for "as much intra-theater airlift as possible," but in battle, airmobile troops would be supported by fire from organic Army attack aircraft, both fixed- and rotary-wing.[14] The Board concluded that Air Force C-130 transports would be unable to operate from the rough forward strips from which the airmobile troops would enter the battle. And that those troops would, therefore, best be served by fixed- and rotary-wing transport aircraft also provided by the Army itself.[15]

Some aviation enthusiasts within the Army may have desired a fully airmobile force, but the Howze deliberations suggested a continuing requirement for conventional formations, enhanced by airmobile units.[16] The Board, therefore, recommended a partial "airmobilization" of the Army by the conversion of five out of the Army's then current peacetime strength of sixteen divisions to airmobile "Air Assault Divisions." The eleven unconverted divisions would remain as conventional formations with augmentation by additional aircraft. Such a proposal had the merit of conforming to McNamara's apparent requirement for radical innovation while still appearing to be a compromise between the Army's adherence to the principles of conventional mechanized warfare and the new airmobility doctrine. The conversion of the divisions to airmobility would also be a gradual process phased over a period of five years or so.[17]

The timing of the emergence of airmobility was apposite in that it occurred at about the same time the Army was undergoing a process of conversion from the "Pentomic" (for "pentagonal atomic") structure of the late 1950s that had emphasized nuclear over conventional war fighting capabilities, consistent with the Eisenhower administration's policy of "massive retaliation," to a structure that emphasized conventional over nuclear war fighting capabilities and counterinsurgency, consistent with McNamara's own policy of "flexible response." The new reorganization objective, army divisions (ROAD) were to be more maneuverable than their Pentomic forbears, they were to have more organic aircraft and there was to be a greater emphasis on air transportability. The Howze Board took the ROAD organization as its starting point, recommending a force structure that combined air assault and ROAD divisions where the air assault divisions were organized on the same principle as the ROAD divisions.[18] Thus, while the Howze Board's airmobility concept represented dramatic doctrinal developments and the massive expansion of Army aviation, it had at its core the more efficient realization of McNamara's own established policy objectives, and it remained compatible with the Army's ROAD reorganization.

Each of the new Air Assault Divisions would have some 459 fixed- and rotary-wing aircraft, including enough transport aircraft to lift one third of its combat strength in a single lift. To make this possible, the new division, as McNamara had hoped, would have approximately only one third as many ground vehicles as a conventional infantry division. It would also have less artillery, but in order to compensate for the shortfall in fire support, each Air Assault Division would have its own organic air support in the shape of 36 UH-1B rocket-armed attack helicopters and 24 AV-1 Mohawk fixed-wing attack aircraft. If the Howze proposals were fully implemented, the Army's aviation inventory would rise from 4,887 aircraft in 1962—a figure about which the Air Force was already vexed—to 10,608 aircraft in the period 1963 to 1968, a dramatic increase in the Army's aviation assets.[19]

In the Howze Board's airmobile concept, Air Assault Divisions would establish secure bases supported by the Air Force's Air Transport Command. From these bases, small Army tactical transport aircraft, both fixed- and rotary-wing, would supply rough forward air strips up to one hundred kilometers away, from which would operate the division's airmobile brigade task forces, flown into battle by Army helicopters and supported by fire from organic Army attack aircraft—again both fixed- and rotary-wing.[20]

In addition to new airmobile formations and the aviation augmentation of existing formations, the Howze Board also discussed the development of a new family of aircraft to equip these units. The backbone of the Army's aviation assets in the period 1963 to 1968 would be provided by variants of the UH-1 utility helicopter. Of these, the UH-1B attack helicopter would be available in 1963, with the AH-1G Cobra attack helicopter becoming available in 1964. The latter aircraft would use the engines and many other common components from the UH-1 helicopter, but in a completely redesigned airframe with an extensive weapons fit to produce the first truly dedicated attack helicopter.

In the shape of the Cobra, the Army would have a real "helicopter fighter," but even this was likely to be replaced by a future "SA" or Surveillance Attack V/STOL aircraft that would also replace the O/AV-1 Mohawk fixed-wing aircraft. The Board anticipated that a number of 1960s aircraft research programs might contribute data to the SA, an aircraft that would have a maximum speed of mach 0.9. These programs included the British Hawker Siddely P-1127 jet V/STOL project, later developed as the Harrier combat aircraft, acquired by the British Royal Air Force and other world armed services including the United States Marine Corps. Thus, the Board was anticipating the use by the Army of dedicated "fighter" helicopters and jet-powered, V/STOL fixed-wing fighter aircraft.

For the transport role between its secure bases and forward strips, the Army would, in the immediate future, use its CH-47 Chinook helicopters and its CV-2 Caribou fixed-wing transport planes, plus its UH-1 utility helicopters. The use of the CV-2 in Vietnam was to prove particularly galling for Air Force officers, many of which believed Air Force transport aircraft could better fulfill its role and that, in any case, all fixed-wing aircraft should be operated by the Air Force. The dispute over the CV-2 was to result in the 1966 decision by which the Army renounced its CV-2s to the Air Force (where they were re-designated C-7s) in return for the Army's retention of the armed helicopter.

However, in the early 1960s, the Army had no intention of getting out of the fixed-wing business. The Rogers Board had declared that the ideal transport aircraft would combine the best attributes of the CH-47 helicopter and the CV-2 fixed-wing transport aircraft in a V/STOL airframe, but since these were then new aircraft, the Board deemed it too early to specify a replacement. As a result, the Army became involved in a tri-service V/STOL research program designed to yield what the Board described as a medium tactical transport (MTT) V/STOL aircraft which it hoped would replace the CH-47 and CV-2 around 1970.[21] The resulting three- to five-ton (US) aircraft was unlikely to be a conventional helicopter and one of the research programs involved a "tilt-wing" design, a principle subsequently adopted by the Marine Corps with its V-22 Osprey transport aircraft.

The Board also anticipated a light tactical transport (LTT) V/TOL aircraft which might use similar technology and which would replace the entire UH-1 utility helicopter fleet from about 1973 onwards. Thus, the Board suggested the replacement of the most numerous and important Army aircraft types by a family of aircraft, few of which might actually be helicopters in the conventional sense, including jet V/STOL fixed-wing aircraft and various other V/STOL designs such as tilting wings, tilting ducts, and gimballing propellers.

Most radically, the Board anticipated the development of an entirely new type of aircraft: the Artillery V/TOL platform, essentially a flying artillery piece it would provide the airmobile formations with indirect fire support from ground sites from which it could be rapidly re-deployed. To be available in the mid-1970s, the artillery V/TOL platform would have a secondary mission of providing direct fire support for ground units, both from the ground and from the air, furnishing the Army with yet another combat aircraft.[22]

The drafters of the Howze Report were clearly aware that, in proposing a massive increase in Army aviation, including the use of organic Army fixed- and rotary-wing aircraft in the attack role, they were treading on extremely sensitive ground with regard to the division of roles and missions between the services, specifically between the Army and the Air Force. The Board was, therefore, at pains to point out that should the Army concept be adopted, the Air Force "will retain practically all of the vitally important functions it now carries with respect to the support of the land battle . . . "[23] This was really a polite way of acknowledging that the Air Force would lose at least some of those functions.

Here, the Board's conclusions may have been influenced by the Army's long-standing dissatisfaction with the quality of the close air support it received from the Air Force. Indeed, the Board suggested, by implication, the Air Force had failed to fulfill certain close air support functions and that these should, therefore, more properly be taken over by the Army. Andrew F. Krepinevich has argued that this was one of the driving forces behind airmobility, but not necessarily in the sense that the Army insisted on assuming the close support role in the first instance. Rather airmobility's justification of Army attack aircraft served as a threat to force the Air Force into providing a better close air support service, or face the prospect of renouncing the role entirely.[24]

According to the Howze Board, existing Air Force aircraft and command and control systems were not optimized for close air support, and they believed that the very high performance of Air Force aircraft detracted from their ability to provide effective close air support, while slower-moving Army aircraft might be better suited to the role. They, therefore, recommended that studies be made of the requirement for "intermediate performance fighter-bombers in joint operations," but insisted that this "should not delay the incorporation of light attack aircraft into the Army structure," as recommended elsewhere in the report.[25]

Whatever the truth of Krepinevich's claims, the Howze Board preferred to suggest that Air Force concerns about Army duplication of its roles and missions were actually groundless. These concerns, said the Board, had only led to the creation of a vacuum in close air support where neither service operated, but where, if released from artificial limitations on weight and firepower, Army aircraft would be most suitable.

The Howze Board insisted that Air Force fighter-bombers would still be required to support the Army on the ground, but the Board's conception of this support was at once both broad and limited. It was broad in the sense that the Board interpreted support of the ground battle to include air defense, interdiction of the combat area and deep reconnaissance. It was limited in the sense that while the Board believed Air Force fighter-bombers should continue to provide close air support to ground troops in contact with the enemy, it had reservations about the Air Force's ability to completely fulfill the Army's requirements for this role.

The members of the Howze Board agreed that the Air Force command and control system provided the "very desirable capability" for concentration of airpower on a "single target system." However, they also felt that this was not necessarily consistent with the close air support needs of the Army, many of which could only be provided by organic Army aircraft whose relationship with the supported units must inevitably be more intimate than could ever be achieved by aircraft from a separate service. Thus, in the Board's view, while "the Army should remain dependent on the Air Force for the greater part of the weight of close air support," airborne firepower should be, in accordance with the Air Force view, concentrated where it was required the most.[26] This was an attempt by the Howze Board to both have its aviation cake and eat it, too. For it could mean the concentration of both Air Force and Army aircraft in support of ground troops in contact with the enemy, but the Army would be under no similar obligation to support Air Force operations away from the ground combat zone with its own aircraft.

46

The good performance of airmobile units in counterinsurgency warfare—an aspect of "special warfare" in Army parlance—that seemed to be indicated by the tests, war games and analysis carried out by the Howze Board, prompted it to drop another bombshell for the Air Force by insisting that "counterinsurgency operations are basically an aspect of land warfare" to which "Army aircraft are particularly well suited." It followed, therefore, said the Board, that the Army should be charged with the supervision and training of foreign personnel employing these types of aircraft whether they are assigned to the local army or air force."[27]

Not surprisingly, the Air Force's senior leadership was shocked by the Howze Board proposals. The resulting controversy triggered Congressional debate and, incidentally, heightened opposition to the airmobile concept from Army conservatives.[28] Naturally, the Air Force rejected the Howze Board's rationale for the introduction of its concept of airmobility, with its concomitant encroachment on Air Force roles and missions, and responded by commissioning its own tactical air support study under General Gabriel P. Disosway.

## THE DISOSWAY REPORT

The Air Force's Tactical Air Support Evaluation Board saw the Howze Report as a wholesale assault on Air Force roles and missions. To the members of the Air Force Board it seemed that the Army was seeking to gain control of the intra-theater airlift, close air support, escort and even interdiction roles from the Air Force.[29] The Board rejected the idea of specialized Army airmobile units with their own organic air support on the grounds that this contravened the tenet of the centralization of airpower under single (Air Force) control that had been a founding principle of the United States Air Force.

The Disosway Board drew attention to Howze's proposal for an Air Transport Brigade. This was a corps-level unit intended to support divisions to which it was not organic. The Disosway Board argued that this flew in the face of the Army's own argument that aviation assets could only be really responsive if they were organic to specific Army formations. For the Disosway Board, this raised the prospect that if the Army was to develop an aviation capability of the magnitude envisioned by the Howze Report, it would soon metamorphose into another centrally controlled "air force" in direct competition with the USAF.[30]

Despite the Howze Board's claims that Army aircraft were less vulnerable than had previously been thought, Disosway and his colleagues found nothing in the Howze Report to contradict their belief that the Air Force's high performance aircraft were both more flexible and more likely to survive combat than the Army's lower-performance machines.[31] For the Disosway Board, the tactical deployment of large numbers of ground troops by helicopter in the face of the intense air defense environment presented by the Warsaw Pact's forces would be quite impossible without unacceptable losses.[32]

The dispute between the Army and the Air Force over helicopters was long-standing and was especially bitter over the Army's arming of rotary-wing aircraft. For many Air Force officers, the adoption of helicopters by the Army was an underhanded move to cash in on the fact that the roles of helicopters, were less-clearly defined than those of fixed-wing aircraft, but while they did not want the Army to take over Air Force missions with helicopters they also did not themselves want these slow and ungainly vehicles. It seemed to the Disosway Board that the Army was merely using the helicopter as a "stepping stone" toward grabbing control of established Air Force missions.[33]

Perhaps even more controversial was the Army's use of fixed-wing aircraft in roles far removed from the Army cooperation missions to which they had originally been confined. The Air Force was bitterly opposed to the Army's CV-2 and O/AV-1 programs, but worse, appeared to be on the horizon in the shape of the Army's Surveillance Attack aircraft. This would clearly be a jet aircraft and, given Army interest in the P-1127 for the role, the Air Force was concerned that the Army might even be considering the planned supersonic derivative of this aircraft—the P-1154—for its post-1968 plans.[34]

Disosway questioned Army specifications for fixed-wing aircraft on the grounds that existing Air Force aircraft could already provide tactical airmobility in the combat zone. According to the Board, the Air Force's C-130 Hercules and C-123 Provider transport aircraft were already capable of distributing supplies and troops to the type of forward airstrips envisioned by the Howze Board.[35] From there, they could be shuttled into battle by a limited number of helicopters. The Board held that 168 Air Force C-130s could provide the same support that, in Howze's concept, required 106 Air Force C-130s plus 775 Army fixed- and rotary-wing transport aircraft.[36]

Disosway rejected the Howze Board's claims that Air Force transport aircraft often would be unable to land close enough to Army units in the field, and in the Air Force's defense, pointed out that Howze himself had praised the "exceptional STOL characteristics" of the C-130 that "should be fully exploited in combat operations." This was disingenuous. While the Howze report did include praise for the C-130's capabilities, it still found in favor of the Army's own CV-2—a considerably smaller aircraft—for the supply of rough sites in the field. In a more telling criticism, the Disosway Board raised the question of the massive logistical problem in terms of petroleum, oil and lubricants, which might be raised by the Army's deployment of the thousands of aircraft required to realize its airmobility mission.[38]

Accepting the Army's use of helicopters for limited reconnaissance and utility purposes, the Disosway Board rejected the service's use of actual combat aircraft, especially jets. The Board felt that these were roles in which the Air Force already had an ample capability, and which would only be duplicated under the Army's scheme.[39] The Board argued that Air Force fixed-wing, high-performance aircraft were quite capable of providing close air support and were more likely to survive the ordeal than Army machines. The Disosway Board asserted that the AV-1, proposed by Howze as the Army's fixed-wing attack aircraft, compared very unfavorably with the F-4C Phantom the Air Force was then acquiring.

The Air Force Board also considered helicopters too slow, fragile and unstable for the combat role. The reliance of Army airmobile units on helicopters would, it was argued, be impractical in all but low-intensity warfare like that in Vietnam. The Disosway Board held that Howze's emphasis on counterinsurgency represented little more than a cynical attempt to exploit President John F. Kennedy's interest in the subject in order to establish an air support role for Army aviation.[40] In 1962, all the US armed forces saw Vietnam as an aberration from the real business of general war with the Warsaw Pact, Kennedy's Green Berets, notwithstanding. Therefore, in the Disosway Board's view, the Howze formulation would be of narrow application in addition to being prohibitively expensive. Furthermore, it rejected Howze's request for exclusive Army responsibility for counterinsurgency aviation operations on the grounds that the Air Force already had a counterinsurgency capability.[41]

Disosway sought to invalidate the Howze proposals by refuting most of them, but his report was slightly subtler than this. To some extent, Disosway accepted the challenge presented by the Howze Report by responding with two main proposals: he acknowledged that the Army was dissatisfied with the Air Force's provision of close air support and recommended the provision of more Air Force tactical fighter wings along with an accelerated program of F-4C Phantom procurement. The report even proposed the adoption by the Air Force of a V/STOL aircraft for tactical air support purposes.

Disosway's second major proposal was that the Air Force should develop its own airmobility concept. In the Howze Board's conception, the Army would adopt organic aviation and thus, "the Army would get an air force." The Air Force concept was, by contrast, less radical as it did not involve the "Air Force getting an army"—though that idea was not entirely without precedent. As Disosway pointed out, the Howze Board had not considered ways in which Air Force aircraft might contribute to increases in Army tactical mobility. Instead, Howze had interpreted his brief from the Secretary of Defense as requiring exclusive reliance on Army aviation resources.[42]

In the Air Force plan, regular Army divisions would have their mobility and effectiveness enhanced by the addition of Air Force units. This would leave the divisions in possession of all their vehicles and artillery should the tactical situation require them. Since this did not involve "over-specialization" of the augmented divisions, the Air Force argued that it was both, more efficient and economical than the Army concept. Significantly, in order to integrate the Air Force support with the Army ground units, Army divisions employing the Air Force concept would require a joint command element.[43]

Ultimately, Disosway recommended that the studies of airmobility should continue with the involvement of both the Army and the Air Force. According to the Disosway Board, joint testing of both airmobility proposals should take place and procurement of CV-2s and O/AV-1s should cease immediately.

This would only be necessary if the Howze Report successfully ran the gauntlet of the Army's senior commanders who were not naturally disposed to airmobility. Once again, it was Colonel Robert Williams who was able to presume upon Army Chief of Staff, General Earle Wheeler, to act upon the report's main recommendations.[44] Given the origins of the report in the Secretary of Defense's office, it is also quite likely that McNamara's influence was also important here.

The Howze Board's "single conclusion" was that the "adoption by the Army of the airmobile concept . . . is necessary and desirable," but the report was ambiguous as to how the Army should proceed.[45] As we have seen, the Board recommended that the Army convert five of its existing sixteen divisions to "Air Assault Divisions" between 1963 and 1968. This implied that the Army undertake an immediate commitment to airmobility, in accordance with the outline laid out in the Howze Report, and begin converting its existing divisions to airmobile formations at once.

This was the view taken by Howze himself. In late 1962, he tried to convince Secretary of the Army, Cyrus Vance, and General Wheeler to begin the process by converting the 82nd Airborne Division into an Air Assault Division while retaining its parachute capability. However, the Howze Board had also recommended a continued program of field tests and war games to perfect the airmobile concept. Howze believed that his Board had conducted enough tests to prove the validity of the Army airmobility concept, but Vance and Wheeler informed Howze that McNamara required more evidence as a prerequisite for its adoption.[46]

McNamara had supported Army airmobility in the creation of a Tactical Mobility Requirements Board predisposed to finding in its favor. He would continue to support the concept in its official adoption by the Army, but it is probable that he did not fully appreciate the full significance and possible consequences of his 1962 airmobility memoranda. As we have seen, the Howze Report recommended the conversion to air assault status of nearly one third of the Army's front-line strength. This would have involved a dramatic increase in Army aviation, and the adoption of the associated doctrine threatened an explosion of the simmering roles and missions dispute with the Air Force. Moreover, despite claims to the contrary, "airmobilization" was unlikely to be cost neutral.[47] McNamara's office, therefore, began to express reservations about the Howze recommendations and, although he praised the Howze Report, McNamara himself also expressed some public criticisms before the House of Representatives in February 1963.[48] Of particular concern to the OSD was the Howze recommendations' reliance on helicopters when light fixed-wing aircraft might have done the job more efficiently, the small payload of the Army CV-2 transport compared with the Air Force C-130 transport, and the roles and missions controversy over the O/AV-1. In the latter case the OSD was concerned about the clash between the different management philosophies of the two services, specifically centralized versus decentralized control of airpower assets.[49] Consequently, McNamara rejected Howze's recommendation for further testing of the Army concept in parallel with its adoption by the service.

Instead, the Army was to form an experimental Air Assault Division as a test bed for the Howze airmobility concept. This unit was designated the 11th Air Assault Division and placed under the command of General Harry O. Kinnard, a logical choice for the job, having been a long-time proponent of Army aviation, particularly, the Army's use of the helicopters.[50] Despite Howze's opposition to a further period of testing, Wheeler wanted him to continue to lead the Army's airmobility project by assuming command of the Test Evaluation and Control Group that would oversee the 11th Air Assault Division tests. However, the Cuban Missile Crisis of October 1962 resulted in Howze's recall to his corps. Wheeler, therefore, selected Williams, now a Brigadier General, for the role.[51] Thus, the person principally responsible for stimulating the examination of airmobility by the Army was also given the responsibility for evaluating the performance of the concept in field exercises.

Both the 11th Air Assault Division and the Test Evaluation and Control group were placed under the authority of the Commanding General of the US 3rd Army, Lieutenant General C.W.G. Rich, who established an exercise direction group for the tests designated Field Project TEAM (provisional) (Test Evaluation of Air Mobility).

The 11th Air Assault Division tests were unilateral Army exercises, although they did involve the provision of some support by Air Force units. The Joint Chiefs of Staff, however, given the Department of Defense's developing reservations about the Howze Report, committed themselves to testing both the Army airmobility concept arising from the Howze Board, and the Air Force alternative arising from the Disosway Board, in comparative divisional exercises under the authority of Strike Command. The Strike Command was a joint Army-Air Force command established to carry out joint exercises, recommend joint doctrine and manage the deployment of Army and Air Force units based in the United States.[52] The two services shared the commanding general and deputy commanding general slots in Strike Command. Army General Paul Adams was Commanding General of Strike Command at the time.

## TESTING THE COMPETING AIRMOBILITY CONCEPTS

During 1963, Strike Command prepared a Test and Evaluation Plan assuming a comparative evaluation by the Command of both the Army and the Air Force airmobility concepts. The Joint Chiefs approved this on 23 August 1963, but in December, the Secretary of Defense cut the Command's Joint Test and Evaluation Task Force's funding for Fiscal Years 1964 and 1965 by more than half. Consequently, Strike Command produced a revised Test and Evaluation Plan in which the main emphasis remained joint field-testing of both the Army and Air Force airmobilty concepts. The new plan of January 1964 was the Command's best effort to retain as much of the original test and evaluation programs as possible, including the goal of comparative evaluation of both the Army and Air Force concepts.[53]

Here, it is important to note the distinction between "joint" and "comparative" testing. Joint testing involved the joint administration of either of the two competing airmobile concepts by both services through the joint-service Strike Command. Comparative testing involved the comparison of tests of both airmobile concepts. These tests might involve the participation of forces from both services, but they need not necessarily be jointly administered. They might be unilaterally administered by one service as in the case of the 11th Air Assault Division tests.

Having committed themselves to testing the Army's airmobility vision arising out of the Howze Board, the Army Chiefs were concerned that

Disosway's demand for joint testing of both Army and Air Force concepts might be an attempt by the Air Force to simply kill off airmobility at the testing stage. Army Vice Chief of Staff General Barksdale Hamlett said on 11th February 1963 that he was concerned that the Army "be permitted to pursue an orderly program without being forced into joint testing."[54] The Joint Chiefs, therefore, with Air Force Chief of Staff General Curtis E. LeMay dissenting, sought and received permission from the Secretary of Defense for the Army to proceed unilaterally with the testing of its own airmobility concept. Only after these tests would the US Army Chief of Staff recommend to the Joint Chiefs whether any part of the Army concept required joint testing. Based on this information, the Joint Chiefs would then make a final decision on joint testing of the Army concept by Strike Command. In the meantime, Strike Command would proceed with joint testing of the Air Force airmobility concept. These tests would involve two major joint exercises: the brigade- level GOLD FIRE I and the Divisional-level GOLD FIRE II.

The Joint Chiefs did order Strike Command to "observe actively" the Army's unilateral tests, with a view to the possibility of the Command testing and evaluating the Army concept in 1965. In accordance with the new instructions from the Joint Chiefs, Strike Command prepared a new Test and Evaluation Plan. This involved provision, if so directed by the Joint Chiefs, for the comparative, joint testing and evaluation of both the Army and Air Force airmobility concepts in two exercises: GOLD FIRE II which would examine the Howze proposal and GOLD FIRE II ALPHA which would examine the Disosway proposal. No joint testing of the Army concept by Strike Command was to precede the approval of the Joint Chiefs.[55]

In September 1963, the 11th Air Assault Division began a series of tests culminating in a battalion-size field exercise called AIR ASSAULT I. This took place on 20 April 1964 at Fort Stewart, Georgia. The object of this phase of the testing was to perfect the coordination of battalion-level airmobile operations along with such required concomitant airmobile techniques as flying command posts, landing zone fire suppression and air assault doctrine. General Williams's Test Evaluation and Control Group deemed the exercises such a success that the Army cancelled a brigade-level exercise scheduled for June 1964 and, instead, pressed on with plans for a full-scale divisional exercise: AIR ASSAULT II to be held in October.

The month before this exercise was due to take place, the Secretary of Defense ordered Strike Command to prepare its own report on it for submission to the Joint Chiefs and his own office. As Strike Command was about to conduct its own field test of the Air Force airmobility scheme in Exercise GOLD FIRE I, the Secretary reasoned that a comparison of its reports on both exercises would constitute a comparative evaluation of an Air Assault Division and a conventional division enhanced by the Air Force concept.[56]

These orders provoked complaints from General Adams who argued that the same team would need to observe both exercises for such an evaluation to be truly comparative. Unfortunately, this was not possible as AIR ASSAULT II was due to take place between 11 October and 15 November 1964, while GOLD FIRE I was scheduled to take place simultaneously between 25 October and 13 November. Adams requested that AIR ASSAULT II be postponed so that the same team could see at least two weeks of each exercise, but the Army Chief of Staff rejected this on the grounds that the 11th Air Assault Division was already deployed in the exercise area. Adams responded that a real comparative evaluation was therefore impossible, but Strike Command did compile a report on AIR ASSAULT II.[57] Adams might also have added the objection that the two exercises were perhaps not truly comparable in any case: AIR ASSAULT II being a division-level exercise while GOLD FIRE I was only brigade level.

The divisional level test of the 11th Air Assault Division took place between 14 October 1964 and 12 November 1964 and involved two brigades of the division operating against the 82d Airborne Division. A third airmobile brigade was simulated in the exercise, the Air Assault Division having not yet been brought up to full strength. In their after action report, the umpires and unit commanders involved in the tests deemed the 11th Air Assault Division's performance in AIR ASSAULT II a success, considering it extremely useful for controlling large areas in low-intensity war environments. The exercise suggested that in a high-intensity conflict the division would make a good reserve screening force, but might otherwise be hampered by weakness in the face of enemy armored forces. The division, of course, had no armored units of its own.

The tests did reveal some other problems with the experimental division: while the division was especially mobile in the sense that its units could patrol and concentrate by air, its lack of ground vehicles meant that once on the ground, its units were actually peculiarly immobile in the absence of helicopter airlift. The division's mobility was drastically reduced in bad weather. Its aircraft were not all-weather capable and during the exercise air operations had been restricted for five days due to storms. Also, the division's efficiency appeared to decline rapidly in sustained operations.[58]

Strike Command's report of AIR ASSAULT II also suggested flaws in the Army airmobility concept in areas involving cooperation between the Army and the Air Force, including Air Force fire support, tactical air reconnaissance, battlefield surveillance by both the Army and the Air Force, compatibility of the Army and Strike Command air traffic systems, and the use of the C-130 Air Force transport aircraft in support of the Air Assault Division. Adams argued, therefore, that further evaluation of the new formation was necessary and he recommended to the Joint Chiefs that the 11th Air Assault Division be subjected to a further test exercise, this time, a joint one under the auspices of Strike Command.[59]

Strike Command's test of the Air Force airmobility concept, Joint Exercise GOLD FIRE I, took place in the area of Fort Leonard Wood, Missouri, using two brigades of the 1st Infantry Division, one performing as the enemy, with Air Force aircraft providing reconnaissance, close air support and troop airlift, including the use of sixteen CH-3C helicopters. Planning for the exercise itself had not proceeded without some interservice difficulty. The Army had been reluctant to furnish the Air Force with elements of a conventional infantry division for the exercise on the basis that such a division was "an approved organization not subject to modification for test purposes." Instead, the Army offered elements of its own experimental airmobile unit, the 11th Air Assault Division, for training with the Air Force for one month in the summer of 1964. This was unacceptable to the Air Force. After Adams had complained to the Joint Chiefs, the impasse was resolved in a meeting at Strike Command headquarters on 2 March 1964, when the Army agreed to provide units of the 1st Infantry Division for the Air Force tests.[60]

Adams pronounced Exercise GOLD FIRE I a success, claiming that the Air Force concept involved the 'generous and whole-hearted accomplishment of tasks that have long been the responsibility of the tactical air forces." He wanted to proceed with a full-scale divisional test of the Air Force airmobility concept—Exercise GOLD FIRE II—but he also declared that GOLD FIRE I was sufficient evidence alone of its validity. As with the Army tests, however, the GOLD FIRE I evaluators did detect a number of problems with the application of the Air Force airmobility concept, which would require corrections in order to realize its full potential.

The evaluators believed the Army would need to develop more equipment compatible with the Air Force's preferred transport aircraft, the C-130 and C-141 Starlifter, much current Army equipment being only compatible with the C-123 and C-133 Cargomaster. Subsequently, the Army's Continental Army Command also criticized the evaluators' "admission" that the Air Force concept was only compatible with infantry divisions, it being impossible to air transport much of the equipment of armored and mechanized divisions.[61] Actually, this was hardly a failing by comparison with the Army scheme as it, too, was only really capable of application to converted infantry or airborne divisions, the resulting "air assault" or "airmobile," division having no armored component. The Army could convert an armored division to an airmobile formation, but the resulting specialized unit would no longer be an armored division.

Following the 1964 airmobility exercises, General Rich reported to the Army's Combat Developments Command that, based on the data assembled in the Army airmobility exercises, an Air Assault Division should become a formal part of the Army table of organization. The command endorsed this recommendation in February 1965.[62] The Department of the Army then proposed that the 11th Air Assault Division be formally absorbed into the Army's order of battle. Satisfied that the 11th Air Assault Division tests were sufficient justification for the adoption of the Army airmobile concept, the Army also requested that the Air Force cancel its upcoming GOLD FIRE II exercise. The Joint Chiefs concurred and recommended that the 11th Air Assault Division be retained and GOLD FIRE II cancelled with the disclaimer that this was "without prejudice to the . . . refinement of Army and Air Force concepts in future joint exercises."[63]

In fact, the cancellation of GOLD FIRE II sounded the death knell for the Air Force airmobility concept and effectively declared the Army's the winner of the competition. Again, the Joint Chiefs were not unanimous on the issue, the Air Force's General LeMay dissenting "because he believes that a sound decision on the subject requires a more thorough evaluation of a tested procedure and available capabilities which would provide a highly effective and economical basis for enhancing Army mobility without the need to establish a less capable division"—in other words, the Air Force's mobility enhancement concept.[64] McNamara, however, approved and the 11th Air Assault Division entered the US Army order of battle on 1 July 1965, re-designated as the 1st Cavalry Division (Airmobile). On the 28th of the same month, the Secretary ordered the division to Vietnam.

In 1962, Army airmobility proponents, unrepresentative of the more conservative views held by the service's most senior commanders, found themselves in positions within the Office of the Secretary of Defense where they were able to use their influence to get McNamara to issue his April 1962 airmobility memoranda. From this perspective, Colonel Robert Williams is probably the single most significant individual in the process by which the US Army came to adopt airmobility.

The activities and conclusions of the Howze Board were deeply parochial. The Board members interpreted their brief as exploiting the opportunities presented by new aviation technology almost exclusively in terms of the Army's own resources. While close air support by the Air Force still featured in the Army's plans, virtually no thought was given to ways in which the Air

Force might contribute towards increasing Army mobility. Instead, the Army chose to drastically increase its own aviation assets in terms of both fixed- and rotary-wing aircraft.

The core of Air Force objections to the Howze Board proposals, as expressed in the Disosway Report, concerned roles and missions. It was an article of faith among most Air Force officers that their service should retain exclusive responsibility for all aspects of military aviation excepting a few observation and utility tasks that could be carried out by the Army in a few unsophisticated aircraft. Airmobility, however, as envisioned by the Army, threatened a massive increase in Army aviation such that the Army would assume an aviation role almost as important as that of the Air Force itself.

Whether out of an intent to kill off the Army's airmobility concept, or out of genuine concern, the Disosway Report criticized the reliance of the Army airmobility scheme on the fragile helicopter. This question of helicopter vulnerability was to become a prominent feature of the Army-Air Force debate over tactical air support in Vietnam.

Even more serious in Air Force eyes than the inclusion in the Army's order of battle of thousands of helicopters was the fact that many of these aircraft would be armed. Worse still was the inclusion of fixed-wing attack aircraft in the Howze proposals. While there might be some confusion about which service should have responsibility for helicopters, there was no doubt in the Air Force's view that it should have sole responsibility for fixed-wing fighter-bombers, and though no self-respecting Air Force pilot would want to fly an aircraft with the performance of the AV-1, this twin-turboprop clearly had become a fighter-bomber in Howze's scheme.

The Army's airmobility concept, if fully realized, certainly did pose a threat to the Air Force's roles, missions and budgets. The Air Force took steps to head off this threat by commissioning its own airmobility study which was, not surprisingly, deeply critical of the Howze Report. While the Disosway Report did acknowledge the weakness of existing Air Force close air support provision for the Army, this was not enough to halt the progress of the Army's airmobility bandwagon, though it might have influenced McNamara's decision to subject the concept to further tests.

The Howze Report acknowledged that some of its proposals represented contraventions of existing agreements on roles and missions, but the Army's point of view was that these should be revised in the light of new technological and doctrinal developments that had been emerging over the last decade or so. The end result, so Army aviation proponents believed, would be an enhancement of the capability of the US Army specifically and the US armed forces generally. Naturally, the Air Force argued that the reverse was actually the case and that the expansion of Army aviation would lead to an undesirable dilution of airpower resources and tie up a sizable chunk of airpower assets in roles from which they could not easily be diverted, should the need arise.

In addition to the technological developments that lay behind the Howze Report, and the doctrinal developments it represented, Army thinking on airmobility was also profoundly influenced by its experience at the hands of the Air Force. It seems clear that the Howze Board's call for organic close air support was not dictated exclusively by a shortfall in artillery support brought on by the novel nature of airmobile formations. Clearly, the Army perceived the existence of its own attack aircraft as an inherent good which might be applied to all its units, not just the airmobile ones, and of course the very existence of Army attack aircraft made their use irresistible whether the supported unit was airmobile or not. Indeed, very early on in its Vietnam experience the Army found that it could not resist using its OV-1 observation aircraft in the close air support role.[65]

The development of Army airmobility highlighted the deep philosophical divisions between it and its sister service. Within the Army, the belief persisted that the point of military decision lay on the ground where the opposing armies clashed. The Air Force, by contrast, believed that tactical air operations were secondary to the strategic missions that absorbed most of its interest, energies and budget. Furthermore, the Air Force's very existence was inextricably entwined with the concept of the centralization of airpower. The Air Force believed that all aviation assets should be centrally controlled so that they could most effectively be concentrated at the point of decision. Naturally, the coordination of this airpower, regardless of the service of origin, should lay with the real airpower experts: Air Force officers.

Both the Army and Air Force airmobility concepts were tested in major field exercises and, despite some apparent problems, both were deemed successful by their partisan evaluators, but McNamara's decision to approve the Army scheme was not based on a truly comparative evaluation with that of the Air Force, for none was ever conducted. While the Air Force airmobility concept may have been merely a ploy to defuse the Army's aviation plans, its details have tended to be obscured by the Army's airmobility success. This suggests that the victors set not only the policy, but also the historical agenda, for the Air Force airmobility concept was certainly not devoid of merit. It was truly interservice and its application to conventional divisions may have actually offered more flexibility than the highly specialized Army scheme. It was also more flexible in that any aircraft allotted to tactical air support tasks within the scheme would still be available for use within the centralized Air Force Tactical Air Control System (TACS), while decentralized Army air assets would be permanently denied to the TACS.

It should be noted, however, that even the Army airmobility aviation proponents did not get it all their own way. Army airmobility appealed to McNamara because it appeared consistent with his established policies of flexible response and the extension of the principles of rationalism and efficiency to the defense community. However, the Howze Board recommendations proved too dramatic and divisive for McNamara to implement them in their entirety. He moderated his support for them somewhat, extending the period of testing and converting only one division to the new role, rather than the five recommended by the Howze Board.

Ultimately, the events surrounding the development of the Army's airmobility concept in the Howze Board's deliberations, the Disosway Board's criticism of them and the field tests of the two competing concepts did nothing to resolve interservice disputes over aviation roles and missions. They were to continue to fester in Vietnam itself where arguments for and against Army aviation raged from the arrival of the first two Army helicopter companies in December 1961.

# NOTES

1. Hamilton H. Howze, "The Requirement for Air Fighting Units," The Rogers Board Report (1960), quoted in Hamilton H. Howze, A Cavalryman's Story: Memoirs of a Twentieth Century Army General (Washington, DC, 1996), 235.

2. Hamilton H. Howze, "The Howze Board," Army (February, 1974), 14.

3. Frederic A. Bergerson, The Army Gets an Air Force: Tactics of Insurgent Bureaucratic Politics (Baltimore, 1980), 110.

4. Barbara A. Sorrill & Constance J. Suwalsky, "The Origins, Deliberations, and Recommendations of the US Army Tactical Mobility Requirements Board" (Fort Leavenworth, Kansas: US Army Combat Developments Command Historical Monograph, April 1969), 8-9, US Army Center of Military History, Washington, DC (hereinafter referred to as CMH).

5. Robert R. Williams, LTG, Interview, Senior Officer Oral History Program, US Army Military History Institute (hereinafter referred to as MHI), Carlisle Barracks, PA (1978), tape 2, transcript, 47.

6. Edwin L. Powell, BG, Interview, Senior Officer Oral History Program, MHI, (1978), tape 1, transcript, 46-50.

7. Williams, op cit, tape 2, transcript, 53-57.

8. Secretary of Defense, memo for Mr Stahr (19 April 1962) in Alain C. Enthoven & K. Wayne Smith, How Much is Enough: Shaping the Defense Program, 1961-1969 (New York, 1972), 103.

9. Secretary of Defense, memo for the Secretary of the Army, & memo for Mr Stahr (19 April 1962), ibid, 101-104.

10. Sorrill & Suwalsky, op cit, 71-73.

11. Ibid., 75 & US Army Tactical Mobility Requirements Board, "Final Report" (hereinafter referred to as the Howze Report), (Fort Bragg, NC, 20 August 1962), 4-6, CMH.

12. Sorrill & Suwalsky, op cit, 77-79.

13. "Howze Report," 78-79.

14. Ibid., 18.

15. Ibid., 29.

16. While Director of Army Aviation Howze himself had refused publication of an article entitled "Air Fighting Army" by BG. Carl Hutton, on the grounds that his proposal for something approaching a fully airmobile army was likely to be a political liability. The commander of the Army Aviation School at Fort Rucker, AL, Hutton had been one of the Army's unofficial experimenters with armed helicopters. Howze, "The Howze Board," 12-13.

17. The Howze Report, 88-91.

18. John L. Romjue, "The Evolution of American Army Doctrine" (Fort Monroe, VA, Military History Office, US Army Training and Doctrine Command, March 1996), 13-14.

19. "The Howze Report," 88-91.

20. Ibid., 36-40 & 47.

21. Williams, op cit, tape 2, transcript, 51-52.

22. "The Howze Report," 62-64 & 66-68.

23. Ibid., 72.

24. Andrew F. Krepinevich, The Army and Vietnam (Baltimore, 1986), 114-115.

25. "The Howze Report," 70-72.

26. Ibid., 71.

27. Ibid., 72.

28. John J. Tolson, LTG, Interview, Senior Officer Oral History Program, MHI (1977), 18-24.

29. AFORQ Presentation on the Howze Report (1962), Air Force Historical Research Agency, Maxwell AFB, AL (hereinafter referred to as AFHRA), K177.1512-7, 9 & 16.

30. US Air Force Tactical Air Support Evaluation Board, Report (hereinafter referred to as the "Disosway Report"), (14 August 1962), AFHRA, K177.1512-2, 24 & Disosway, memo to LeMay (14 August 1962), 7-11 (included in report)

31. Disosway Report, 14 & AFORQ Presentation on the Howze Report, 47.

32. Disosway Report, Attachment 1, 1.

33. AFORQ Presentation on the Howze Report, 36.

34. Ibid., 22-23 & 37-38.

35. Disosway Report, Attachment 1, 2.

36. AFORQ Presentation on the Howze Report, 5.

37. Disosway Report, 16; see also 17-18 for performance figures dealing with this issue.

38. Ibid., Attachment 2, 1.

39. Gabriel P Disosway, Gen, USAF, Interview, US Air Force Oral History Project, AFHRA, K239.0512-974, 177-178.

40. Disosway Report, Attachment 3, 1-3.

41. Ibid., 7 & 21-22.

42. Disosway Report, Disosway, memo to LeMay (14 August 1962), 12.

43. Continental Army Command (CONARC), Command History 1964, CMH, 272 & 286.

44. Williams, op cit., tape 2, transcript, 57.

45. "Howze Report," 95.

46. Hamilton H. Howze, "Winding up a Great Show," Army (April 1974), 23-24 & Sorrill & Suwalsky, op cit., 120-121.

47. Harry W.O. Kinnard, LTG, Interview, Senior Officer Oral History Program, MHI (1977). Although one of the Howze Board's working groups satisfied itself that the replacement of ground transportation by aircraft would not be prohibitively expensive except in Europe where the density of the ground transport network made ground vehicles much more economical, the Board also estimated the cost for an air assault division for initial equipment and five years operating costs at $987M while the comparable costs for a ROAD infantry division and an

armored division were $693M and $863M respectively. Howze Report, 85 & Sorrill & Suwalsky, op cit, 87.

48. Richard G. Davis, The 31 Initiatives: A Study in Air Force – Army Cooperation (Washington, DC, Office of Air Force History, 1987), 18.

49. Howze disagreed with the criticisms of the O/AV-1 despite his acknowledgement that it was an interim aircraft pending the development of helicopters that could perform the same role more efficiently. He disagreed with the criticisms regarding the CV-2 arguing that short field performance was vital and that here the CV-2 definitely did outperform the C-130. The implication here is that whatever the payload limitations of CV-2s, Howze believed their short field performance made them worth having. Even better, in Howze's view, would be V/TOL performance for which the convertiplane would be the answer. Unsurprisingly, Howze also favored the Army's decentralized approach where air assets were devolved to division. Hamilton H. Howze, Gen, Senior Officer Oral History Program, MHI (1977), 2-6.

50. When at the Air Command and Staff College at Maxwell AFB in the late 1940s, Kinnard had written his thesis on the military future of the helicopter. Kinnard, op cit, 4.

51. Williams, op cit, tape 2, transcript, 57.

52. William W. Momyer, Airpower in Three Wars (New York, 1980), 65.

53. United States Strike Command, Command History 1964, (an in-house publication), CMH, 50-52.

54. Quoted in Scott W. Lackey, ed, "Four Divisional Test Beds," from "Initial Impressions Report: Changing the Army" (Fort Leavenworth, Kansas, CAC History Office, Center for Army Lessons Learned, US Army Combined Arms Command, 1994), http://call.army.mil:100/call/exfor/specrpt/chp5.htm, 7/10/97, 1.

55. Strike Command, op cit, 59-62.

56. Ibid., 63.

57. Ibid., 63-65.

58. "Four Divisional Test Beds," 2-3.

59. CONARC, op cit, 278-279.

60. Strike Command, op cit, 54-55.

61. CONARC, op cit, 287.

62. Ibid., 277 & 283.

63. JCS, Memo for the Secretary of Defense (20 March 1965), CMH, 1-2.

64. Ibid., 3.

65. Originally, OV-1s operating in the battlefield surveillance role in Vietnam were armed with .50 caliber machine guns that were to be used only in self-defense. This became a source of considerable frustration to the ground commanders because the OV-1s, with their long loiter time and ability to carry a wider variety of weapons, offered a close air support capability that had the potential for much faster reaction times than that provided by the Air Force. Given the capabilities of the aircraft, its increasing use in the close air support role was inevitable. John J. Tolson, Vietnam Studies, Airmobility (Washington DC: Department of the Army, 1973), 40-44.

# CHAPTER 3

# COMMAND AND CONTROL

**Command and Control:** *The Exercise of authority and direction by a properly designated commander over assigned forces in the accomplishment of the mission. Command and control functions are performed through an arrangement of personnel, equipment, communications, facilities, and procedures which are employed by a commander in planning, directing, coordinating, and controlling forces and operations in the accomplishment of the mission.*[1]

As a result of the particular historical circumstances under which the United States became ever more deeply involved in the Second Indochina War, responsibility for the execution of American military policy at the theater level became fragmented between the Commander in Chief Pacific (CINCPAC) and the Military Assistance Command Vietnam (MACV). Interservice rivalry contributed to the development of this complex arrangement and was a continuing factor in the relationship, both between the two commands, and their various subordinate agencies. This fragmentation of command authority at the theater level was reflected in a similar dispersal of responsibility for the air power resources committed to the war.

The United States' Army and Air Force entered the Vietnam War with unresolved doctrinal differences regarding command arrangements and appropriate strategies for limited war. They pursued their own agendas in Southeast Asia, and the persistence of such rivalry within the context of the war was inherently inefficient, but they did so in the conviction that their own designs provided the swiftest route to victory. In hindsight, the costs were failure to arrive at optimal senior command arrangements or strategies for the war, with a consequent dissipation of air resources, but the individual service efforts were not always entirely incompatible.

Interservice rivalry also emerged at the operational level of control of United States air power resources in Vietnam. This debate centered on Air Force efforts to bring the air power assets of the other services, particularly the Army and the Marine Corps, under the umbrella of its own Tactical Air Control System (TACS). The Air Force sought to assert its responsibility, however indirect, for all air power assets, while the Army and the Marines sought to retain the unique responsiveness of their own organic aviation resources to the requirements of their ground forces. There are arguments, both pro and con, for each service's position with regard to operational control of air assets, but the full realization of the Air Force's objectives had potentially serious, and perhaps even fatal, institutional consequences for Army and Marine organic aviation.

## THE THEATER LEVEL

Theater-level responsibility for the execution of United States military policy in the Second Indochina War is difficult to pin down with precision. Technically, CINCPAC was the commander of all American forces engaged in the war, but the name of Admiral Ulysses S. Grant Sharp is not often associated with the conflict in the informed public's mind, whereas that of Army General William C. Westmoreland more frequently is. This is indicative of the fragmented nature of the senior command arrangements for the United States' role in the conflict. While CINCPAC's headquarters was in Honolulu, 6,000 miles from the seat of the fighting, Westmoreland's MACV was based in Saigon. Yet the Commander US Military Assistance Command Vietnam (COMUSMACV) did not have sole command authority for all US military units participating in the war.

MACV was not, in fact, a theater command. With few exceptions, its writ did not extend beyond the borders of South Vietnam. Those United States forces engaged in the war but which did not fall within MACV's remit reported directly to CINCPAC. Under the nominal authority of CINCPAC, MACV's responsibility was the management of the United States war effort inside South Vietnam—the so-called "in country" war. The command was not a prefabricated product of contingency planning simply plucked off the dusty shelves in some Pentagon basement room and set down in Saigon. In fact, MACV was much more of an ad hoc arrangement that evolved in response to the developing situation in Southeast Asia, changing United States' roles with respect to that situation and institutional pressures within the American armed forces.

The word "assistance" in the very title of the US command explains some of the confusion. MACV had its origins in structures designed not for war, but for assistance short of war. The command had started life, not as an operational military headquarters, but as a body for the coordination of military assistance; first to the French and then to the infant state of Vietnam. When MACV came into being on 8 February 1962, it did so as a reorganization of the earlier Military Assistance Advisory Group Vietnam (MAAG). MAAG's gestation went right back to the First Indochina War of

1946 to 1954 when France had battled the communist nationalists for control of its Indochinese colonies in Vietnam, Laos, and Cambodia.

Convinced that communism must be contained in Indochina, Secretary of State, Dean Acheson, announced the provision of military and economic aid both to France, for her own use in the region, and directly to the "Associated States" of Vietnam, Cambodia, and Laos, on 8 May 1950.[2] United States containment strategy for Indochina came to rest on the establishment of a pro-American state of Vietnam of sufficient strength to resist external attack and internal subversion. However, while Washington's strategy did involve an independent Vietnam, a continued French presence was also necessary to provide short-term security for the infant state. Therefore, the Truman administration encouraged the French to stay in Indochina, while at the same time urging upon them real concessions to the Bao Dai regime preparatory to complete withdrawal. For France, however, the Indochina War remained a colonial war. The French were not prepared to withdraw from Indochina after expending so much effort to defeat the Viet Minh.[3]

The members of the Joint Mutual Defense Assistance Program Survey Mission, which visited Indochina in July and August of 1950, appreciated the contradictions of the United States' Indochina strategy, but few alternatives presented themselves and the mission recommended more aid to the French and the establishment of a United States Military Assistance Advisory Group for Indochina to oversee the application of this aid. The first personnel for the MAAG began arriving in South Vietnam in September of 1950.[4]

Despite the largesse of American assistance that, by the end of the First Indochina War was accounting for 80% of the French war effort, France was defeated and Vietnam divided at the 17th parallel between a communist north and a non-communist south. For a time, the French retained a presence in the south, but the United States gradually supplanted them as the sponsor of the new southern State of Vietnam and, in October 1954, President Dwight D. Eisenhower committed the United States to the security of the region when he offered South Vietnam's then Prime Minister, Ngo Dinh Diem, direct American assistance which would not be channeled through the French. This was to include the training of a small South Vietnamese army for internal security purposes and Diem formally requested American instructors for this purpose on 10 May 1955. On 28 April 1956, MAAG assumed responsibility for the training of the Army of the Republic of Vietnam (ARVN). Thus, the US had now assumed an advisory role, in addition to that of providing military aid in the form of money and equipment.

As one might expect, American advisors served in conventional training roles in the bases established for the new army. They also assumed a more operational role, being appointed to shadow South Vietnamese officers in the field. This meant that from 1957, as Diem moved against the remaining Viet Minh enclaves within South Vietnam and as a new communist-led insurgency developed within the South, they became increasingly exposed to potential combat situations. The first American advisors were wounded in South Vietnam in 1958 and the first American serviceman was killed in action there in 1961.

While it may have been "undeclared," the United States was, very definitely, at war in South Vietnam in 1965, but it cannot be said that the USA was so definitely at peace before that year. At some time before 1965, what had been an advisory and assistance role for the United States shaded gradually over to more of a belligerent one, and almost absentmindedly, the United States suddenly found itself at war in South Vietnam. It was MACV, ostensibly an advisory command that oversaw the United States' part in this "in country war" from 1962, and MAAG before that.

By the end of 1961, there were more than 3,000 American advisors —mainly US Army personnel—in South Vietnam, including US Army Special Forces Troops (Green Berets). An Army general led MAAG and the vast majority of his staff were from that service. They, and their South Vietnamese counterparts, cooperated in waging a ground war that had, at the outset, no significant air component. The Communists never deployed any significant air power in South Vietnam throughout the entire war, and in the early days, the South Vietnamese, forbidden under the terms of the Geneva agreement to possess military jet aircraft, disposed of only a relatively tiny, unsophisticated, embryonic air arm.

United States Army officers, however, both in the USA and in Vietnam, did not ignore the third dimension of warfare. Vietnam was, of course, a helicopter war. The UH-1 "Huey" helicopter's distinctive shape, perhaps along with that of the B-52 heavy bomber, became one of the key symbols of the United States in Vietnam. As we know, the US Army had been conducting experiments in the integration of helicopters with its ground forces since the 1950s, and in the early 1960s, was refining its airmobility concept. The latter development proceeded in lockstep with the escalation of the war in Vietnam.

The development—in parallel with the war in Vietnam—of the Army's airmobility concept involved the necessary assumption that aircraft were a legitimate form of transport in the US Army of the late 20th century. According to Army aviation enthusiasts, a helicopter in Army service was little different to a jeep. Furthermore, many Army officers, including the commanding general of MAAG Vietnam (and later MACV) General Paul

D. Harkins believed that as a counterinsurgency campaign, the war in South Vietnam was a ground campaign and should, therefore, be predominately an Army responsibility. As we have seen, the Howze Report argued precisely this. This line of thinking had two possible consequences: First, it could be used to justify the monopolization, by the Army, of senior slots within the command organization for the war in Vietnam. Second, it could be used to justify the virtually complete exclusion of the other services from Vietnam, except to the extent that the Army required them in a completely supporting role.

Of the first of these possibilities, more details follow later in this chapter. As to the second, in 1961, the US Army had not yet deployed major ground units to South Vietnam. The service was principally involved in aiding and advising the ARVN, and conducting counterinsurgency operations with small numbers of Special Forces troops. Clearly, these efforts would require some kind of air support, but in 1961, it seemed that this might need to be mainly logistic. This could be provided by the Air Force, supplemented by Army helicopters and fixed-wing transport aircraft.

As the pioneer in the field the Army could, of course, provide the ARVN with a measure of airmobility and, to this end, the first US Army helicopters arrived in South Vietnam in December 1961, when two Army aviation companies began operating in support of the ARVN, including the transport of troops directly into combat. The arrival of the helicopter companies meant that the US Army had, not for the last time, more aircraft in South Vietnam than the US Air Force. While this arrangement might seem, at first sight, somewhat anomalous, the ARVN's close air support demands were limited in the early days of the Vietnam War, and could be filled by the expanding Vietnamese Air Force (VNAF). Given the US Army's perspective on its exclusive responsibility for counterinsurgency warfare, and the permissive South Vietnamese air defense environment, the Vietnam War seemed a perfect opportunity for the service to provide some of its own air support with its OV-1 Mohawk fixed-wing aircraft and its armed helicopters. A very real question emerges, therefore, as to whether the Army felt it required a US Air Force combat role in South Vietnam in 1961—for it did not ask for one —and indeed, whether one was actually necessary.

Certainly, the US Air Force thought it was, and during the course of 1961 lobbied the Department of Defense for an increased role in Vietnam. Despite his and his service's traditional preoccupation with strategic air warfare, Air Force Chief of Staff General Curtis E. LeMay seems to have became increasingly concerned that the Army's virtual monopoly of the low-intensity conflict in South Vietnam would deprive the Air Force of valuable opportunities likely to accrue from significant participation in the war. Mindful of the emphasis on low-intensity warfare in the Kennedy administration's policy of "flexible response," it was at LeMay's initiative that the Air Force began the development of counterinsurgency techniques, or in Air Force parlance: Special Air Warfare.[5]

As a consequence, under the code name JUNGLE JIM, the 4400th Combat Crew Training Squadron (CCTS) was established in April 1961.[6] Among the 4400 CCTS's tasks were the development of counterinsurgency tactics and hardware and, as the name suggests, the training of third country air forces in these techniques. It seems clear that the Air Force had developed the 4400 CCTS with the Vietnam conflict in mind, and in October 1961, in response to Air Force initiatives, the President approved the deployment of a detachment from the unit, code-named FARM GATE, to Bien Hoa in South Vietnam.[7]

Despite an assertion by President Kennedy that FARM GATE was to fulfill an exclusively advisory and training role, the members of the 4400 CCTS, or "Air Commandos" as they were known, were soon employing their aging piston-engine aircraft in clandestine combat missions. On 4 December 1961, Secretary of Defense Robert S. McNamara agreed to the use of Air Commando aircraft on combat missions provided at least one member of the crew was South Vietnamese.[8] Thus, in the shape of the Air Commandoes, the Air Force had significantly expanded its advisory role and staked out the beginnings of a combat role for itself in South Vietnam.

The arrival of the Air Commandos in Southeast Asia represented the establishment of an air component within MACV, with a corresponding requirement for a higher Air Force command agency in South Vietnam. Thus, in November 1961, the 2d Advanced Echelon (2d ADVON), of the 13th Air Force assumed control of Air Force combat operations in South Vietnam. As the role of the US Air Force expanded in South Vietnam, 2d ADVON became the 2d Air Division and, finally, the 7th Air Force.

7th Air Force was to be a divided command. Its commanding general established headquarters in Saigon to oversee the air war in South Vietnam, but his deputy was based in Thailand. The reason for this peculiar arrangement lay in the widening of the war that had begun in the summer of 1964. Following the Gulf of Tonkin incidents in early August of that year, the United States began conducting a separate air war over North Vietnam from that over the south. The first US air strikes against North Vietnam added the US Navy's air arm to those of the Army and the Air Force with a combat role in Southeast Asia. Further retaliatory strikes in response to the incident at Pleiku in early February 1965 sent 7th Air Force and the Republic of Vietnam's Air Force

(VNAF) north of the 17th parallel. On 2 March 1965, the 7th Air Force and the 7th Fleet's Task Force 77, operating from the Gulf of Tonkin, began a sustained campaign against the north code named ROLLING THUNDER.

The Air Force had never been happy with the Army's counterinsurgency strategy in South Vietnam, but rather than be left out of the war completely, it developed Special Air Warfare capability and secured a role within that strategy. However, the Air Force still believed that the war required an *air strategy* rather than an Air Force role dictated by the Army's strategy in South Vietnam. The official US government position was that the war in South Vietnam was not an internal insurgency—a civil war in which the US had no right to intervene—but was in fact instigated and sustained by North Vietnam. It was then, in the government's perspective, an attack by one sovereign nation—the Communist Democratic Republic of Vietnam in the north—on another sovereign nation—the non-communist Republic of Vietnam in the South—and the US was, therefore, fully justified in going to the aid of its South Vietnamese ally. If the root cause of the war lay in the north, as the government's White Paper of February 1965 maintained, then, said the Air Force, the most direct method of concluding the war successfully lay in attacking the source of the problem.[9] In the Air Force's view, the most economical way of doing this in terms of US (and North Vietnamese) casualties would be by unleashing the Air Force against North Vietnam, and any ground campaign in the South beyond a holding action, was largely superfluous. The Air Force, therefore, drew up a list of 92 key targets in North Vietnam, the prompt destruction of which, it believed, would bring the country to its knees and force it to desist from sustaining the insurgents in the south. In fact, the extent to which ROLLING THUNDER ever conformed to the Air Force's preferred strategy remains moot, but it was clearly more to the Air Force's taste than its role in the south. Thus, 7th Air Force came to be engaged upon two different air campaigns: one in support of the Army in South Vietnam and the other over North Vietnam.

As we have seen, the Army, by contrast, believed, at least initially, that the war in Vietnam was an insurgency and that counterinsurgency operations should be its exclusive preserve. Its officers always maintained that whatever the nature of the war, the point of decision was on the ground. Political considerations restricted ground operations to South Vietnam and the Army, therefore, planned a strategy for victory in the south, though it did make periodic proposals for limited amphibious operations against North Vietnam.

In 1965, Army plans did not include an air campaign against North Vietnam. General Westmoreland thought that such a campaign would actually further undermine the already fragile security of South Vietnam. Later, Westmoreland sincerely came to endorse the air campaign against North Vietnam and made a number of public statements to this effect, but only as an adjunct to what he saw as, the more important ground campaign in the south.[10] This begs the question: in 1965, as in 1961, was there sufficient justification for an Air Force combat role in the Vietnam War, given that, with the exception of the Air Commandoes and the air defense of South Vietnam, this was, first and foremost, directed towards attacks on North Vietnam?[11]

President Lyndon B. Johnson approved such a role in the face of lobbying by the Air Force for attacks on North Vietnam alongside Army plans to Americanize the ground war. The fact that he did so may have been the result of bureaucratic compromise between competing military institutions rather than a decision based on the operational situation in Southeast Asia. Alternatively, the decision to initiate the air campaign against North Vietnam may have had different political motivations. The President may have felt that public opinion considerations dictated he "try" the "economical" air option, whatever his views about how successful it might be, before he escalated the ground war.

Even if one accepts the requirement for an air offensive against North Vietnam, one could still question the Navy's role in it, or at least the persistent use of the Navy's expensive carrier air arm long after sophisticated land air-basing facilities had become available both in South Vietnam and Thailand. Certainly the Air Force did question the division of North Vietnam into separate "Route Packages" in which either the navy or the Air Force had exclusive responsibility. This, too, was a bureaucratic compromise designed to ease the complexities that would otherwise result from joint operations throughout North Vietnam.

Ironically, the beginning of the air offensive against North Vietnam provided the justification for the dispatch of major United States ground units to South Vietnam. The first units of the 9th Marine Expeditionary Brigade began to deploy to South Vietnam in March 1965, initially to guard the air base at Da Nang, but the Marines were soon involved in aggressive patrolling and a fully fledged US ground war was soon under way in South Vietnam. The following month, the first Marine jet fighter-bombers flew to Da Nang and on 6 May, the III Marine Expeditionary Force (III MEF) was established in South Vietnam though the name was soon changed to III Marine Amphibious Force (III MAF).[12] On 11 May, the Marine air component in South Vietnam was established as the I Marine Air Wing (I MAW).

In fact, the Marines had already established an aviation role for themselves in South Vietnam when, on 15 April 1962, the Marine Corps "seized the opportunity" provided by the Secretary of Defense's approval of the deployment of another helicopter unit beyond the three companies then already deployed to Vietnam by the Army.[13] The squadron of Marine transport helicopters, then dispatched to Soc Trang in the Mekong Delta area, formed the basis of Marine Task Unit SHUFLY. In September 1962, this unit moved to Da Nang in the northernmost, or First Corps, Tactical Zone of South Vietnam where the Marines were to concentrate their operations until their departure from the country in 1970. In December 1963, SHUFLY was renamed Marine Unit Vietnam (MUV); it was integrated with the 9th Marine Expeditionary Brigade when that arrived in 1965.

While COMUSMACV controlled the Marines in South Vietnam, he did not have full control of the total allied forces committed to the Second Indochina War. Nominally, MACV was a "unified" command—that is one in which all three services are supposed to share an equitable division of responsibilities and offices. This was the US military establishment's model for the conduct of combined warfare based on its experience in the Second World War where the US had employed a strategy based, at least in theory, on teamwork between the three services. General Paul D. Harkins, COMUSMACV until General Westmoreland took over in 1964, however, favored a different kind of command arrangement known as "specified." As the name suggests, this involved the dominance of a specified service—in this case the Army. Harkins's rationale for this was that the war in South Vietnam was a counterinsurgency campaign and, as such, a ground campaign for which the Army must be primarily responsible.

Harkins argued along these lines up until May of 1964 when he made a formal request that MACV be made a specified command, but at the urging of Admiral Sharp, the JCS rejected Harkins's suggestion and elected to retain the unified nature of the command.[14] Creation of a specified MACV may have been difficult for the JCS. Acceptance of the seniority of the Army required the Chiefs to disregard the individual service interests they had always followed, in favor of a wider view they were rarely called upon to take. A specified Army command would deny the other services their right to an equal division of the roles and missions in Vietnam, and perhaps even have an impact on their funding levels. Whether for operational or bureaucratic reasons, this was a risk the Chiefs dare not take. Thus, when faced with the task of creating a command for Vietnam, the JCS's preferred option was to clone itself to form the unified MACV, and given its bureaucratic inclinations, it was, perhaps, institutionally incapable of doing anything more.[15]

Thus far, we have referred to MACV as the command authority for the war in South Vietnam, but it is important to realize that the war in Southeast

Asia was not confined to South Vietnam. In fact, the title "Second Indochina War" is a much better description of the conflict fought out in the 1960s and 1970s in Southeast Asia than the more common "Vietnam War." Indeed, the war was very much a resumption of unfinished business from the French, or First Indochina War of the late 1940s and early 1950s. Of course, the bulk of the ground combat did take place in South Vietnam, but during the course of the war, fighting spread throughout the entire Indochina region. As the foregoing has shown, in addition to the fighting in the south, the United States also waged an air campaign over North Vietnam. Aircraft engaged in ROLLING THUNDER were based outside South Vietnam; those from 7th Air Force flew from Thailand, while 7th Fleet aircraft flew from the carriers of Task Force 77 on "YANKEE STATION" in the Gulf of Tonkin.

In addition to the campaigns over North and South Vietnam, the air war was further complicated by subsidiary operations in northern Laos and Cambodia. From the early 1960s, the CIA front airline, Air America, began to airlift arms and equipment for royalist Lao troops in their war with the communist Pathet Lao and North Vietnamese Army (NVA). Later, US armed forces aircraft became directly involved in supporting royalists, neutralists, and Meo tribesmen in Laos with airlift and attack missions. Again, 7th Air Force aircraft, operating from bases in Thailand, flew many of these missions.

Obviously, these "out-of-country" air operations over North Vietnam and Laos were designed to have some kind of an impact on the war in South Vietnam. By knocking North Vietnam out of the war with sustained air attacks, the Air Force hoped to end the war in the south at a stroke, while at the same time providing the ultimate validation of the classical air power theory which was the service's *raison d'être*. Subsequently, the Air Force complained that ROLLING THUNDER never conformed to the letter of its preferred strategy, but even the more limited ROLLING THUNDER campaign, as imposed by the politicians, was meant to improve South Vietnamese morale and interdict northern troops and supplies before they could affect the war in the south. As such, it might be said that the reality of ROLLING THUNDER, as a "deep interdiction" campaign, was meant to affect the war in South Vietnam more directly, at least in the operational sense, than the more truly strategic 94-target list Air Force dream campaign. Yet, despite the fact that all of this US air activity was part of the same war, it was not all controlled by MACV. Thus, while Southeast Asia might be described as a single theater, and South Vietnam only one element within that theater, MACV was not a theater command. In fact, COMUSMACV had no authority whatsoever for operations anywhere else in Southeast Asia, including North Vietnam, Laos, and Cambodia.[16]

Before 1964, neither the JCS nor the White House saw Vietnam as sufficiently important to justify the establishment of a theater command in Saigon, but as the United States' role escalated, the argument for such a command became increasingly strong. However, political and institutional considerations may have colored Washington's view of the situation. Reestablishment of MACV as a Southeast Asia theater command would have considerably reduced the forces commanded by CINCPAC, and removed the ultimate responsibility for a major war effort from a Navy admiral in favor of an Army general who had formally been his subordinate. Clearly, this would have been an unattractive prospect for the Navy.

As MACV itself was under the authority of the unified CINCPAC, it was, more correctly, a "sub-unified" rather than a unified command. It was CINCPAC who controlled the air war over North Vietnam. He controlled the carrier-borne air power of Task Force 77 through the Commander in Chief Pacific Fleet (CINCPACFLT), and the tactical aircraft of the 7th Air Force based in Thailand through the Commander in Chief Pacific Air Forces (CINCPACAF). COMUSMACV enjoyed responsibility only for that part of the 7th Air Force actually based inside South Vietnam.

Westmoreland has subsequently admitted that he would have preferred to head a "Southeast Asia Command" with responsibility for the entire Southeast Asian "theater."[17] At the time, he did request that the entire resources of 7th Air Force be placed at his disposal for operations inside South Vietnam, but CINCPACAF General Hunter Harris refused claiming other commitments in Southeast Asia and throughout the Pacific generally. Westmoreland's attempts to gain control of the Air Force's C-130 transport fleet in the Pacific also met with failure.[18]

Naturally, Westmoreland's reasoning behind these attempts to gain control of more air resources for the war in South Vietnam lay in his conviction that the ground war was the point of decision. Air Force officers, by contrast, believed that an air campaign against North Vietnam was the best way to conclude the war successfully. CINCPACAF was, therefore, reluctant to commit more resources directly to the war in South Vietnam for fear that, should an air campaign be approved that complied with the Air Force's views, it might then be difficult to secure the release of precious air resources which had already been committed to the war in the south. This reluctance on the part of CINCPACAF to commit more resources directly to the war in South Vietnam may have damaged the Air Force's reputation with the Army.[19]

Placing the entire responsibility for the Second Indochina War in the hands of COMUSMACV as a single Southeast Asia Theater Commander was certainly logical from the operational point of view, but it also carried political difficulties. In its rationale for participation in the war, the US government had presented itself as coming to the aid of a peace-loving, democratic, sovereign nation, the Republic of Vietnam, against which another sovereign nation: the communist Democratic Republic of Vietnam, was waging aggressive war.[20] This justified US action within South and North Vietnam, but against the background of world opinion and the Cold War, the US wanted to keep the war limited and did not want to appear too aggressive. This meant that the US must not be seen to be widening the war elsewhere in Indochina, whatever the reality of the situation. In furtherance of these objectives, it was convenient to restrict the ground commander's (COMUSMACV's) responsibility to South Vietnam. Thus, political considerations reinforced institutional proclivities to retain MACV as a sub-unified command under CINCPAC. In any case, having established MACV as such, the temptation must have been to leave it that way, whatever the developing military situation in Southeast Asia, and this is what Washington did.

Political considerations also militated against establishing MACV as a combined command with responsibility for South Vietnam's forces. Thus, in addition to having little responsibility for United States forces committed to the war outside of South Vietnam, COMUSMACV did not even have full responsibility for all the allied forces inside South Vietnam. Publicly, Westmoreland accepted the political necessity of maintaining Vietnamese sovereignty by excluding the republic's forces from the United States' chain of command. COMUSMACV did retain responsibility for other so-called "free world" forces including the important Australasian and South Korean contingents, although he was limited in the area in which the ROK forces could be deployed.

The B-52 heavy bombers of the 8th Air Force, which began operating in a tactical role over South Vietnam from June 1965 under the code name ARC LIGHT; also lay outside COMUSMACV's direct authority. These aircraft remained under the control of Strategic Air Command. Again, the Air Force feared that, once committed to MACV, it might be difficult to reclaim the B-52s should circumstances permit their use over North Vietnam. The Air Force successfully argued for the retention of these aircraft under SAC on the grounds that their wider role as part of the US nuclear deterrent triad required they might be withdrawn at a moment's notice should a national security emergency arise. MACV was able to pick the majority of targets for the giant bombers and prepare prioritized lists of targets from all sources, but final mission approval for the giant bombers lay in Washington.[21] Here, a measure of intraservice rivalry emerged. From July 1966, the commander of the 7th Air Force General Momyer began to call for the attachment of 8th Air Force's Advanced Echelon, which was responsible for the B-52s, to his own headquarters, an arrangement which finally went into operation in January of the following year.[22]

Both Harkins and Westmoreland were, however, able to make the Army's position within MACV stronger than the unified nature of the command might suggest it should be. Obviously, even the most perfect unified command has some built-in bias in the sense that its commanding general can come from only one service. Normally, the JCS allotted unified commands to a general of the most represented service. Clearly, throughout most of the Vietnam War, this was the Army and the position of COMUSMACV always went to an Army general.

If the spirit of a unified command is to be fully realized, and the command slots distributed as fairly as possible, then the command should be relatively equally divided among a number of service "component commands." Within MACV, the Air Force component was 2d Air Division—later the 7th Air Force—which had its own staff subordinate to COMUSMACV. There was no Army component command. According to Westmoreland, in the early days of the war, Air Force strength and responsibilities were such that they actually justified a separate Air Force component command before the US Army build-up justified a separate Army command.[23] What this meant, in practice, was that the multiservice MACV controlled the ground war directly by serving—effectively—as the Army component staff. When COMUSMACV finally did institute a MACV Army command: US Army Vietnam (USARV), he perpetuated the existing arrangement by serving as his own Army Component Commander. Thus, MACV continued to perform as the Army Component Commander's staff.[24]

According to the Air Force, the net effect of COMUSMACV acting as his own Army component commander was a reduction in the authority of the Air Force representatives at MACV. Few of these Air Force officers were familiar with the Army-orientated tasks that comprised most MACV staff work. In practice, therefore, Army officers exercised dominant authority even over those MACV functions nominally under the control of Air Force officers. Though Harkins failed to make MACV an official specified command, the effect of his and Westmoreland's decision to act as their Army component commanders was to make MACV a unified command "in name only."[25]

The issue of its relative under representation in MACV caused concern within the Air Force throughout the Vietnam War. In an effort to redress this imbalance, the Air Force Chief-of-Staff, General Curtis E. LeMay, while visiting Vietnam in April 1962, proposed that an Air Force officer become deputy commander of MACV. This was to be a similar position to that held by the British Royal Air Force's Air Chief Marshal Tedder in the Second World War Supreme Headquarters Allied Expeditionary Force, Europe.

The commander of the 2d Air Division, Major General Rollen H. Anthis, also felt strongly that COMUSMACV's deputy should be an Air Force general.[26] In January 1963, he went over Harkins's head to appeal directly to the Secretary of the Air Force Eugene Zuckert for an Air Force officer as overall deputy of COMUSMACV, and he reiterated his displeasure regarding the under representation of the USAF in the MACV staff to the Commander in Chief Pacific Air Force General Jacob E. Smart in November of the same year.[27] Harkins, however, insisted that the MACV deputy should be an Army officer and Secretary of Defense Robert S. McNamara supported him.

Initially, Harkins was equally opposed to the idea that he appoint an "air deputy" with duties confined to air operations alone, but Harkins later changed his mind and proposed that his air component commander become Deputy Commander of MACV for Air Operations. Following Harkins's return to the United States, Westmoreland made a number of similar offers. While the concept of an "air deputy" was less than ideal for the Air Force, it did hold out the potential for providing the service with some real authority. The new commander of PACAF, General Hunter Harris, felt that it offered the prospect of bringing all air power assets in Vietnam—Army, Navy and Marine Corps—under the authority of the Air Force in the way that the 5th Air Force had exercised control over Marine and Navy aircraft during the Korean War.[28] Nevertheless, LeMay and the air staff held out for an Air Force officer as full deputy commander of MACV for all operations and Westmoreland continued to resist on the grounds, he has subsequently implied, that the war in Vietnam was primarily a ground war for which only the Army had the expertise required of the senior commander. Following this logic, as Westmoreland's deputy might have to succeed him, he must be an Army officer.[29] Only after the retirement of the stubborn LeMay did his replacement, General John P. McConnell, accept Westmoreland's offer as the best he was likely to get. Thus, the commander of the 2d Air Division, General Joseph H. Moore, became MACV air deputy in June 1965.

The disputes over which service should occupy the post of deputy COMUSMACV and whether there should be a deputy for air operations concerned the Chairman of the JCS General Earle Wheeler lest the debate attract Congressional interest. Wheeler favored offering the Air Force the MACV Deputy for Personnel and Deputy for Communication—Electronics positions by way of concessions, but was opposed by Westmoreland. After a few months in post, Westmoreland's first deputy, Lt. General John L. Throckmorton, was forced to return to the United States for surgery on a slipped disc. In a message to COMUMACV, Throckmorton reported his view that Westmoreland's new choice for MACV overall deputy, General John A. Heintges, had only been approved by the JCS, "because he was top of your [Westmoreland's] list and not in recognition of the fact that the war . . . is predominantly a series of ground battles and that the deputy slot should logically go to an Army type."[30]

As they emerged in practice, the arrangements for the theater-level command of US forces during the Vietnam War suited neither the Army nor the Air Force. Clearly, the Army would have preferred MACV to be a true theater command with responsibility for the entire resources committed to the war in Southeast Asia, including all of 7th Air Force, Task Force-77 and SAC's B-52s. No doubt the Army would also have preferred that this "Southeast Asia Command" be a specified formation under Army authority, an arrangement for which Harkins did argue on the basis that the conflict in Vietnam resulted from a guerrilla insurgency for which the Army should have primary responsibility.

Taken to its ultimate conclusion, the logic of this argument suggested that there might be no need for a significant USAF presence at all in Vietnam. Furthermore, new Army formations, with greatly expanded air assets, could do the job unaided. In the event the USAF resisted the threat of its virtual exclusion from Vietnam and the Army was obliged to settle for the sub-unified MACV whose writ was essentially confined to those forces actually based in South Vietnam and which included a sizable and growing Air Force component.

The USAF's dream theater-level command arrangement would also have involved MACV being a true theater command, but it would also have been a truly unified arrangement in which the USAF component enjoyed equal status with that of the Army, and in which the USAF exercised its doctrinal requirement for centralized control—or single management—of all the command's air assets. The Air Force complained that it was not able to secure centralized control of all air assets and that this mirrored the US command arrangements for the prosecution of the Vietnam War which were, as we have seen, fragmented. By centralized control of all air assets, the USAF meant the establishment of USAF control over Marine and Army air power. In fact, the precedents for Air Force control of Army air power were moot. It might also be said that, to some extent, the USAF actually contributed to the fragmentation of air power by seeking to reserve its 7th

Air Force assets in Thailand and its 8th Air Force B-52s outside MACV in order to keep them available for operations against North Vietnam which were more in keeping with the service's doctrinal proclivities.

Air Force responsibility, even for its own units, engaged in the war in Southeast Asia, was divided. On the one hand, the service prosecuted an air campaign against North Vietnam, while on the other, it was expected to support the Army's efforts in South Vietnam. While the Air Force believed the central pillar of a proper air strategy to be a campaign against North Vietnam, it has argued that ROLLING THUNDER did not conform to the model that it, as the air power experts, would have preferred. The validity of this position is, however, beyond the scope of the present study.

It has also been suggested that, in the eyes of the Johnson administration, the air campaign against North Vietnam began as no more than a political smoke screen designed to conceal the Americanization of the ground war, which, it concluded, was the only option likely to produce favorable results in Vietnam. Such a campaign would prove to the American people that the supposedly low casualty high-tech air option had been tried before the ground troops went in and they could then be introduced stealthily, first as "security" forces to guard US air bases from which the raids against the north were being launched.[31] Were this highly speculative theory found to have any basis in fact, then it would call into question the need for the campaign against the north in the same way that the validity of Army theories about counterinsurgency call into question the requirement for any Air Force presence in South Vietnam to speak of in the early 1960s.

Despite Westmoreland's early opposition to ROLLING THUNDER, which is a matter of record, the air campaign went on to develop its own raison d'être. At the very least, the administration was reluctant to back away from a campaign it had insisted was so important and that might actually be doing some good, though there was precious little evidence of this in South Vietnam. Westmoreland, it seems, sincerely changed his tune about the need for the bombing of the north, though at times he did have to be prodded by Washington to talk up the bombing in suitably public forums.

In regard to the war in South Vietnam, the Air Force was obliged to get on, not with pursuing its own air strategy, but with supporting the Army's ground campaign and this involved making itself more responsive to the requirements of the Army. While, then, it may be that the Air Force sought to impose its own doctrinal inclination towards a strategic air campaign against North Vietnam on the war in Southeast Asia, it was less than entirely successful and, indeed, found itself measuring its effectiveness in terms of the efficiency with which it performed tasks for the Army—a yardstick which, by the service's definition, could not equate with the effective use of airpower.[32]

The Army sought to make the best of its command in South Vietnam and increase its grip on MACV by making the command "more specified" in practice. This led to what the Air Force saw as its relative under representation in MACV. In its turn, the Air Force sought to move closer to its desired command arrangements by redressing this perceived imbalance within MACV. Ideally, this would have involved the establishment of an Air Force general as a true deputy commander of MACV with real power. Instead, the Air Force was obliged to settle for the post of deputy commander with responsibility for air operations only, in the hope that such a role would maximize the centralization of air assets under Air Force control. Whether this arrangement provided the Air Force with a measure of real power can only be established by looking at the service's efforts to bring all allied air assets under a common—Air Force managed—air control system.

## THE OPERATIONAL LEVEL

Interservice rivalry also emerged at the operational level of US air power resources. This debate centered on the Air Force's efforts to bring the air power assets of the other services, particularly those of the Army and the Marine Corps, under the umbrella of its own Tactical Air Control System (TACS). The Air Force sought to assert its responsibility, however indirect, for all air power assets, while the Army and the Marines strove to retain the unique responsiveness of their own organic aviation resources to the requirements of their ground forces.

The rationale behind the USAF TACS was the control of all air power resources by a single management authority vested in the Air Force Component Commander (AFCC), regardless of the service of origin. As such, the TACS incurred early opposition from the Army on account of its implied threat to that service's preferred decentralization of its own air power resources. While the Army was unable to prevent the establishment of the TACS, it was largely successful in retaining operational control of its own air power resources outside the system.

Efforts by the Air Force to bring both the Marine and Army air power resources under the TACS umbrella served only to underline the weakness of the AFCC's position as the coordinating authority for air operations in the face of determined opposition from the other services. As an Army General, COMUSMACV did not have any desire to turn over control of Army aviation to the Air Force; nor did CINCPAC, a Navy admiral, wish to renounce Marine Corps control of its own air power to the Air Force.

Prior to the introduction of US Air Force, ground support aircraft into South Vietnam in 1961, all fixed-wing air support for the Army of the Republic of Vietnam (ARVN), was provided by South Vietnam's small air force: the VNAF. Requests for preplanned air support missions were passed from divisional headquarters to the Corps Tactical Operations Center where there was a VNAF Air Liaison Officer. Those requests, approved at the corps level, were then sent to the Joint General Staff's Joint Operations Center in Saigon, which also included VNAF, and later also USAF officers. Here, the details of the mission and the resources to be allotted to it were worked out before being passed to the VNAF Air Operations Center—which had a USAF officer as deputy director—for execution.[33] VNAF air units were parceled out to the corps commanders, limiting the resources available for use in each corps area and the degree to which those resources could be shifted about South Vietnam.

The US Air Force regarded this system as unresponsive and lacking in adequate air force representation.[34] Consequently, with the arrival of the FARM GATE detachment, the USAF set about establishing its own Tactical Air Control System to control and coordinate its growing air resources in South Vietnam. United States Air Force doctrine demanded that this involve the centralization of all air power assets committed to a theater under a single authority—the USAF Air Component Commander—so that he could shift these resources about the theater in accordance with the dictates of the operational situation.[35] This implied the USAF's desire to bring the air assets of other services operating in the theater under its, and therefore the AFCC's, control, an arrangement which it described as "single management." The United States Air Force was to make repeated requests that the TACS become the sole management agency for all air assets in South Vietnam, regardless of their service of origin.

Thus, from the earliest days of United States involvement in the Second Indochina War, the USAF sought to centralize all air assets under its own control. Essentially, in 1961, the USAF was engaged in building the new VNAF; the closeness of the relationship between the USAF and the VNAF resulted in the inclusion of the latter service's resources in the TACS from its inception, though they remained, rigidly divided among the Corps commands for the duration of the war. Ironically, however, while the VNAF participated in the USAF TACS, the US Army, with its growing aviation presence in South Vietnam—both rotary- and fixed-wing—remained aloof from the system. During his trip to South Vietnam in April 1962, LeMay called on Harkins to centralize all air assets in South Vietnam, including the Army's helicopters and fixed-wing aircraft, through the mechanism of the USAF's TACS which was then in the process of assembly.

Harkins, of course, was hostile to such a development, but he sought to kill the issue with a seemingly positive response to LeMay's demands that would leave the ultimate authority for the control of Army aviation in his own hands. He agreed that there was a case for the better coordination of all air assets, including the Army's aviation companies which were supporting South Vietnamese operations in the field, and designated the Air Force Component Commander as the authority for the coordination of all VNAF and US air activity in South Vietnam, including that conducted by the Army and the Marines.[36]

While the USAF hoped that Harkins's directive would further the principle of unity of command, as they understood it, by placing all air resources under single—Air Force—management, Army officers believed it to contravene their interpretation of unity of command by interfering with the corps advisers' authority over the use of Army aviation assets.[37] Army doctrine called for the decentralization, rather than centralization, of air power assets. The Army believed air resources should be devolved to local ground commanders for their direct application to the decisive ground battle. In the context of Vietnam, in 1961, this meant that US air assets should be placed under the operational control of the senior US Army advisers to the ARVN corps commanders, while VNAF aircraft should come directly under the operational control of the Corps commander.[38]

Presumably to assuage Army fears that they were about to completely lose control of their own air assets, Harkins introduced an Army element into the Air Operation Center that was to function as the senior element of the USAF's TACS. (It was later to be replaced by dedicated Tactical Air Control Centers). In practice, however, the Army retained operational control of its aircraft under the corps advisers, where they might be allocated to even lower levels of command for employment by individual ground commanders as they saw fit. Army aircraft were not, in the main, coordinated with the AFCC through the mechanism of the TACS.[39] Nor was the USAF able to do much about this in the face of Army resistance.

Harkins's directive had been quite specific that the Air Force Component Commander could not order agreement on matters of air coordination, for which ultimate authority lay with himself as COMUSMACV.[40] This was consistent with the "Dictionary of United States Military Terms for Joint Usage" which states that a "coordinating authority" has the right "to require consultation between . . . agencies, but . . . not the authority to compel agreement. In the event he is unable to obtain essential agreement, he shall refer the matter to the appropriate authority."[41]

Naturally, this did not satisfy the AFCC, General Anthis. He did not believe that the corps advisers' staffs were sufficiently trained to control helicopter operations in support of South Vietnamese forces. When Anthis's successor, General Moore, became air deputy, he also suggested that Army aircraft come under the USAF TACS. However, the directive establishing the air deputy contained no reference to Army aviation and Westmoreland was no more prepared to surrender Army aircraft to the USAF than his predecessor at MACV.[42]

While the Army was able to retain its aircraft outside the TACS in the short term, it was unable to prevent the actual establishment of the USAF system with its implied threat to Army air autonomy; the first elements of the TACS began deploying to South Vietnam before the end of 1961, and a basic system was in place by the end of the following year. The establishment of the TACS highlighted the doctrinal dispute over tactical air power raging between the two services in the early 1960s. Representatives of the Air Force's 2d Air Division in Southeast Asia suggested that it was deliberate US Army policy to use its own aircraft in preference to those of the Air Force, while the ARVN reserved the right to select between the use of Air Force aircraft or US Army aircraft as it saw fit. This resulted, they said, in the use of Army aircraft in roles for which Air Force types would have been more appropriate. In the main, this type of complaint centered upon the ARVN's use of US Army armed helicopters for a variety of missions, including transport helicopter escort, close air support and even attack missions independent of ground forces in contact with the enemy. In addition, the absence of Army aircraft, whether rotary- or fixed-wing, from the TACS led to what 2d Air Division saw as lamentably poor control and coordination of air assets. Second Air Division maintained that the use of these "uncontrolled" Army aircraft represented a flying safety hazard both to themselves and to any "properly coordinated" Air Force aircraft operating in the same area. They even went so far as to suggest that the use of Army aircraft outside of the TACS sometimes led directly to friendly-fire casualties.[43]

In making these complaints about the Army's command and control of air power, 2d Air Division drew on an Operational Test and Evaluation of the Vietnam TACS conducted by HQ PACAF between 1 June and 31 August 1963. It was, of course, perfectly reasonable that a new and important system such as the Vietnam TACS should undergo a period of testing early in its life. However, it is also quite possible that part of PACAF's intention behind conducting a test of the TACS was to "prove" conclusively USAF concepts regarding tactical airpower, while providing a forum for the criticism of the Army's use of the medium. As such, the operational test and evaluation report provided convenient ammunition for the USAF's use in its dispute with the Army over command, control and centralization of air power.[44]

Harkins seems to have sensed this (perhaps he was already aware); assuming that the TACS report would be critical of Army air procedures he launched a preemptive strike before it was released on 25 February 1964. On the 17th, he disingenuously insisted to CINCPAC that any indication of an interservice dispute between the US Army and the USAF over their respective air control systems was an "illusion" resulting from the "heat generated in honest argument" and pointed out that the two services "cooperated splendidly when committed to operations."[45] The real problem, said Harkins, was more a function of a lack of cooperation between the ARVN and the VNAF and that this was why the ARVN preferred to call on US Army and Marine Corps air support in preference to that of the VNAF.[46]

However, in the same memo, Harkins's inability to resist putting the Army's case indicates that in fact the interservice dispute over command and control of air power was anything but an "illusion." Harkins acknowledged that there were "two discrete systems" for the allocation and control of aviation in Vietnam, but he insisted that "there is, repeat is, an operational requirement for two systems . . ." He went on to argue that since Air Force and Army aviation resources had different capabilities they were, therefore, "complementary" rather than competing; this implied that, in Harkins's view, 1) The Army had a legitimate close air support role and 2) Army aircraft should remain outside the Air Force air control system. Both ideas were anathema to the USAF.[47]

In fact, while Harkins insisted that two air control systems were justified, his arguments also suggest that he believed one system might be adequate. The two systems reflected individual service doctrine, but Harkins said that individual service doctrine should be disregarded in favor of the most effective solutions to the special close air support problems raised by counterinsurgency operations. Apparently, this would involve a review of current procedures, both Army and USAF, and presumably this could result in an abandonment of those procedures found wanting. For whatever reasons, as of February 1964, Harkins believed the Air Force TACS "more cumbersome" than that of the Army so that when it came down to "immediate air requests"— that is requests for air support by troops in contact with the enemy—the local ground commander must be free to decide which air control system to use.[48] Given both this, and Harkins's well-established belief in Army primacy for counterinsurgency warfare, Harkins's expression of his views to CINCPAC can also be interpreted as a thinly veiled plea for the possible abandonment of the Air Force system in favor of exclusive Army control of air operations in South Vietnam.

Not surprisingly, when the TACS report was finally released it represented an endorsement of the USAF system, an attack on the Army one and an argument in favor of the abandonment of the latter in favor of the centralization of air resources under the former.[49] The report's authors argued that the operation of Army and Marine aircraft outside the TACS resulted in poor coordination of air assets and represented a serious air safety hazard. They observed that while the TACS had been designed to control all air operations, during the period of the test, more than half of the total aircraft committed to South Vietnam operated independently of the TACS and the numbers were rising.[50]

The TACS report was, in its turn, criticized by Army sources. The commander of the Army Concept Team in Vietnam (ACTIV), Paul L. Bogen, attacked the unilateral nature of the test despite the fact that this was clearly an area of common interest between the services. For Bogen, the very fact that fewer than half the aircraft in South Vietnam operated under the TACS meant that "any conclusion as to the effectiveness of TACS to control all air resources in Vietnam is based on conjecture and ignores the strikingly different requirements posed by the employment of Army aircraft." Furthermore, Bogen asserted that the report's conclusions that the TACS provided an effective system for the provision of close air support, tactical air reconnaissance and logistic air support in South Vietnam, without any requirement for modification of its concept or structures, were "not supported by the discussion" therein. Bogen argued that the USAF's demands for the centralization of all "air forces," including Army air assets, under a single—USAF command—missed the point that Army aircraft did not constitute an "air force" since they were integrated with the ground forces, and he made no secret of his own belief that USAF aircraft should themselves be more closely integrated with the ground forces. Bogen reiterated Harkins's claims that the ARVN preferred to request air support through Army or Marine channels and he worried that the TACS was ineffective for close air support missions, hinting that this might be a product of the Air Force's doctrinal preference for strategic air warfare. In any case, Bogen doubted that the TACS actually could control all air assets in South Vietnam, including those of the Army and he noted that Army aircraft tended to operate at very low altitudes where TACS communications were poor. Like Harkins, Bogen recommended a joint evaluation of the TACS and the ARVN/US Army air control systems.[51]

Bogen's sensitivity to the TACS report is easy to understand. ACTIV had been established initially to study the application of the Howze Report on airmobility to Vietnam. As such, it was directly concerned with the operational testing of armed fixed- and rotary-wing Army aircraft in support of Army airmobile forces, and as we have already seen, the Howze Report came down firmly on the side of exclusive Army responsibility for counterinsurgency warfare.

In fact, the USAF subsequently acknowledged in a 1973 report that the South Vietnam TACS, established in 1962, was not really a "viable" system until the end of 1964. There were also problems coping with the rapid expansion of the air war and that it "was not as responsive to the immediate needs of the ground commander" as it should have been.[52] Communications, the report acknowledged, were also a problem. As a result, various efforts were made to increase the responsiveness of the system to the needs of the ground commander between 1964 and 1966 with, the report's authors believed, some success, but:

> Despite these improvements, the Army still lacked confidence in the ability of tactical air operations to deliver ordinance in a timely manner, especially for troops-in-contact situations. This resulted in the Army tendency to use preplanned close air support as combat air cover in an effort to provide constant coverage during ground operations.[53]

With the establishment of the USAF TACS in 1962, there were two tactical air control systems in South Vietnam. The arrival of the I Marine Air Wing in June of 1965 further complicated the issue. When the decision was taken to add a Marine Expeditionary Brigade to MACV, CINCPAC Admiral Ulysses S. Grant Sharp declared that COMUSMACV would exercise operational control over the Marines through the commander of the MEB and the AFCC, that is the commander of 2d Air Division, would be the "coordinating authority" for all air matters including the use of the MEB's associated Marine Air Wing. As such, Sharp complied with the recommendations of the Tactical Air Support Procedures Board instituted by his predecessor at CINCPAC Admiral Harry D. Felt in 1963. Felt's then Assistant Chief of Staff for Operations, Marine General Keith B. McCutcheon, who was later to be I MAW's first commander in Vietnam, had been the chairman of this board.[54]

The 1963 Tactical Air Support Procedures Board's report acknowledged that each service had air assets which were essential for the support of its mission and accepted that they would exercise individual command and control over them, though the Board deliberately excluded itself from any effort to resolve the debate between the Army and the USAF over the Army's provision of its own close air support. However, the board added the proviso that these individual service efforts must be coordinated and the board decided that this coordinating authority would be exercised by one of the service component commanders.[55]

Felt neither rejected nor endorsed the findings of the 1963 Board, but COMUSACV went beyond its recommendations by informing CINCPAC that I MAW's jet aircraft would be placed under the operational control of the AFCC—to be exercised through the TACS—though Westmoreland stressed that the Marines could expect support from their own aircraft in combat. Sharp, however, upheld the letter of the 1963 Board's report by not approving the subordination of I MAW to the USAF and allowing the Marines to establish their own air control system: the Marine Air Command and Control System whose Tactical Air Direction Center was established at Da Nang in June 1965. This system was used by the Marines to allot their aircraft to individual missions and monitor the activity of all Marine aircraft. Thus, in that month, Westmoreland revised his directive for the control of his air assets by ordering that the commander of the III Marine Amphibious Force would exercise operational control of all Marine air power committed to Vietnam, except in the event of an emergency, when COMUSMACV reserved the right to order the AFCC to take-over operational control. The commander of III MAF was also instructed by Westmoreland to identify any Marine aircraft sorties that were surplus to the immediate requirements of III MAF so that they could be reallocated by 7th Air Force to other missions, including the support of forces other than the Marines.[56]

The USAF argued that the existence of three competing air control systems in South Vietnam contravened the military principle of unity of command enshrined in the service's doctrine of the centralization of air power under its own control. As we have seen, the Army opposed this view on the grounds that USAF doctrine was flawed for the purposes of close air support. By contrast, Army doctrine called for the decentralization of air resources. The Marines agreed with the Army. Their doctrine emphasized the concept of an "air-ground team" where their air power was closely integrated with the Marine ground forces and their close air support requirements. The Marines, therefore, resisted the notion of placing their own aircraft under the Air Force TACS that would likely involve their use in support of other non-Marine forces. They preferred to use their own air control system to control Marine aircraft in exclusive support of Marine ground forces. It may be argued that the 1963 CINCPAC Tactical Air Support Procedures Board did indirectly support the bringing of Marine aircraft into the TACS inasmuch as the MACV AFCC, as "coordinating authority" wished it, but as we have already seen, such a coordinating authority could not compel agreement. In the face of resistance from a subordinate agency, its only recourse was to refer the matter to a higher authority.

This is precisely what occurred in 1965. 7th Air Force's commander as the "coordinating authority" for air operations wanted to bring I MAW's aircraft under his operational control through the TACS, but the USMC, as was its right, did not feel compelled to contravene its doctrine by accepting this arrangement. Westmoreland, although commander of a "semispecified" command, was willing to accede to USAF wishes with regard to the Marines (though not to the Army), but CINCPAC, as the ultimate authority, supported the Marines. It should be noted that, as a Navy officer, Admiral Sharp might have been expected to be somewhat more sympathetic to their case.

The matter did not, however, end there. The USAF continued to press for the bringing of as much of the Marine air effort as possible under its own operational control through the TACS. If he could not gain control of all Marine aircraft, Second Air Division's commander General Moore decided to try for at least part of it by requesting that his command assume overall operational control of all air defense resources.

MACV's air defenses were never tested in any significant degree during the Vietnam War, but the command retained an air defense capability mainly as a result of the slight threat posed by the North Vietnamese Air Force's IL-44 light bombers. These represented an "air force in being," while they existed there was always the threat, however slight, that they might mount raids against MACV's large and vulnerable installations in the south. In fact, the IL-44s never came south, but their existence forced MACV to maintain air defense forces of fighters and surface-to-air missiles. Part of these air defense forces were provided by the Marines, indeed, it will be recalled that the Marines' original mission in 1965 was the defense of the Da Nang air base, and the first Marine unit to arrive in South Vietnam was a Hawk surface-to-air missile battery.

Naturally, the Marines were no more enthusiastic about losing operational control of their air defense resources than they were of losing control of any other aspect of their air assets, and this was particularly true of actual air combat units. The Marine fighter squadrons in South Vietnam operated the F-4 Phantom aircraft and McCutcheon's early rationale for refusing Moore's overtures was that the F-4 was a multirole aircraft with a substantial attack role. It could not, therefore, be regarded exclusively as an air defense aircraft. Nevertheless, the Marines finally did compromise with the USAF. In August 1965, they agreed that the overall responsibility for air defense should pass to 7th Air Force, including that for the Marines' area of responsibility in the I, or northernmost, Corps Tactical Zone of South Vietnam, and the commander of I MAW would designate Marine air resources to be used by a USAF air defense commander.[57]

Having gained a measure of control over a small aspect of Marine air operations, the USAF continued to argue that all Marine air resources should follow suit. Westmoreland gave them another opportunity to plead their case when he asked General Moore to examine the advantages that might accrue from placing Marine air power under the control of 2d Air Division. General Moore responded by citing events during the recent ARVN/USMC combined operation HARVEST MOON, held between 8 and 18 December 1965. This, he said, indicated that Marine air power should come under one commander and be controlled through the TACS.[58]

According to Moore, and to a subsequent USAF Contemporary Historical Examination of Current Operations (CHECO) report on the operation, the Marines experienced an almost complete breakdown of air power coordination during HARVEST MOON. Despite requests for his admission, the USAF Air Liaison Officer with the ARVN 2d Division—one of the units involved in the operation—was excluded from the planning sessions held between III MAF and the ARVN I Corps.[59] Orders for HARVEST MOON included the provision of US Marine Corps artillery and air support to both ARVN and Marine ground units, but they did not include USAF or VNAF support.

Marine air support was to be coordinated by an airborne Direct Air Support Center with positive control of air strikes by ground forward observers and airborne Forward Air Controllers (FACs) in helicopters and Army light aircraft.[60] Moore and the CHECO report claim that the Marines had difficulty coordinating air support for the operation. Apparently, Marine forward observers suffered from poor communications with the airborne Direct Air Support Center and USAF FACs "saved the day" by stepping in to control Marine air strikes and diverting USAF and Marine preplanned sorties to the support of the ARVN through the TACS. The Air Force FACS even warned retreating ground troops of Viet Cong ambushes visible from the air. Having taken a hand in directing the air support effort, USAF FACS controlling USMC aircraft found themselves subject to interruptions by other Marine aircraft making uncoordinated strikes.[61] These sources even suggest that on the 10th, apparently as a result of the problems experienced with the Marine coordination of air support, the ARVN 2d Division commander announced that, henceforth, he would use only VNAF/USAF air support for the remainder of the operation.[62]

Most of the evidence for Moore's and the CHECO Report's assessment of the Marine air performance during HARVEST MOON comes from USAF Air Liaison Officers (ALOs), a not necessarily entirely unbiased source. As might be expected, the tenor of ARVN and USMC after action reports—again, not necessarily entirely unbiased sources—is not completely in accord with those sources originating with the Air Force. The drafters of these reports professed themselves generally satisfied with the air support during the operation, whatever its source or controlling authority, and much to the USAF's chagrin, they do not even mention the role of USAF FAC aircraft. Perhaps most curiously, the ARVN decision to withdraw from the Marine air control system does not feature in the ARVN 2d Division's after action report.

The USAF found further support for its demands for single management of all air resources in subsequent Marine operations, including Operations HICKORY and NEUTRALIZE, both in 1967. In the wake of the former operation, the USAF's Deputy Director of its Tactical Air Control Center, Colonel Hagemann, reiterated USAF recommendations that future joint operations should come under the command and control of the Air Force Component Commander.[63]

There were serious deficiencies in the planning of the air support for Operation HICKORY. United States Marine and Air Force personnel who were to have key responsibilities for the control and coordination of air power during the operation were excluded from the briefing process and only learned about the operation from unofficial sources.[64] Target materials prepared according to individual service procedures turned out to be incompatible and, in any case, some of these materials were not distributed in a timely manner.[65]

The lack of coordination in the planning process manifested itself during the operation when there was confusion between the USAF and the USMC as to the exact border between their areas of responsibility.[66] A further serious problem occurred with the introduction into the operation of a Marine helicopter borne special landing force from naval units off the coast. Originally, III MAF and the Navy had requested a carrier task group provide the necessary air support for the landing, but the Air Force insisted the Marines support the landing from their own air resources.[67] Reluctantly, the Marines agreed, however, so secret was the planning of this phase of the operation that I MAW does not seem to have been informed of the actual timing of the landing. Major Allen C. Getz, Officer in Charge, Detachment Bravo, MAS reports that the first I MAW knew of the actual landing was at 0730 on 18 May when, with the landing force already ashore, "they called us on the radio and requested emergency FAC and fixed-wing because they were in pretty deep trouble."[68]

Nor does it seem that USAF FACS were officially informed of the addition of an extra 100 US Navy sorties to their remit. These extra sorties merely contributed to an *embarrassment de riches* for the FACS, who were overloaded with too many sorties in too small an area.[69] Colonel Hagemann opined that the main cause of the problem was the late inclusion of the Navy sorties in the operation. This left too little time for the timely dissemination of target data to the Navy. As a consequence most of the Navy sorties were simply handed over to the control of USAF FACs, but the necessity of coordinating the carrier launch cycle with timing of USAF sorties does not seem to have been appreciated by the operation's planners, leading to saturation of the airspace in the target area. According to Hagemann, most of the problems contributing to this saturation had been resolved after a day or so, suggesting that a better coordination effort might have preempted them altogether.[70]

The USAF's CHECO Report on Operation HICKORY implies that part of the difficulty with the Navy sorties emerged from the delays involved in 7th Air Force having to obtain CINCPAC's approval for the use of the carrier air group from Task Force 77.[71] In fact, it took some three days from the point where 7th Air Force decided to request the supplementing of its forces for the operation with a carrier air group to the point where the TACC learned the request had been approved. This was at 1645 on the afternoon of 17 May with the operation due to begin the following morning.[72]

Three USAF wings participated in the operation and, of course, there was no requirement for 7th Air Force to request these—its own resources—from CINCPAC through COMUSMACV. Clearly then, Navy aircraft would have been available more quickly had they been permanently under the operational control of the AFCC, in other words: under "single management" as the Air Force understood it.

In the USAF view, some of the same command and control problems which had dogged Operation HICKORY re-emerged in Operation NEUTRALIZE, and for the same reasons: a duplication of air control systems and the lack of an interface between those two systems.[73] Operation NEUTRALIZE was an intensive air campaign designed by 7th Air Force to suppress North Vietnamese artillery positions dug in just above the DMZ. During 1967, these positions had been bringing a series of Marine 175mm fire-bases in the I Corps region of South Vietnam under an increasingly heavy fire. The operation involved the pooling of III MAF, 7th Air Force and MACV intelligence resources; Marine, Navy and USAF fighter-bombers, and SAC B-52s took part.[74]

The 7th Air Force Commander, General Momyer, was satisfied that the operation successfully "broke the siege of these northern bases . . . [and] relieved pressure on the northern two provinces," but in his service's estimation, NEUTRALIZE was also yet another confirmation of its long-running argument for single management.[75] The Marines, of course, felt that the preservation of their air-ground team was more important than any benefits the USAF perceived in single management and, interestingly enough, a measure of Marine dissatisfaction with the operation was centered on the Air Force's performance rather than any lack of coordination resulting from the existence of two air control systems in I Corps.[76]

According to the US Air Force then, allied airpower suffered from particular control and coordination problems in the I Corps area, and the main reasons for this were the existence of two distinct "air forces" in the region: the Marines' I MAW and the USAF's 7th Air Force, both of which operated through different—and incompatible—air control systems. The situation was further complicated by the periodic use of aircraft from the Navy's Task Force 77 in the area. These operated only at the request of 7th Air Force and through the Air Force air control system, but prior approval had to be obtained from CINCPAC before their use. Navy procedures, which differed from those of the Air Force, led to a lack of flexibility in the use of Navy aircraft and further coordination problems. Of course, the VNAF also operated in the area, but the South Vietnamese service was much more closely coordinated with the US Air Force and used the same air control system. What United States airpower needed in order to realize its full efficiency and potential, said the Air Force, was single management, under the control of the Air Force Component Commander.

United States Air Force demands for single management of all air power resources derived from precedent in the Second World War and Korea. The validity of this precedent must be regarded as moot in the Army case. Army airmobile forces differed vastly in quality and purpose from their distant airborne ancestors; as we will see elsewhere, an argument can be made—and at least in the case of helicopters was eventually accepted by the Air Force in Vietnam—that Army organic airborne fire support performed a different, but compatible, role to that of the Air Force's fighter-bombers, for which decentralization may have been an essential prerequisite. In any case, the Air Force was at a distinct disadvantage in pressing its claim to bring Army aviation under the TACS, because as only the coordinating authority for air operations it must first convince COMUSMACV, an Army general, of the rightness of its case, and Army doctrine maintained that its aviation assets were part of the ground forces, not therefore, air power resources per se.

The Air Force case for bringing Marine air under its operational control was stronger, but still largely unsuccessful before 1968. During the Korean War, the Air Force gained control of Marine air power and in Vietnam, with the two services aircraft, plus those of the Navy, operating in I Corps, there obviously were coordination problems that the Air Force lost little opportunity to document. Clearly single management would reduce these problems, but of course it could only do so at the expense of Marine doctrinal requirements—that is at the expense of the Marine air-ground team. Single management was clearly more responsive and efficient regarding the doctrinal inclinations of the Air Force, but this does not prove the doctrine correct. For their part, the Marines believed the preservation of their air-ground team more important than any advantages the Air Force thought likely to accrue from single management.

Responsibility for the execution of United States military policy in the Second Indochina War was fragmented between CINCPAC and MACV; this fragmentation was reflected in a complex dispersal of command authority for air power resources committed to the war. The reasons for this phenomenon lay, in part, in the historical gestation of the command arrangements for the United States role in the conflict, and one factor here does seem to have been interservice rivalry within the US military establishment.

While the Air Force was the major critic of this fragmentation of air resources, it actually contributed to the phenomenon in Vietnam. Its commanders desired a unified command for Vietnam in which the Air Force Component Commander would enjoy equal responsibility with his Army counterpart, but they also wanted to keep MACV subordinate to CINCPAC in order to retain tighter control over 7th and 8th Air Force resources for use in a strategic campaign against North Vietnam. The Air Force achieved the second of these objectives in that MACV remained a sub-unified command subordinate to CINCPAC, but its efforts to achieve the first were less successful.

Political factors served to reinforce the institutional pressures conspiring against MACV becoming either a theater or a combined command. The Joint Chiefs and President Johnson may also have been wary of making Westmoreland too powerful, lest he become a political liability in the way that General Douglas MacArthur had during the Korean War.

Once committed to the war in Vietnam, both the US Army and Air Force sought to bend the senior command arrangements for US forces to conform more closely to their own doctrinal inclinations. These were invariably consistent with each service's institutional advantage, but there is no evidence to suggest that the officers concerned did not believe sincerely in the validity of their own service's particular doctrine.

At their most extreme, the divergent doctrines of the Army and the Air Force pointed towards exclusionary command arrangements and strategies for the Vietnam War. Army counterinsurgency and airmobile theory pointed to a specified Army theater command with little or no place for an Air Force Component, while USAF doctrine argued that a strategic air campaign against North Vietnam, independent of MACV, was the most appropriate solution to America's Vietnam dilemma. Washington rejected both of these extremes, but carefully ensured that all services had an appreciable stake in the war. While this may have preserved the United States from whole-hearted endorsement of ill-conceived, and possibly disastrous military schemes, it clearly produced a command arrangement that was excessively bureaucratic, and a mediocre strategy that, as we know, was ultimately unsuccessful.

Regarding the operational control of air power resources in the Vietnam War between 1960 and the beginning of 1968, again interservice rivalry emerged. The Army and the Air Force clashed over the best way to control Army aviation for doctrinal reasons; this was largely an argument about control rather than command, but it had potentially far-reaching consequences. The Air Force was not very interested in the contribution that helicopters or the low-performance Army fixed-wing aircraft were likely to make to the sum of the airpower equation in Vietnam; it believed them to have only limited application as tactical transports and weapons systems for close air support tasks, even in South Vietnam's permissive air defense environment. The important point for the Air Force was to assert its responsibility, however indirect, for all air power assets.

There were advantages and disadvantages to Air Force control of Army aircraft through the TACS. On the debit side, it would likely have reduced the responsiveness of armed Army aircraft to the requirements of ground troops because it would have required that the Army use the TACS request procedure for Army air support and this clearly did take longer than the Army's decentralized system. It would also have meant that the Air Force officers operating the TACS, not the Army officers making the requests, would have had the choice of responding to pre-planned or immediate requests for support with either Army aircraft or Air Force fighter-bombers, and this brings us back to the question of which was the better or most appropriate weapon system for a given set of circumstances. The Army felt that it was often the helicopter or the slow-moving OV-1, either by virtue of their unique capabilities, or simply because they were organic to Army units, while the Air Force felt that these aircraft were rarely the appropriate weapon systems. On the credit side, control of Army aircraft through the TACS would likely have speeded the availability of fixed-wing air support, where this proved necessary, because it would have deprived the Army of the opportunity to try its own organic air support before it took recourse to the Air Force option. Also, it almost certainly would have improved air safety standards for both Army and Air Force aircraft, but lower safety standards was a price the Army was willing to pay for the easy availability of its own organic air support.[77]

More fundamentally, if in Vietnam, Army aircraft under the TACS were to be less responsive to the ground commander's needs and, if there was no guarantee that Army aircraft, with their unique characteristics, would be provided by the TACS, in response to requests for sir support, then this called into question the very concept of having Army aircraft for close air support purposes and reopened the interservice doctrinal dispute about the basic right of the Army to operate armed aircraft, or at least aircraft armed for anything other than self defense. The Army successfully defended its organic aviation against this potential threat by never allowing it to come under the authority of the Air Force TACS. No doubt, the Army enjoyed a considerable advantage here in that in order to win the argument the Air Force must convince COMUSMACV, and COMUSMACV was an Army general.

The Air Force also clashed with the Marines over their aviation arm. The Air Force wanted to bring Marine aircraft under its control through the TACS in the manner that 5th Air Force had controlled Marine aircraft during the Korean War, and the full realization of its objectives would have spelled the end of the Marine air-ground team in Vietnam. In some ways, this was a commendable objective. The Marines designed their air support system to supplement the firepower of their lightly armed formations during amphibious assaults, but by 1968, the Marines had been in I Corps for three years. The permanent availability of Army artillery support compensated for Marine deficiencies in this arm, yet the Marines continued to operate their air power as if conducting an amphibious assault. United States Air Force control of Marine aircraft through the TACS would undoubtedly have resulted in a more flexible and equitable use of Marine resources throughout I Corps in support of both Marine and the increasing number of Army units assembling in the region from the end of 1967. Undoubtedly, it would also have reduced the coordination problems that clearly existed between the two services as a result of their different doctrines and air control systems.

However, it was also likely to reduce the amount and responsiveness of Marine aviation available to support Marine ground forces and as such could have had a severe impact on the unique nature of Marine air power as part of their air-ground team, and if there was to be no air-ground team what was the point in having a Marine air arm? The Marines might just as well have drawn their air support from the USAF which is, of course, just what the Air Force wanted them to do. The dispute between the USAF and the Marines in I Corps had, therefore, potentially far-reaching, institutional, consequences. It threatened the Marine air-ground team in Vietnam and thus the very existence of an organic Marine air arm. Consequently, the Marines also fought back. This debate was to reach its height during the Khe Sanh crisis of early 1968.

# NOTES

1.  Department of Defense Dictionary of Military and Associated Terms (1979) quoted in John J. Lane Jr., *Command and Control and Communications Structures in Southeast Asia* (Maxwell AFB, AL, Air War College, 1981).
2.  Ronald H. Spector, *Advice and Support, The Early Years of the US Army in Vietnam, 1941-1960* (New York, 1985), 110.
3.  See Ian Horwood, The United States and Indochina in the Truman Years, Unpublished MA thesis (University of Missouri-Columbia, 1993).
4.  Spector, *op cit.*, 114-115.
5.  Earle H. Tilford, *Setup: What the Air Force Did in Vietnam and Why* (Maxwell AFB, AL, 1991), 62.
6.  Robert F. Futrell, *The United State Air Force in Southeast Asia: The Advisory Years to 1965* (Washington, DC, Office of Air Force History, 1981), 79.
7.  Ibid., 79-80.
8.  In fact the Air Commandos had already fired some shots in anger during some early familiarization flights. Ibid., 80-82.
9.  US Government White Paper (February 1965), Marvin E. Gettleman, ed., *Vietnam: History, Documents, and Opinions on a Major World Crisis* (Greenwich, CT, 1965), 284-316.
10. Plans and Policy Division, Office of the Chief of Information, "Analysis of Public Statements on Ten Selected Issues of Gen. W.C. Westmoreland" (July 1968), Box 1 & Memo for Rostow (24 October 1966), Box 12, Westmoreland v CBS Litigation Collection, US National Archives (hereinafter referred to as USNA) College Park, MD., RG 407. It should also be noted that, in 1967, Westmoreland was actually ordered by the Chairman of the JCS to make some positive public statements about the bombing. Wheeler to Westmoreland (March 1967), Westmoreland Papers, Box 13, Folder 363, USNA RG 319.
11. Robert Thompson, "Lessons from the Vietnam War," Report of a seminar held at the Royal United Services Institute, London, Westmoreland Papers, Box 3, Folder 77, 2.
12. The name was changed due to the colonial connotations attached by the Vietnamese to the word "expeditionary," a title that the French had given to their own forces during the First Indochina War.
13. Keith B. McCutcheon, "Marine Aviation in Vietnam, 1962-1970," *US Naval Institute Proceedings, Naval Review 1971*, 164.
14. William W. Momyer, *Airpower in Three Wars* (New York, 1980), 76-77.
15. See Edward Luttwak, *The Pentagon and the Art of War* (New York, 1985), 24-27, 43, 86 & 272 for a discussion of the nature of the JCS.
16. With the exception of the southernmost portion of North Vietnam, or Route Pack One, which was deemed to be an extension of the southern

battlefield on account of the fact that the North Vietnamese emplaced artillery there which was capable of firing into South Vietnam.

17. William C. Westmoreland, *A Soldier Reports* (New York, 1980), 96.

18. John Schlight, *The United States Air Force in Southeast Asia, The War in South Vietnam, The Years of the Offensive: 1965-1968* (Washington, DC, Office of Air Force History, 1988), 10.

19. Ibid, 10.

20. US Government "White Paper" (February 1965), Gettleman, op cit., 284-316.

21. Momyer, *Airpower in Three Wars*, 99-104.

22. Ibid., 99-104.

23. Westmoreland, *op cit.*, 94.

24. While perhaps not entirely in accord with the spirit of unified command, considerable precedent exists for this arrangement. During the Korean War General Douglas MacArthur acted as his own Army component commander in the technically unified FECOM. General Dwight D. Eisenhower reserved the same role for himself in the Second World War SHAEF.

25. Schlight, *op cit.*, 10-11.

26. Rollen H. Anthis, MG (USAF), Interview (US Air Force Oral History Collection, 17 November 1969), US Air Force Historical Research Agency [hereinafter referred to as AFHRA], K239.0512-240, 42.

27. Anthis to Zuckert (9 January 1963), & Anthis to Smart (25 November 1963), Miscellaneous Correspondence, AFHRA, K526.

28. Hunter Harris, Gen (USAF), Interview (8 February 1967), AFHRA, K239.0512-377, 19-20.

29. Westmoreland, *op cit.*, 95.

30. Throckmorton to Westmoreland, (131822Z, November 1965), Westmoreland Papers, Box 12, Folder 358b, Message File COMUSMACV (1 October-December 1965), USNA RG 319.

31. Robert L. Gallucci, "United States Military Policy in Vietnam: A View from the Bureaucratic Perspective" (Ph.D. diss., Brandeis University, 1974), 107.

32. See J. Taylor Sink, *Rethinking the Air Operations Center: Air Force Command and Control in Conventional War* (Maxwell AFB, AL, 1994), 13-22.

33. William W. Momyer, *USAF Southeast Asia Monograph Series, Vol. III, Monograph 4, The Vietnamese Air Force, 1951-1975, An Analysis of its Role in Combat* (Washington, DC, Office of Air Force History, 1985), 10.

34. Ibid., 10.

35. Lawrence J. Hickey, "Operation HICKORY – Special Report," Contemporary Historical Examination of Current Operations [CHECO] Report (24 July 1967), AFHRA, K717.0413-18, 1.

36. MACV Directive 34, "Air Operations Center" (18 August 1962), in 2d Air Division, "Discussion of MACV Directives Relating to Control and Coordination of Air," 18 August 1962-November 1963), AFHRA, K526.549-1.

37. George S. Eckhardt, *Vietnam Studies, Command and Control* (Washington, DC, Department of the Army, 1974), 37-38.

38. Momyer, *The Vietnamese Air Force*, 4-8.

39. 2d Air Division, "Discussion of MACV Directives Relating to Control and Coordination of Air."

40. MACV Directive 34, "Air Operations Center" (18 August 1962), 2d Air Div.,"Discussion of MACV Directives Relating to Control and Coordination of Air."

41. McCutcheon, "Marine Aviation in Vietnam," 175.

42. Momyer, *Airpower in Three Wars*, 73-81.

43. "Discussion of MACV Directives Relating to Control and Coordination of Air."

44. HQ 2d Air Division, "Final Report: Operational Test and Evaluation Vietnam TACS" (25 February, 1964), AFHRA, K526.45011-1.

45. COMUSMACV to CINCPAC, "Air Support Arrangements in Vietnam" (17 February 1964), AFHRA, K526.45011-3, 1-7 &, 23.

46. Ibid., 15, 18 & 22.

47. Ibid., 7.

48. Ibid., 7, 15, 18 & 22-24.

49. HQ 2d Air Division, "Final Report: Operational Test and Evaluation Vietnam TACS," iii-iv.

50. Ibid., 21.

51. Paul L. Bogen to Director JRATA, "Comments on the Final Report Operational Test and Evaluation TACS in RVN" (5 May 1964), AFHRA, K526.45011-2, 1-3.

52. Corona Harvest Report, "Command and Control of Southeast Asia Air Operations, 1 January 1965-31 March 1968" (January 1973), AFHRA, K239.034-4, 25-27.

53. Ibid., 27.

54. The twelve-man board had included representatives from CINCPAC's staff and the three Pacific Command component commands. McCutcheon, "Marine Aviation in Vietnam," 174.

55. CINCPAC Tactical Air support Procedures Board Report (December 1963), McCutcheon Papers, US Marine Corps Historical Center, Washington, DC.

56. McCutcheon, "Marine Aviation in Vietnam," 175-176 & 178.

57. Keith B. McCutcheon, LG. (USMC), Interview (22 April 1971), AFHRA, K239.0512-1164, 5 & McCutcheon, "Marine Aviation in Vietnam," 176.

58. 2d Air Division to CINCPACAF (1 Feb 1966), Doc 6, Kenneth Sams, "Operation HARVEST MOON, 8-18 December 1965 – Special Report," CHECO Report (3 March 1966), AFHRA, K717.0413-3, 1.

59. 2d Air Div to CINCPACAF (1 February 1965), Doc. Sams, op cit., 1.

60. Sams, op cit., 3-4.

61. After Action Report, LIEN KIET 18 (HARVEST MOON), ALO 5th Regt. ARVN, n.d., Doc. 2, Sams, op cit. According to the ALO the US Army advisor with ARVN 1/5 said that "if it had not been for the [USAF] O-1Es the

VC would have over-run their position" on 9 December. [paraphrase by ALO] & Sams, op cit., 5-7.

62. Sams, op cit., 2. This information furnished by I Corps ALO, but otherwise unconfirmed.

63. Report, TACD [Hagemann] to 7th Air Force, Subject: "7th Air Force Participation in III MAF Operation HICKORY" (26 May 1967), Doc. 2, Hickey, op cit., 3 & Report, 26.

64. Interview with Henly (7AF ALO with I MAW), (24 May 1967), Interview with Newell & Interview with Capt. H. Campbell [Tally Ho FAC], Hickey, op cit., Docs: 1, Item 2 (1), 4 (5) & 6 (1-2).

65. Hickey, 6-12.

66. Interview with Campbell (Tally Ho FAC); Interview with Newell & Letter TACD (Hagemann) to 7th Air Force, Subject: "7th Air Force Participation in III MAF Operation HICKORY" (20 May 1967), Hickey, op cit., Docs: 3 (1-2), 4 (1-2) & 6 (2-4).

67. Letter, TACD to 7th Air Force, Subject: "7th Air Force Participation in III MAF Operation HICKORY" (20 May 1967), Doc. 3, Hickey, op cit., 2.

68. Interview with Getz, Item 1, p1 & Interview with Henly, Item 2, 3, Doc 1, Hickey, op cit., Doc. 1, Items: 1 (1) & 2 (3).

69. Interview with Maj. W. Newell (Operations Officer, Task Force Tally Ho), Interview with Campbell [Tally Ho FAC] & Message, 20 TASS to 7th Air Force, Subject: "Special Report - ABCCC Hillsboro Operations Activities, Tally Ho/Tiger Hound" (18 May 1967), Hickey, op cit., Docs.: 4 (3-4), 6 (4-5) & 7.

70. Report, TACD [Hagemann] to 7th Air Force, Subject: "7th Air Force Participation in III MAF Operation HICKORY" (26 May 1967), Letter, TACD [Hagemann] to 7th Air Force, Subject: "7AF Participation in III MAF Operation Hickory" (20 May 1967), Hickey, op cit., Docs: 2 (3), 3 (3) & Report, 9 & 20-24.

71. Hickey, op cit., 7-9.

72. Letter, TACD [Hagemann] to 7th Air Force, Subject: "7th Air Force Participation in III MAF Operation HICKORY" (20 May 1967), Hickey, op cit., Doc. 3, 1-2.

73. "Command and Control of Southeast Asia Air Operations," 25-27.

74. COMUSMACV to Johnson [Acting CJCS] and Sharp [CINCPAC] (27 September 1967), Westmoreland Papers, Box 13, Folder 365, Message File.

75. Momyer, *Air Power in Three Wars*, 304-306.

76. MG. John R. Chaison [USMC] has argued that the USAF's sortie rate was poor by comparison with that of I MAW's aircraft and that the NVA artillery may have been dispersed rather than destroyed. Interview (19 November 1969), USMC Oral History Collection, US Marine Corps Historical Center, Washington, DC

77. General Hamilton H. Howze, head of the 1962 Army Tactical Mobility Requirements Board may have summed up part of the Army's attitude to aviation in describing flying with the service in the 1950s: "Our accident rate was terrible . . . We took prudent measures to lessen accidents, but deemed it

very unwise to decrease the accident rate by lessening our exposure . . . we were experimenting with low-level flight maneuvers and rough terrain landing and takeoff techniques which, when they went slightly awry, would roll up an aircraft. Of course, an Army helicopter might land and take off twenty times as often as an Air Force jet, habitually flirting with the tree tops: and it is well-known that accidents occur at low altitudes." "The Howze Board," Army, Vol. 24 (February 1974), 10-11.

# CHAPTER 4

## TACTICAL AIRLIFT IN VIETNAM

*From a comprehensive standpoint, the possession*
*of organic aviation has increased the combat potential*
*of Army ground units tremendously. According to Army*
*sources, organic aviation assets multiplied friendly*
*troop numbers. A few commanders considered their*
*units—with helicopters—could carry out operations*
*with the same effect as ground units, as much as fifteen*
*times as large, but without aviation. Others believed*
*six or eight to one, was a more realistic figure.*[1]

After Vietnam, it is difficult to talk about tactical airlift as a discrete subject—at least in the context of the United States. This is because the seemingly clear distinction between tactical airlift and close air support operations was complicated in South Vietnam by the US Army's introduction of airmobility.

Fundamentally, airmobility could be described as a developed form of tactical airlift—or more correctly, a developed form of "assault airlift." Although the subject of debate, the Air Force had borne primary responsibility for this role, but in the years between 1962 and 1964, the Army had won the right to develop extensive organic aviation resources to provide its soldiers with the new form of mobility. Thus, a burgeoning area of tactical airlift had become a major Army—not Air Force—responsibility.

For its newfound airmobility, Army units relied not only on organic helicopters, but also on a fleet of Army fixed-wing light tactical transport aircraft. While the Air Force could perhaps tolerate large numbers of Army utility helicopters, the existence of the Army's CV-2 Caribou light tactical transport aircraft was a much harder pill to swallow as it seemed to compete very closely with the Air Force's own tactical transport force.

The picture was further complicated by the fact that airmobility brought in its train new requirements for close air support, especially in the assault phase of airmobile operations, and the Army sought to fill this vacuum with its own organic helicopter gunships and fixed-wing AV-1 Mohawk close air support aircraft. Eventually, in South Vietnam, the Army even hung guns on most of its utility and transport helicopters. Thus, close air support in Vietnam is inextricably entwined with airmobility which itself is a developed form of tactical airlift.

In the early 1960s, United States Army aviation consisted of both a helicopter program and an extensive fixed-wing aircraft program. The objectives of the latter went far beyond the light aircraft that the Army had traditionally used for artillery observation and liaison purposes. Despite the increasing significance of helicopters, there were no indications that rotary-wing aircraft would entirely supplant fixed-wing aircraft in the Army aviation inventory for the foreseeable future. Important Army fixed-wing aircraft projects continued in the shape of the O/AV-1 Mohawk surveillance/close support aircraft and the CV-2 Caribou light tactical transport. Both the Army helicopter and fixed-wing programs competed with the Air Force for key airpower roles and missions, but while the Army's helicopters are still with us, the service's ambitious fixed-wing program did not survive the decade.

The Vietnam War forced the developmental pace of both airpower doctrine and technology. The resulting hothouse atmosphere exacerbated existing differences between the US armed services over airpower roles and missions. By 1966, the dispute between the Army and the Air Force had become so emotive that it began to attract the attention of both the Secretary of Defense and Congress. This led to a series of talks on roles and missions between the Air Force and Army Chiefs of Staff from which there emerged a formal agreement between the services on 6 April 1966.

In subscribing to this agreement, Army Chief of Staff, General Harold K. Johnson, wished to end the threat posed by Air Force opposition to the Army aviation program in general and to its helicopters in particular. To achieve this central objective General Johnson felt it necessary to give up the service's CV-2 fixed-wing light tactical transport to the Air Force, but he hoped to do so in such a way as to have some prospect of retaining the special capabilities of these, and any follow-on replacement aircraft, at the disposal of the Army. Johnson also wished to placate conservative Army officers by curtailing some of the more ambitious, and therefore inflammatory, expectations of Army aviation proponents, particularly in regards their demands for the increasingly capable fixed-wing aircraft that so clearly impinged on Air Force roles and capabilities.

As a result of the talks with his opposite number—Air Force General John P. McConnell—General Johnson achieved his objective of securing the Army's helicopter program for the future at the expense of surrendering the Army's CV-2 transports to the Air Force. For his part, General McConnell established the Air Force's exclusive right to operate fixed-wing tactical transport aircraft at the cost of renouncing any further claims to helicopters.[2]

The Air Force, however, was to renege on its promise—implicit in the McConnell-Johnson Agreement—to retain within its inventory light tactical transports, like the CV-2, for the support of the Army. The service also acted contrary to the spirit of the agreement by applying to it a strict interpretation that permitted continued Air Force criticism of the Army's helicopter program. However, Air Force protests were ineffective in halting the expansion of the Army's helicopter force.

The expansion of the Army helicopter program after the Korean War had already led to clashes between the Air Force and the Army over the latter service's organic aviation. In the Air Force's view, the Army had adopted the helicopter, not so much because of its unique capabilities—which the Air Force did not rate highly—but because the very novelty of rotary-wing technology made the helicopter an anomaly for which service responsibility was not yet clearly defined. Thus, Air Force officers feared that the Army was attempting to usurp established Air Force roles and missions by the "back door."

Combat experience in Vietnam stimulated the Army's development of the armed helicopter. As early as autumn 1962, the Army's disingenuously named Utility Tactical Transport Company began to experiment with helicopter gunships in Vietnam. These helicopters undertook what can only be described as close air support missions, a role from which Army aircraft were clearly excluded by established policy.[3]

The Utility Tactical Transport Company flew armed versions of the UH-1 Iroquois (Huey) helicopter, as did the Air Cavalry companies in the Army's ROAD divisions and the Aerial Rocket Artillery of the Army's new airmobile division, the 1st Air Cavalry. The early UH-1 gunship helicopters originally used by the US Army in Vietnam were actually conversions of a utility helicopter not originally intended for the armed role. However, on 7 September 1965, the Bell Helicopter Company flew the first prototype of a helicopter specifically designed to provide close air support: the AH-1 Cobra. During the Howze Board's deliberations, Bell proposed the idea of developing such an aircraft quickly by mating the UH-1's engines and drive train with a completely new airframe optimized for air-to-ground combat. The Howze Board recommended development of the AH-1 despite the fact that the Army had no official requirement for a dedicated "attack" helicopter. In this event, Bell built the AH-1 prototype as a private venture. On 11 March 1966, the Army announced that it would purchase large numbers of the new helicopter, the AH-1 becoming operational with the Army in Vietnam in November 1967.[4]

Vietnam experience also generated an Army desire to arm its troop-carrying helicopters, a development which Secretary McNamara sanctioned on 11 September 1965.[5] As we have seen, the Army had employed "gunship" helicopters for some years, but doubtless, both the Army and the Department of Defense were reluctant to aggravate Air Force roles and missions sensitivities by extending the principle of armed Army aircraft still further without a more clearly demonstrable justification. This development coincided with the beginning of airmobile operations in Vietnam by wholly US Army units rather than ARVN units supported by US Army helicopters.[6]

While the Air Force opposed these developments, it did not confine its complaints about Army aviation solely to the use of helicopters. Some of the most serious disputes involved Army fixed-wing aircraft. In December 1963, Director of Army Aviation, General John J. Tolson, briefed Air Force Chief of Staff General Thomas D. White on the Army's aviation program. During the briefing White warned that an Army-Air Force clash might occur over two of the Army's fixed-wing aircraft: the O/AV-1 and the CV-2, because of their considerable size. In fact, while both aircraft did exceed, by considerable margins, the weight limit established for Army aircraft by Secretary of Defense Charles E. Wilson's 1956 Roles and Missions memorandum, such weight restrictions had been subject to exemptions since the 1952 Pace-Finletter Agreement. Secretary Wilson had already specifically exempted both the CV-2 and the OV-1 from the theoretical 5,000-pound weight limit on Army fixed-wing aircraft at the time of the White briefing.[7] Other Air Force officers at the White briefing also expressed concern about the Army's testing of jet fixed-wing aircraft for deep surveillance. Army Chief of Staff General George H. Decker closed the discussion with the warning that pressure existed within the Army for the service's seizure of exclusive control of certain aviation functions, though Decker insisted that he personally was not of this mind.[8]

The origins of the Army's O/AV-1 program lay in an Army requirement for a long-range reconnaissance aircraft. Existing Army light observation aircraft were insufficiently capable for the role and the Army therefore experimented with a series of possible contenders including Air Force trainers: the piston-engine T-28 Trojan and the jet-powered T-37 Dragonfly, the Navy A-4 Skyhawk and the Italian G-91 jet light strike aircraft. The latter two aircraft were, incidentally, also theoretically capable of carrying nuclear weapons.

The jet aircraft incurred strong opposition from the Air Force and the Army eventually settled on the OV-1, a turbo-prop powered follow-on proposal for the same role, developed in association with the Marine Corps. While the OV-1 was originally conceived only as a reconnaissance aircraft, the Marines insisted that the design incorporate machine guns and weapons hard-points. After the Marines pulled out of the program, it proved cheaper to fare over the hard-points than design them out of the airframe. Thus, the Army inherited an aircraft that could be armed quite easily and from the outset those OV-1s serving in Vietnam were equipped with 0.50 caliber machine guns, though these were to be used for self defense only.[9]

There is little evidence that the Army adopted the OV-1 as a way of securing a close air support capability by the back door—though a few Army officers clearly were attracted by the aircraft's potential as a weapons platform. However, the existence of the aircraft's self defensive armament, its long loiter time and its ability to carry a variety of other stores became a source of considerable frustration among the ground commanders. It seemed clear to the ground troops that the OV-1s, going about their surveillance tasks overhead, offered a close air support capability that was potentially much more responsive than that provided by Air Force aircraft. Yet, they were only permitted to use their weapons in self defense. Given the aircraft's considerable attributes, the increasing use of the OV-1 in the close air support role was probably inevitable.[10]

The Howze Board also seized upon the OV-1's ability to carry weapons and included 24 copies of an armed variant, the AV-1, along with 36 armed UH-1B helicopters as "Aerial Rocket Artillery" in its proposed Air Assault Division.[11] These aircraft were duly included in the experimental 11th Air Assault Division (Provisional). In the Howze conception then, organic Army close air support was to be provided by both helicopters (UH-1s later to be supplemented by AH-1 Cobras) and fixed-wing aircraft (AV-1s).

Many Army helicopter enthusiasts, including General Howze, saw the armed AV-1 merely as an interim measure pending the development of more capable rotary-wing attack aircraft. However, it is likely that the Army would have persevered with fixed-wing aircraft for organic close air support had it not encountered such strong opposition from the Air Force. The development of a truly dedicated attack helicopter was always going to be a long way in the future and, as we have seen, the Howze Board argued that both the UH-1B and the AV-1 should be replaced by a projected Surveillance Attack (SA) aircraft to which a number of 1960s aircraft research programs might contribute, including the British P-1127 jet, fixed-wing, vertical take-off and landing (VTOL) aircraft.[12] This suggests that it is likely the SA, as envisaged in the Howze Report, would have been a fixed-wing aircraft, especially given that its projected maximum speed of mach 0.9 was well beyond the capability of projected helicopter designs.

In 1960, the Rogers Board took the decision to move to an all-helicopter force for the light observation role, but this incurred considerable criticism from many Army aviation proponents who favored the higher performance, lower complexity and cheapness of fixed-wing aircraft compared with helicopters.[13] Obviously, the O/AV-1 did not have the performance of the Air Force's favored multirole jet fighter-bombers, but the Air Force itself invalidated this criticism to some extent by operating its own low-performance Second World War vintage aircraft in South Vietnam between 1961 and 1965.

While it is probably true that most Air Force jet pilots had little desire to fly the slow and awkward-looking, turbo-prop powered OV-1, a number of their colleagues did enthusiastically fly the similar Air Commando T-28 Trojans, A-26 Invaders and A-1 Skyraiders. Air Force Chief of Staff General Curtis E. LeMay, however, pushed for the introduction into South Vietnam of the more sophisticated aircraft in the service's inventory.[14] It seemed only logical, therefore, that if the OV-1 remained unopposed, it would only be a matter of time before the Army graduated to more sophisticated fixed-wing aircraft of its own. As we have seen, the Army had already tested a number high-performance jet aircraft for the role filled by the OV-1 and Army pilots were participating in a tri-national evaluation squadron's tests of the British P-1127 VTOL aircraft.

The Air Force's lack of its own requirement for an armed helicopter tended to focus the service's animosity on the armed OV-1. Armed helicopters posed a threat to Air Force roles and mission, but in the short term, they seemed a lesser one than the O/AV-1 because their performance appeared so poor when compared with the Air Force's jet fighter-bombers. The O/AV-1, however, not only duplicated, Air Force roles and capabilities, it was actually a rather close relative of the types of low-performance aircraft the Air Force was obliged to operate in Vietnam before 1965.

Such was the level of Air Force animosity toward the armed O/AV-1 that the Army eventually decided to delete the armed contingent from its new airmobile division for fear that these aircraft would jeopardize the Army's entire airmobility program and none were sent to South Vietnam when the 1st Air Cavalry (Airmobile) became the first Army "ground" combat unit ordered to that country in July 1965.[15]

Apart from the O/AV-1, the other Army fixed-wing aircraft that was singled out for special criticism by the Air Force at General White's December 1963 briefing was the CV-2 light tactical transport. Large quantities of CV-2s supported the Army's effort in Vietnam and it was to these aircraft that Air Force attention turned following the deletion of the Army's AV-1.

Experience with airborne forces in the Second World War had alerted the Army to the vulnerability of its all-wooden gliders. The Army, therefore, developed an all-metal glider that metamorphosed into the C-122 powered assault transport. Further refinements led to the C-123 Provider. However, as part of the agreement creating the independent air force, the Army had to buy its aircraft through the new service. Having no requirement of its own for an assault transport, the Air Force over-developed the C-123 into a much heavier replacement for its C-119 Flying Boxcar.[16] Consequently, the Army claimed that the C-123 was unsuitable for the small, minimally prepared airstrips from which the Army intended it to operate. The Army decided, therefore, to purchase the already-developed DHC-4 Caribou transport from DeHavilland Canada which it re-designated the CV-2.

The Army-Air Force dispute over the employment of fixed-wing tactical airlift in Vietnam appeared to revolve around the relative performances of the two services' transport aircraft. These primarily technical issues obscured the fact that the services were most seriously at variance on matters of fundamental doctrine. Both the Army and the Air Force found evidence in their Vietnam experience to support their contending cases, but they were both trying to achieve different objectives and, as a consequence, spoke different languages, precluding effective interservice communication. Only the threat of Congressional and Department of Defense intervention contrived to force the service chiefs to seek a resolution of their ongoing differences.

The Air Force maintained that for maximum efficiency all intratheater airlift assets should be centralized under its own control. In Vietnam, the Air Force sought to do this through its tactical airlift system known as the Southeast Asia Airlift System (SEAAS) that supported airlift requirements in South Vietnam and Thailand with directly assigned C-123 aircraft. At the request of Military Assistance Command Vietnam (MACV), these were regularly augmented by numbers of heavier C-130 Hercules transports from outside South Vietnam. Among the tactical airlift system's tasks was the direct support of the US Army in the field in what were known as "assault airlift" operations.[17]

Certain that the Air Force would not provide all the airlift requirements necessary for the support of its airmobile forces in the field, the Army supplemented Air Force tactical airlift support in Vietnam with its own CV-2s operating outside Air Force control. In the Air Force's view, however, the Army's CV-2s could not supplement the SEAAS because they represented a second, and therefore, by definition competing, tactical airlift system. In truth, the Air Force believed the very concept of an "assault transport" to be inherently inefficient. Events in South Vietnam confirmed this view to the Air Force's satisfaction. The Air Force complained, for example, that around 70% of theater airlift capacity, including the Army CV-2s, was operating on an "on-call" basis.[18] The Air Force, however, preferred to operate a regular airlift service based on planned forecasts and believed that this would most efficiently be achieved with the larger Air Force transports alone. The Army CV-2s were therefore surplus to requirements, and in the Air Force view, the existence of this separate Army fixed-wing transport force should be dispensed with on operational grounds, quite apart from the demarcation issue.

Army officers, however, were much less interested in running a scheduled airlift service. They argued that the CV-2 fleet improved the Army's tactical flexibility. Because the CV-2s were organic aircraft outside the Air Force's airlift system they were, therefore, at the exclusive disposal of the Army. Also, the CV-2's excellent short-field performance meant that it could operate into shorter, more austere tactical airstrips than could the Air Force's transports.

Establishing meaningful comparative performance figures for transport aircraft is difficult because of the large number of variables involved. Broadly speaking, Air Force intratheater transports could carry larger maximum payloads than the Army's CV-2s, but the latter aircraft had better short- and soft-field performance.

An average mission payload for the C-123B was approximately 11,000 pounds compared with 6,000 pounds for the CV-2. The take-off rolls for these payloads were 4,670 and 1,200 feet, respectively. The later C-123K model had a considerably improved short-field performance as a result of the installation of auxiliary jet engines, though at 2,800 feet, this was still a good deal more runway than the CV-2 required.[19] Of course, the Air Force could improve short-field performance for individual missions by flying with reduced payloads. Despite the differences in the performance of both aircraft, Air Force officers claimed that the Army's operation of the CV-2 was a contravention of earlier demarcation agreements and a duplication of roles already carried out by the C-123.[20]

The Air Force accepted that the CV-2 had a better short-field performance than any of its own transports, but it criticized the aircraft's small payload and it also argued that in South Vietnam, the CV-2 rarely operated from airstrips that could not accommodate the C-123. The Air Force was, however, obliged to admit its reluctance to use its own C-130 transports from the numerous Army tactical airstrips of 1,500 feet or less. The Air Force objected to using these austere airfields because of safety considerations, a lack of suitably qualified pilots and because they took a serious toll of the C-130s in terms of structural and maintenance problems. Furthermore, the Air Force disliked the reduced C-130 payloads required by operation into these tactical strips because of the concomitant reduction in airlift efficiency. Nevertheless, the Air Force did make an effort to improve the short-field performance of its aircraft while at the same time pressing the Army to build longer strips in the 3,000-foot class, into which the C-130 could operate more comfortably.[21]

Naturally, Army sources disagreed with the Air Force's contention that their CV-2s rarely operated from strips that could not accommodate the C-123. Army General Robert R. Williams estimated that at any one time, the CV-2 could operate from approximately four times as many fields in South Vietnam as the Air Force C-130 medium tactical transport, and twice as many fields as the Air Force C-123. General Johnson believed that judging from his own experience, when flying in C-123s, "there were quite a number" of very rough and short strips in Vietnam where the Air Force crews either would not or could not land, though Army CV-2s did operate from them.[22]

Also, the Army saw the small load of the CV-2 as a positive advantage. It meant that an "adequate" payload for the CV-2 was actually quite small, whereas the Air Force was reluctant to fly a C-130 sortie unless it carried what the Air Force saw as its (much larger) adequate payload and there was also the prospect of an appreciable return payload. Even the Air Force's readiness to operate with a less than adequate payload increased with smaller aircraft, making them more ready to fly such missions with the C-123 and even more so with the C-7 (as CV-2s in Air Force service were designated) than with the C-130.

The Air Force argued that all transport aircraft, including those of the South Vietnamese Air Force (VNAF) and the USA's "third country" allies, should be incorporated into the tactical airlift system, but the Army refused to participate. Only the Royal Australian Air Force (RAAF), which incidentally also operated DHC-4s (CV-2s) in South Vietnam, joined the US Air Force in SEAAS. The number of RAAF aircraft was small; usually about three to six DHC-4s at any one time, but an Air Force report of 1967 found that since January 1966, the utilization rate of Army CV-2s was "slightly less" than that of RAAF CV-2s serving with the Air Force tactical airlift system.[23]

The argument over service responsibility for tactical air transport became increasingly charged with the dispatch of the 1st Cavalry Division to Vietnam in 1965 because of the airmobile unit's operational reliance on an aerial line-of-communications. In the face of mounting Congressional criticism, and with Secretary McNamara about to intervene, the argument threatened to spill over into other areas of dispute between the Army and the Air Force over aviation roles and missions.[24]

Both the feuding services had much to lose. The Army had its airmobility program and the Air Force its tactical air support roles. Unwilling to risk so much, the Chiefs of Staff of the Air Force and the Army, Generals McConnell and Johnson, respectively, agreed to hold a series of closed talks. On 6 April 1966, they reached a compromise agreement, to be implemented by the beginning of the new year.

Under the terms of this agreement, the Army would surrender its fleet of approximately 160 CV-2s, plus a few examples of the follow-on CV-7 Buffalo, to the Air Force and abstain from any further employment of organic fixed-wing tactical transports. In return, the Air Force would renounce its claims to responsibility for all helicopters operating in the intratheater movement, fire support and supply of Army forces roles.[25] The Air Force would continue to operate helicopters in the search and rescue and special air warfare roles and for administrative purposes. General McConnell promised that the Air Force would retain the CV-2 and CV-7 in its inventory and consult with the Army regarding changes in the number of these aircraft and their replacement. He also agreed that, where necessary, the Air Force would attach light tactical transport aircraft to Army units below the army level.[26]

Naturally, General Johnson's decision to give up the CV-2 to the Air Force aroused severe criticism amongst the Army's organic aviation proponents. For example, after Secretary of Defense Robert S. McNamara had expressed to General Johnson a reluctance to fund "two tactical air forces," the Chief of Staff had sought the opinion of Army aviation specialist Colonel Delbert Bristol as to whether the Army really needed its own "air force." Bristol's attitude was not untypical within the Army aviation fraternity. He replied that he did not think the independent air force should have been created in the first place and that he believed the Army should have both its own tactical transport aircraft and its own close air support aircraft. Following the signing of the McConnell-Johnson Agreement, Colonel Bristol went so far as to write a personal letter to McNamara in an effort to stop the CV-2 transfer to the Air Force, an action which led to calls from some quarters for the Colonel's resignation.[27]

General Johnson had two reasons for handing over the Army's CV-2s to the Air Force. First, the Army was already experiencing difficulty in securing replacement CV-2s and Johnson believed that this was because the Office of the Secretary of Defense already accepted the Air Force's view that its own C-130 Hercules transport aircraft could best fulfill the intratheater airlift requirements of both services. He therefore decided that it was better to trade the Army's CV-2s in return for concessions from the Air Force regarding the Army's use of the helicopter, rather than risk losing the CV-2 by Secretary McNamara's executive decision.

Johnson's other reason for trading the CV-2, and one that he must have been much more reluctant to share with colleagues at the time, was to curtail the ambitions of those very people within the Army who complained so bitterly about its loss: the service's aviation proponents. He subsequently acknowledged that the Army was "clearly . . . overlapping the role of the Air Force . . ." by procuring increasingly capable airplanes and it was this process that he sought to halt by surrendering the CV-2, at least as far as fixed-wing aircraft were concerned.[28]

In negotiating about the future of the Army's CV-2s with his opposite number, Air Force General McConnell sought to re-establish the principle that his service bore sole responsibility for the operation of fixed-wing aircraft. McConnell also desired to assert the basic Air Force tenet that all air power assets should be centralized under its control. In the Air Force's view, all tactical transports in Southeast Asia, including the CV-2, must be brought into the service's tactical airlift system and flown by its own pilots and not those of the Army.

The Air Force achieved the first of these objectives as the McConnell-Johnson Agreement mandated the transfer of the CV-2s from the Army, effective from the beginning of 1967. It was less successful with its second objective in that the McConnell-Johnson Agreement was a compromise that preserved some vestige of dedicated support for the ground forces by Air Force CV-2s, now re-designated C-7s.

Despite General McConnell's promise to detach C-7s for dedicated use by Army units, however, the Commander of the 7th Air Force General William W. Momyer attempted to bring the aircraft into the tactical airlift system following their acquisition by the Air Force. This was a direct contravention of the McConnell-Johnson Agreement and only after Army protests was the Air Force obliged to accept a compromise form of "dedicated airlift." Under this arrangement, the C-7s were concentrated in three fixed bases where they were under the nominal control of the tactical airlift system, but ground commands could request dedicated C-7 support on a daily basis by specifying their mission requirements. 7th Air Force would then allot "dedicated" C-7s to be managed by the ground command concerned, subject to diversion in the event of MACV declared emergencies.[29] US Army Divisional Headquarters; Headquarters US Army, Vietnam (USARV); the Special Forces and corps headquarters (including the Marines) were the main requestors of such dedicated airlift; with the supported forces usually receiving between five and ten aircraft daily.

According to Johnson, these arrangements were "largely satisfactory to the Army, although there were some complaints."[30] Certainly, the C-7 utilization rate did increase after January 1967 and some ground commanders praised the Air Force's use of the aircraft over that by the Army. However, other Army officers argued that not only had demands on the air transport system risen since 1966, but the exclusive availability of the C-7 to the Army had actually fallen, leading to a compensatory increase in the utilization rate of the Army's CH-47 Chinook medium lift helicopters which were more expensive to operate.[31]

Furthermore, the Army claimed that the transfer of the CV-2s to the Air Force proved that its own decentralized aviation system was inherently more efficient than the Air Force's centralized one. According to the Army, it simply plugged its aircraft into its existing logistics system, whereas the centralized Air Force system involved a whole new logistical layer to accommodate the C-7s. The end result was that the Air Force required considerably more personnel to operate the same number of C-7s for the same mission than the Army. This naturally meant that the Air Force organization also required more senior officers.[32]

111

Support of ground forces by dedicated airlift elements remained deeply unpopular within the Air Force even after the McConnell-Johnson Agreement had given it a measure of official endorsement. Air Force officers never abandoned the long-term project of fully integrating the C-7 force into the tactical airlift system. Immediately, the Air Force assumed overall responsibility for the C-7s, it allotted a few of the aircraft directly to the tactical airlift system and 7th Air Force officers, assisted, after 1968, by the withdrawal of Army units from South Vietnam, contrived gradually to increase this number.[33] By mid-1971, C-7s operating wholly within the tactical airlift system were involved in more than 50% of the total number of missions flown by the aircraft. Thus, there was some truth in Army claims that the number of C-7s available for dedicated use by Army commands declined.

While General Johnson may have been broadly happy with the performance of the C-7 in Air Force hands, he was much less so with the Air Force approach to the very principle of retaining a fleet of light tactical transport aircraft for the dedicated support of ground units.[34] Though he probably could have predicted as much, it proved no easier to secure C-7 replacements for attrition losses after the agreement than it had done before it. Nor did it prove possible to arrange for the replacement of the C-7 by a follow-on aircraft.

The Air Force did keep a measure of faith with the Army in General McConnell's promise to retain within its inventory light tactical transports for dedicated use by the ground forces, and by requesting replacement C-7s and follow-on aircraft in the same class. Given Air Force opposition to the very concept of dedicated use, and 7th Air Force's efforts in Vietnam to reduce the number of C-7s available for such operations, these requests were, however, never much more than half hearted.

A joint US Army Vietnam-7th Air Force review of C-7 operations in support of the Army did propose an increase in C-7 numbers in April 1968. The review team included Army General Robert R. Williams and found the current C-7 force insufficient to allocate the number of available aircraft envisaged by priorities established in June 1967. Although the fleet was supposed to produce as many as 60 available aircraft per day, there were actually only 51.7 C-7s available per day in June 1967 and attrition had reduced this to 48.4 aircraft per day by February 1968. The reviewers noted that Air Force attempts to make the most efficient use of the remaining C-7s were contrary to the spirit of providing aircraft to the ground commanders for their dedicated use and recommended an increase in the number of C-7 squadrons from six to nine.[35]

Generals Momyer and Westmoreland approved the review's recommendations with the latter pointing out that demands for the C-7's services, or those of some similar follow-on aircraft, were actually rising.[36]

McConnell responded by pointing out that it was unlikely funds for further C-7s would become available, though the Office of the Secretary of Defense had approved the procurement of additional C-130s. Beyond that, the Air Force was now concentrating its efforts on a Light Intratheater Transport (LIT) and McConnell told Momyer that he believed that the Air Force was pursuing the best course with regard to tactical airlift.[37]

McConnell's replacement as Air Force Chief of Staff, General John Ryan, wrote to Westmoreland, now Army Chief of Staff, in August 1969 expressing concern about the attrition to the dedicated airlift force, particularly as it affected Vietnam, but complained that the Air Force could not secure funds for more C-7s from the Office of the Secretary of Defense. This was possibly because "the OSD staff has not recognized dedicated airlift as a special aspect of the tactical airlift mission." If the Army wanted more dedicated airlift, said Ryan, it must support Air Force requests to OSD with a better justification for the role.[38]

The Air Force had long regarded small tactical transports in the C-7 class as inefficient. This view was reinforced by an Air Force Office of Operational Analysis study in the summer of 1969 which showed that 75% of C-7 sorties in South Vietnam were still being flown between airfields of 2,500 feet or longer. This suggested the Air Force claim that most of the work done by C-7s could be done more efficiently by C-123s and perhaps even C-130s remained valid.[39] As the Air Force shifted more C-7s away from dedicated use missions in Southeast Asia, the requirement for aircraft of the same class declined ever further in the service's list of priorities.

The very existence of such an ambitious Army aviation program in the early 1960s was, in itself, testimony to the intense rivalry between the Army and the Air Force over air roles and missions. This rivalry spilled over into the Vietnam War itself in the areas of close air support and tactical airlift. These particular disputes concealed the deeper fundamental doctrinal differences between the two services over centralized versus devolved control of airpower assets.

In the early days of the war, the O/AV-1 was the main focus of Air Force animosity towards Army aviation. Clearly, some of the uses to which the Army put its OV-1 aircraft in Vietnam did impinge on roles that were officially the responsibility of the Air Force. This development persisted with the Army's decision to use the AV-1 as Aerial Rocket Artillery in the airmobile divisions and the extent of Air Force opposition to the project convinced Army Chief of Staff General Johnson to abandon the armed AV-1 as part of a compromise designed to preserve the Army's airmobility program.

However, when the Army removed the AV-1 from its inventory, Air Force attention shifted to the CV-2 light tactical transport. Eventually, the dispute between the two services over this particular aircraft threatened aspects of the aviation programs the services were unprepared to risk. The Army's entire organic airmobility program would surely founder without the helicopter, but it might survive the loss of fixed-wing aircraft. General Johnson was, therefore, prepared to sacrifice the CV-2 for the principle of continued helicopter operation by the Army.

For his part, Air Force Chief of Staff General McConnell sought to re-establish the principle that the Air Force, not the Army, had exclusive responsibility for the tactical airlift role. If successfully achieved, this would necessarily make the Air Force responsible for the CV-2 and its possible successors. General McConnell realized that the cost of such an agreement would be the Air Force's renunciation of rotary-wing aircraft for most roles. Despite the severity of Air Force opposition to Army helicopters, this was, in some ways, relatively easy for an Air Force that had never been attracted to rotary-wing aircraft, and in any case, the battle against the general principle of Army helicopter operation had already been effectively lost in Vietnam. The resulting McConnell-Johnson Agreement of 1966 may have been, in part, prompted by the exigencies of combat in Vietnam, but the threat to individual service programs and budgets posed by the imminent prospect of Congressional and Department of Defense investigation loomed as large. Generals McConnell and Johnson were doubtless also eager to reach a decision before the issue came before the full Joint Chiefs, where the Navy and Marines would have a say.

Not only did the Army surrender its CV-2 fleet to the Air Force, but it also found that the consultative role—regarding fixed-wing light tactical transport aircraft—clearly specified in the McConnell-Johnson Agreement—was a dead letter. The Air Force, having secured control of the CV-2, was less than true to the spirit of the April 1966 agreement. It nibbled away at the "dedicated use," tactical airlift fleet, gradually absorbing the C-7s into its own tactical airlift system and allowing the light tactical transport role to languish, first by failing to provide attrition replacements and then by refusing to procure a follow-on aircraft.

In truth, there was genuine Congressional and OSD reluctance to provide the funds necessary for additional light tactical transports, but in any case, the Air Force preferred to emphasize the C-130 medium tactical transport, the B-1 strategic bomber and fighter production. The Air Force abandoned development of the follow-on LIT tactical transport in 1970, and OSD rejection in 1971 of an Air Force request for four squadrons of an "interim STOL" transport effectively terminated the light tactical transport role in the service.[40] The Air Force eventually handed over its few examples of the CV-7 Buffalo (C-8 in Air Force parlance) to the National Aeronautics

114

and Space Administration.[41] Whatever the reason for the disappearance of the light tactical transport, most Air Force officers found its demise infinitely preferable to continued frustration over the Army's handling of the aircraft.

In part, these developments were driven by the military situation in South Vietnam itself. It was only the actual combat use in Vietnam of light tactical transports by the Army that had induced the Air Force to take any interest in the role in the first place, but after 1968, the United States was withdrawing from Southeast Asia, and with the war winding down, the requirement for this type of aircraft's use in South Vietnam was declining along with budgetary support for new military aircraft projects. Nevertheless, an Army requirement for a new light tactical transport still existed. Even in the absence of war in Vietnam, and the failure to secure the interim STOL transport program can hardly have come as a bitter blow to an Air Force that never wholeheartedly embraced the light tactical transport role. Instead, the run down of the war provided the Air Force with a not unwelcome opportunity to concentrate on projects more closely attuned to its self image.

Without the services of its own CV-2s, the Army in Vietnam was forced to rely on the Air Force centralized air transport system and this did not entirely meet its tactical needs. Consequently, the service was obliged to think increasingly in terms of rotary-wing aircraft for all its organic transport requirements. In this way, the McConnell-Johnson Agreement may be said to have produced an arbitrary "solution" to the interservice dispute over the tactical airlift role, causing the employment of helicopters in Army roles for which fixed-wing aircraft might have been better suited. As a further consequence of the McConnell-Johnson Agreement, the Army may have felt similarly inclined to use helicopters in close air support tasks for which fixed-wing aircraft might actually have been more suitable. Close air support forms the subject of the next chapter.

# NOTES

1. Ernie S. Montagliani, *Army Aviation in RVN – A Case Study – Special Report* (Contemporary Historical Evaluation of Current Operations [CHECO] Report, 11 July 1970), US Air Force Historical Research Agency, Maxwell AFB., AL. (hereinafter referred to as AFHRA), K717.0413-75, 61-62.

2. *Agreement Between Chief of Staff, U.S. Army, and Chief of Staff, U.S. Air Force, 6 April 1966,* (The "McConnell-Johnson Agreement"), Miscellaneous Correspondence Box, AFHRA., K168.7085-33.

3. George P. Seneff, LTG, Interview (1978), 36 & Robert R. Williams, LTG, Interview (1978), tape 1, transcript 8, Senior Officer Oral History Program, US Army Military History Institute (hereinafter referred to as MHI), Carlisle Barracks, PA.

4. Williams, ibid., tape 1, transcript, 9.

5. Richard G. Davis, *The 31 Initiatives: A Study in Air Force-Army Cooperation* (Washington, DC: Office of Air Force History, 1987), 21.

6. The US Army 1st Cavalry Division (Airmobile) went into action in the Ia Drang Valley in October 1965.

7. Memorandum of Understanding Relating to Army Organic Aviation (4 November 1952) [The "1952 Pace-Finletter Agreement"] & Memorandum by the Secretary of Defense for the Members of the Armed Forces Policy Council, Subject: "Clarification of Roles and Missions to Improve the Effectiveness of Operation of the Department of Defense" (26 November 1956), Richard I Wolf, *The United States Air Force, Basic Documents on Roles and Missions* (Washington, DC, Office of Air Force History, 1987), 243-245 & 293-301. The basic unloaded operating weight of the CV-2 was 18,260 pounds. The empty weight of the OV-1 was 9,937 pounds. John W. R. Taylor, ed., *Janes' All the World's Aircraft, 1967-68* (New York, 1967).

8. John J. Tolson, *Vietnam Studies, Airmobility* (Washington, DC: Department of the Army, 1973), 10-14.

9. Williams, *op cit.*, tape 2, transcript, 33 & 35.

10. Tolson, *op cit.*, 40-44; Glenn O. Goodhand, BG., Interview (1978) Senior Officer Oral History Program, MHI, tape 1, transcript 73 & Williams, *op cit.*, tape 2, transcript, 53.

11. US Army Tactical Mobility Requirements Board, Final Report (hereinafter referred to as the "Howze Report"), (20 August 1962), US Army Center of Military History, Washington, DC, 36.

12. According to LTG. George P. Seneff (who had commanded the 11th Aviation Group during the 1964 Air assault Tests and the 1st Aviation Brigade in Vietnam), he and his colleagues saw the armed OV-1 as an interim measure until more capable helicopter gunships became available. Seneff, *op cit.*, 24. 24. Col. Delbert Bristol, a former Director of Army Aviation with Vietnam service, agrees that the armed OV-1 was an interim measure until the rotary-

116

wing Advanced Aerial Fire Support System came along. Delbert Bristol, Col., Interview (1978), Senior Officer Oral History Program, MHI, tape 1, transcript, 64. Hamilton H. Howze, Gen., Interview (1977), Senior Officer Oral History Program, MHI, tape 1, transcript, 3 & "Howze Report," 62a.

13. Goodhand, *op cit.*, tape 1, transcript, 71-72.

14. At a meeting of the Joint Chiefs of Staff on 5 December 1961 Gen. LeMay recommended the deployment of extensive US combat forces to South Vietnam including an Air Force tactical fighter squadron, an Air Force tactical bomber squadron and a Marine air wing. This was less than one month after the deployment of the Air Force Air Commandoes to Vietnam with their Second World War vintage aircraft. Robert F. Futrell, *The United States Air Force in Southeast Asia, the Advisory Years to 1965* (Washington, DC: Office of Air Force History, 1981), 90. In a 1972 interview, LeMay explained that he preferred high-performance aircraft to the types used by the Air Commandoes for close air support. Although he thought the Air Commando aircraft performed well he believed they were too vulnerable to anti-aircraft fire. Curtis E. LeMay, Gen. (USAF), Interview (8 June 1972) USAF Oral History Collection, AFHRA, K239.0512-592.

15. Tolson, *op cit.*, 62 & Seneff, *op cit.*, 23. According to J.D. Coleman, this was the result of a deal struck between Secretary of Defense Robert S. McNamara and the Air Force. J.D. Coleman, *Pleiku, The Dawn of Helicopter Warfare in Vietnam* (New York, 1988), 31.

16. This according to Gen. James Gavin. James Gavin, *War and Peace in the Space Age* (New York, 1958), 109-111.

17. Bernell A. Whitaker & L.E. Paterson, "Assault Airlift Operations – Jan. 1961-Jun. 1966," CHECO Report (23 Feb. 1967), AFHRA, K717.0414-2, 66.

18. Ibid.

19. Source for aircraft performance figures: Ray L. Bowers, *The United States Air Force in Southeast Asia, Tactical Airlift* (Washington, DC: Office of Air Force History, 1983), 34.

20. The Air Force had actually prepared to drop the C-123 from its inventory before Vietnam. Only a request by the Office of the Secretary of Defense that the Air Force turn over its surplus C-123s to the Army for training purposes stimulated the service's rediscovery of a requirement for the transports. It is possible that had things had been left entirely to the Air Force the service might even have abandoned tactical transport aircraft entirely. In the 1950s, economic considerations predisposed the Air Force towards ever-larger transport aircraft and it was, in fact, only Army pressure that ensured the survival of the C-130 programme. Williams, *op cit.*, tape 1, transcript, 3.

21. Whitaker & Paterson, *op cit.*, 55-59 & 98-104.

22. Harold K. Johnson, Gen., Interview (1972-1973), Senior Officer Oral History Program, MHI, Vol. III, Tape 12, transcript, 34.

23. Whitaker & Paterson, *op cit.*, 45 & 98-104.

24. Douglas Kinnard, *The War Managers* (Hanover, NH., 1977), 60.

25. CV-7 was the US Army designation for the DeHavilland, Canada DHC-5, a higher performance development of the Caribou. Despite a very successful evaluation the Army was obliged to cancel orders for the CV-7 after the delivery of only four aircraft.

26. The "McConnell-Johnson Agreement."

27. "Two tactical air forces" are Bristol's own words. Bristol, *op cit.*, tape 1, transcript, 56 & 60-61.

28. Johnson, *op cit.*, Vol. III, tape 12, transcript, 35-36.

29. Bowers, *op cit.*, 358-359.

30. Johnson, *op cit.*, Vol. III, tape 12, transcript, 36.

31. Seneff, *op cit.*, 33 & Kinnard, *op cit*, 17.

32. This report came to the attention of Congress resulting in some criticism of the Army. Williams, *op cit.*, 4-5.

33. Bowers, *op cit.*, 353 & 366-367.

34. Johnson, *op cit.*, tape 12, transcript, 36.

35. Burl W. McLaughlin, BG (USAF) & Robert R. Williams, MG (USA), "Review of Air Force C-7A Operations in Support of the Army," (18 April 1968), Ryan Collection, Miscellaneous Correspondence Box, AFHRA, K168.7085-33.

36. Westmoreland to Sharp (n.d.). & Momyer to McConnell (3 May 1968), Ryan Collection, Miscellaneous correspondence Box, AFHRA, K168.7085-33

37. McConnell to Momyer (1 June 1968), Miscellaneous Correspondence Box, AFHRA, K168.7085-33.

38. Ryan to Westmoreland (1 August 1969), Ryan Collection, Miscellaneous Correspondence Box, AFHRA, K168.7085-33.

39. Bowers, *op cit*, 525.

40. Ibid., 650-651.

41. Johnson complained to the House Armed Services Committee about the Air Force's reluctance to buy more C-7s, or its more capable successor the C-8, to support the Army. John Schlight, *The United States Air Force in Southeast Asia, The War in South Vietnam, The Years of the Offensive: 1965-1968* (Washington, DC, 1988), 123-127, 237-239 & Tolson, *op cit.*, 104-107.

# CHAPTER 5

# CLOSE AIR SUPPORT IN VIETNAM

*They [Army officers] were reluctant to be drawn into a comparison of close air support (CAS) by USAF tactical fighters versus CFS [Close Fire Support] by the gunships, with statements to the effect that it was as if one were trying to compare 'apples and oranges.'*[1]

As we have seen, the 1962 US Army Tactical Mobility Requirements (Howze) Board put forward the view that the Army should have exclusive responsibility for "special"—or "counterinsurgency"—operations, including any related aerial fire-support.[2] In doing so, the Board contributed to an ongoing debate between the United States armed services on this issue.[3] The Army claimed primacy in counterinsurgency operations, and as the war in South Vietnam appeared to fall into this category—at least until about 1964 or 1965—this suggested to some Army officers that there was no requirement for an Air Force presence in the country. However, the Army did not formally win the argument because, as we have seen, the US Military Assistance Advisory Group Vietnam (MAAG Vietnam) and its successor the Military Assistance Command Vietnam (MACV) were constituted as unified commands in which all three services were theoretically equally represented. Nevertheless, the Army did dominate both MAAG Vietnam and MACV, and indeed, early United States participation in the Vietnam War was almost entirely an Army affair.

However, while dedicated to the primacy of strategic air warfare, the senior Air Force leadership was unable to ignore the increasing emphasis of the Kennedy administration on "wars of national liberation." The Air Force, therefore, sought to cash in on the Vietnam conflict's growing potential for prestige and budgetary largesse by carving out a role for itself in Southeast Asia. Ideally, this would involve a strategic campaign against North Vietnam, but in 1961, in the absence of the necessary political will, the Air Force settled for a return to the tactical airpower business in South Vietnam, while keeping its strategic options open.

Once the Air Force had secured the principle of its participation in Vietnam, the stage was set for a direct confrontation between the services as both deployed their own forces for close air support and tactical airlift. These separate air forces were the subject of acrimonious dispute, but—at least in the short term—it does not seem that the Army wished to supplant the Air

Force entirely in its traditional tactical roles. Rather, the Army wished to stake out an area of organic air support, both fixed- and rotary-wing, which would be more responsive to its needs than that provided by the Air Force, but which could be augmented by heavier Air Force assistance when required.

Limited, though they may have been in the short term, there is no doubt that the Army aviation's designs did impinge on formally established Air Force roles and missions, and they also ran counter to Air Force doctrine regarding the centralization of airpower assets under Air Force control. Thus, Army-Air Force technical arguments over the relative short-field performance of their respective tactical transports and the responsiveness of their respective close air support aircraft in South Vietnam disguised more fundamental doctrinal differences.

The interservice debate between the Army and the Air Force over roles and missions became so bitter and so visible in South Vietnam that the service chiefs sought compromise so the dispute did not spiral out of control with consequent serious damage for both services' aviation programs and budgets. Early attempts to reach such a compromise achieved only limited success because the doctrinal differences between the two services meant that they were trying to solve their problems without a common language. Indeed, the Army and the Air Force never resolved their basic doctrinal differences during the Vietnam period. However, they did eventually come to carve out discrete service aviation fiefdoms, support the parallel development of each other's aviation programs (whether they overlapped or not) and develop practical working relationships for joint operations in the field.

Only grudgingly did the Air Force come to accept the Army's right to operate its own rotary-wing close air support. It finally did so under the formulation that this support was actually of a different kind to that provided by the Air Force with which it was actually compatible.

The Air Force continually lost ground to the Army over the issue of the latter's helicopters in Vietnam. First, the Air Force accepted the Army's use of helicopters in the troop transport role; then it accepted the principle of helicopter escorts. Next, Air Force officers found themselves trying to prevent the expansion of the Army's use of armed helicopters beyond the assault phase of airmobile operations.

The 2d Air Division made a number of complaints to the commander of MACV, General Paul D. Harkins much like that of 26 July 1963 which cited three incidents where Army helicopters had operated "offensively." The Air Force complained that this seemed an expansion of the Army's directive on the use of armed helicopters "to include interdiction and close air support missions." Furthermore, 2d Air Division surmised that requests for air support were being met by Army aircraft rather than passed on to the Air Force. The General was unmoved; he referred 2d Air Division to the senior American advisors with the ARVN divisions through the medium of their Air Force Air Liaison Officers (ALOs) because, according to Harkins, the ground commander had ultimate responsibility in these matters.[4] Harkins's replacement, General William C. Westmoreland, confirms that American advisers with ARVN units preferred to request close air support from US Army helicopters because their response times were faster than those of US Air Force and Vietnamese Air Force aircraft.[5]

This pattern persisted despite Air Force protests. Then, in the McConnell-Johnson Agreement of 1966, the Air Force accepted the Army's right to operate helicopters in the fire-support role. Towards the end of the decade, the Air Force was acknowledging the fact of the parallel employment of both its and the Army's aircraft in close air support roles as a function of the different types of support performed by both services.

The United States air effort in Vietnam was fought in two parallel campaigns: one over South Vietnam in support of the war on the ground and the other over the territory of the Democratic Republic of Vietnam (DRV) in the north. Despite the backwardness of Vietnam, the DRV eventually confronted United States forces over the north with the most sophisticated air defenses ever encountered in battle up to that time.

In contrast to this dense network of guns, missiles, radars, and jet interceptors, Communist air defenses in the South Vietnam were far more primitive. In the early days of American involvement in Vietnam, the Army frequently found itself with more aircraft in the country than the Air Force, while initially the Air Force exhibited more interest in applying its full strength to strategic air operations against the north rather than to tactical air operations in the south. This proved a very satisfactory situation for the Army and the service continued to cite the permissiveness of the air defense environment over the South Vietnam as a justification for the maintenance of its virtual monopoly of US airpower responsibilities in the country.

By the end of 1961, there were more than 3,000 American advisors — mainly US Army personnel—in South Vietnam, including US Army Special Forces troops (Green Berets) and two US Army helicopter companies which provided the ARVN with a measure of airmobility, including the transport of troops directly into combat. The arrival of the helicopter companies meant that the US Army had, not for the last time, more aircraft in South Vietnam than the Air Force.

However, despite his and his service's traditional preoccupation with strategic air warfare, Air Force Chief of Staff, General Curtis E. LeMay, had become increasingly concerned about the lack of Air Force capability in sub-limited wars as early as the mid-1950s. It was clear to LeMay that the Army's virtual monopoly of the low-intensity conflict in Vietnam might deprive the Air Force of valuable opportunities likely to accrue from significant participation in the war. Mindful of the emphasis on low-intensity warfare in the Kennedy administration's policy of "flexible response," it was at LeMay's initiative that the Air Force began the development of a unit for the prosecution of counterinsurgency—or in Air Force parlance—"Special Air Warfare" operations.[6]

Under the code name JUNGLE JIM, the 4400th Combat Crew Training Squadron was established in April 1961. Among the 4400 CCTS's tasks were the development of counterinsurgency tactics and hardware and—as the name suggests—the training of third country air forces in these techniques. Despite its innocuous official designation, the 4400 CCTS was developed from the start with a combat role in mind, a fact indicated by its informal title: "Air Commandos."[7]

In a National Security Action Memorandum of May of 1961, the Kennedy administration asked the armed services to develop forces and techniques for the specific purpose of conducting counterinsurgency operations and the 4400 CCTS seemed to fit the bill perfectly.[8] On 5 September 1961, Secretary of Defense Robert S. McNamara informed the armed services that he intended to establish an experimental counterinsurgency combat laboratory in South Vietnam. Clearly, the Air Force had developed the 4400 CCTS with the Vietnam conflict in mind and LeMay, naturally, recommended to Air Force Secretary Eugene M. Zuckert the deployment to Southeast Asia of a detachment of the Air Commandos. Zuckert, in turn, recommended this to McNamara. After the Joint Chiefs of Staff had agreed to the proposal, McNamara put it to Kennedy who approved the deployment on 11 October 1961 of a detachment from the 4400 CCTS to Bien Hoa in South Vietnam under the code name FARM GATE.[9]

LeMay, like most of his Air Force colleagues, believed that once the United States was committed to a conflict, the service should apply maximum force to it. However, in 1961, the United States was not quite wholeheartedly committed to the war in South Vietnam. Officially, the United States' role remained advisory and President Kennedy reserved the right to withdraw from the conflict if he judged the moment propitious. The nature of the Air Commandos' equipment, and confusion about their mission, reflected the ambiguity of the American relationship with South Vietnam at this stage of the war.

Sporting jaunty bush hats and carrying M-16 assault rifles onboard their aircraft, the Air Commandos were, by virtue of their selection and training, an elite unit, but their equipment was not at the cutting- edge of military aviation technology. It was selected with a view to ease of operation and maintenance under austere conditions by third -world air forces like that of South Vietnam, which the 4400 CCTS element was supposed to train. This fact also complied with the United States government's reluctance to use jets in South Vietnam because the South Vietnamese Air Force (VNAF) was specifically forbidden to use them under the terms of the 1954 Geneva Agreement.[10] Thus, the 4400 CCTS was equipped entirely with piston-engine aircraft: an armed version of the T-28 Trojan trainer, the Second World War vintage A-26 Invader attack aircraft and the C-47 Skytrain transport. Later, structural problems with the T-28s and A-26s necessitated their replacement by the more powerful piston-engine A-1 Skyraider that also served with the VNAF. The US Air Force hoped that these low-performance aircraft would not be unduly vulnerable in the primitive air defense environment found in low-intensity warfare.

Despite an assertion by President Kennedy that FARM GATE was to fulfill an exclusively advisory and training role, the Air Commandos were soon engaged in clandestine combat missions. On 4 December 1961, Secretary of Defense, Robert S. McNamara, agreed to the use of Air Commando aircraft on combat missions provided at least one member of the crew was South Vietnamese.[11] Thus, the 4400 CCTS joined the South Vietnamese Air Force in providing air support to the country's ground forces (and their American advisors), and although their aircraft were painted with VNAF markings, the 4400th became the first United States Air Force unit to fly combat missions in South Vietnam.

As the only Air Force unit in South Vietnam equipped with attack aircraft, the 4400 CCTS was, technically, the only United States unit permitted by established policy to provide close air support to ground forces.[12] However, the loss of a number of transport helicopters stimulated the US Army's adoption of its own organic air support in Vietnam. As we have seen, as early as autumn 1962, the Army's Utility Tactical Transport Company had begun to experiment with armed helicopters in Vietnam. Flying an armed version of the UH-1 Iroquois (Huey), the UTTC developed techniques for the escort of transport helicopters and the suppression of enemy fire in the landing zones. An Army Concept Team in Vietnam (ACTIV), established to study the application of the Army Tactical Mobility Requirements (Howze) Board's Report on airmobility to Southeast Asia, undertook further experimentation with helicopter gunships in South Vietnam.

The existence of an independent Army close air support capability in Vietnam was to be a point of contention between the services throughout the war. Air Force officers believed it represented an inefficient duplication of their own service's tactical air power and a contravention of their key doctrinal tenet of the centralization of all air power assets under Air Force control. Not surprisingly then, the appearance of Army helicopter gunships in South Vietnam led to early calls by the commander of the 2d Air Division, General Rollen H. Anthis, for the placing of Army helicopters under Air Force control. Anthis claimed this was not so much to dictate the manner of their use by the Army, but to provide better support for airmobile operations and increase coordination between Army helicopters and Air Force fixed-wing fighter-bombers. The Army refused, on the grounds that whatever Anthis's real intentions, the practical effect of his proposal would be the loss of any advantages accruing from the organic nature of these Army aviation assets. The Commander of MACV (COMUSMACV), General Paul D. Harkins, did not uphold Anthis's request, but in August 1962, he did direct the escort of all helicopter assaults by fixed-wing aircraft and ordered that enemy defenses be suppressed by concentrated air attack before any landings took place.[13]

Obliged to recognize the Army's new helicopter escort mission in Vietnam, the 2d Air Division sought to restrict it by continuing efforts to bring it under at least a limited form of Air Force control. Air Force officers argued that because of their lower approach speeds and altitudes, helicopters were more vulnerable than conventional fixed-wing paratroop transports, and fixed-wing air support was, therefore, even more important in airmobile than in airborne operations. They also argued that the crowded airspace over helicopter landing zones increased the requirement for centralized control.

Consequently, on 27 December 1962, General Anthis announced that Air Force fixed-wing aircraft would guarantee the security of helicopter troop transports until one minute before touchdown, when responsibility would pass to the armed helicopters. Authority for the dispatch of the armed helicopters against targets en route to the landing zone would lie with the fixed-wing pilots.[14] This system corresponded closely with Second World War airborne practice where the Army Air Forces were responsible for the security of Army airborne troops until they were actually on the ground. Not surprisingly, the Army disagreed with the system, not least because it precluded helicopter assaults in the absence of fixed-wing fighter cover.[15]

Air Force officers felt they had secured decisive proof of the urgent need for fixed-wing air support of helicopter-borne assaults and better Army-Air Force coordination in the Battle of Ap Bac which took place in January 1963. At Ap Bac the commander of the ARVN 7th Division and his US

Army adviser, Colonel John P. Vann, decided to go ahead with an airmobile assault in the absence of Air Force fixed-wing air support, using only Army helicopters to suppress the ground defenses. The result was the loss of five helicopters: the largest number shot down in a single action since the beginning of the war. A further nine helicopters were damaged.

As a consequence of Ap Bac, the Commander in Chief, Pacific (CINCPAC) Admiral Harry D. Felt, issued a directive that fixed-wing aircraft support all future helicopter-borne assaults.[16] The commander of ACTIV, Army General Edward L. Rowny, however, argued that the introduction of armed helicopter escorts appeared to resolve the problem of greater helicopter vulnerability that had accompanied increasing National Liberation Front familiarity with rotary-wing aircraft.[17] Ultimately, Felt's and the previous directives to the same effect by Harkins and Anthis were honored more in the breach than in practice.

The Army had already rejected the T-28 in favor of the OV-1 for the long-range reconnaissance role. Compared with this, and the other FARM GATE aircraft, the OV-1 did not have a significantly lower performance. Indeed, it out-performed the equivalent Air Force aircraft in terms of maneuverability and short take-off and landing (STOL) capability, the latter attribute being particularly prized by an Army which wished to closely integrate its supporting aircraft with its ground forces in the field.[18]

Along with the Air Force, the Army also had participated in the multiservice, fixed-wing, light-armed reconnaissance aircraft (LARA) program, for which the T-28 had once again been a contender. This was a specialized form of fixed-wing aircraft for the helicopter escort and forward air control (FAC) missions, whose role sounds suspiciously similar to that envisioned for the Army's armed OV-1s.

Long after the demise of the FARM GATE program, some Air Force officers, mainly ALOs with the ground forces and Forward Air Controllers (FACs), continued to believe in the value of low-performance, fixed-wing aircraft for quick response fire support of ground troops in Vietnam.[19] Air Force FACs and ALOs often argued that their own service's responsiveness to requests for immediate air support could be speeded considerably by arming the low-performance FAC aircraft themselves. This was precisely the kind of aircraft the Army had been developing in the early 1960s, but, from 1965, the Army was precluded from using them itself by a Department of Defense directive forbidding the arming of its fixed-wing aircraft.

The Army had, with some slight justification, described its armed UH-1s and AV-1s in the air assault divisions as artillery as they did compensate for a genuine artillery shortfall brought about by the need to make airmobile formations air transportable. However, the Air Force saw this form of words as a subterfuge designed to obscure the fact that these aircraft impinged on a role which was, technically, an exclusive Air Force responsibility—close air support—and in which the Air Force had an existing capability. Furthermore, the Air Force also opposed both types of aircraft on the grounds that they lacked the performance of the Air Force's fixed-wing, high-performance, multirole jets although, as we have seen, the Air Force itself used lower-performance aircraft during its early days in Vietnam.

Meanwhile, the Air Force at last enjoyed some success in its long quest for the combat use in Vietnam of more sophisticated aircraft from its inventory. Never very enthusiastic about the low-performance aircraft operated by the FARM GATE detachment, Air Force leaders had long been eager to illustrate the conclusive results they thought could be achieved in South Vietnam with more modern aircraft. Attempts to equip both the VNAF and the FARM GATE detachment with an armed version of the T-37 jet trainer amounted to nothing because the Department of Defense believed the South Vietnamese not yet capable of maintaining jet aircraft and because of the limitations imposed upon the VNAF by the 1954 Geneva Agreement, but the NLF attacks on Pleiku in February 1965 prompted a change of heart.[20]

Washington now authorized strikes by B-57 tactical jet bombers that had been based in South Vietnam since the previous August. From this point, US Air Force ground attack aircraft began to operate in their own national markings and the US government revealed for the first time that American aircrews were flying combat missions against the NLF. The requirement for a South Vietnamese crewmember on ground attack missions was also dropped. With the build up of US forces during 1965, higher performance multirole fighter-bombers followed the B-57s.

The absence of a clearly discernible front dictated that all Air Force close air support in South Vietnam took place under the guidance of airborne FACs orbiting the targets in slow, light aircraft. This reduced the risk of friendly and civilian casualties as a result of inaccurate air strikes. Close air support missions in South Vietnam comprised two types: "preplanned" and "immediate." As the name suggests, preplanned missions were scheduled a day in advance, in what were known as fragmentary orders to strike specific targets in general support of the ground campaign. They did not necessarily involve troops in contact with the enemy though they were often flown in support of specific ground maneuvers or air assaults which might be expected to encounter enemy resistance. They might be directed against known or suspected enemy positions, or designed to seal off access routes. Between 1965 and 1968, approximately 70% of 7th Air Force strength was committed to preplanned missions with about 300 such sorties being flown each day.

Immediate missions were flown in direct response to requests for assistance from ground troops who were actually in contact with the enemy, and these represented about 30% of the 7th Air Force effort between 1965 and 1968. Naturally, the key issue for the troops on the ground was the responsiveness of the Air Force to these requests for immediate support. In 1962, Air Force response times for immediate requests could be as long as 90 minutes.[21] However, the expansion of US Army forces in South Vietnam and the concomitant increase in requests for immediate air support led to improvements in the Air Force's Tactical Air Control System, which were largely in place by 1966. The speed with which USAF aircraft could respond to immediate air requests was further facilitated by the development of jet bases within South Vietnam in 1965 and 1966, which brought virtually the entire country within 15 minutes jet flying time.[22]

Apart from their obvious value to the supported ground forces, immediate missions were important in the light of the attritional strategy by which the United States pursued its war in Vietnam. Most operations, at least until 1968, were designed to bring the communist forces to battle and immediate missions, by definition, involved the confirmed presence of enemy troops. Consequently, the Air Force was quite prepared to divert preplanned strikes, already in the air, to cover requests for immediate support. These diverts provided the quickest responses to requests for immediate support. From 1966, diverts were usually over the target area about 20 minutes after the ground forces had requested assistance.

If no preplanned strikes were available to divert, the Air Force would scramble pre-armed aircraft waiting on runway alert. An average of about 40 fighter-bombers were held on runway alert each day between 1965 and 1968 and these usually took about 40 minutes from request to arrival over the target.[23] The reader will note that this is considerably longer than the maximum 15 minutes jet flying time from base to target in South Vietnam. The disparity is due to the operation of the Tactical Air Control System itself, by which requests for support were processed, targets approved and aircraft selected and launched.

The Air Force believed that its close air support effort in Vietnam was a resounding success. A 1969 Air Force report on responses to immediate air requests found that:

> In the course of research for this report, no interview, discussion, letter, or message brought forth any documented evidence that the 7th Air Force Tactical Air Control System was remiss in providing immediate response to requests for air strikes. On the contrary, numerous reports attested to the speed and effectiveness

of tactical air . . . the evidence . . . indicated that the overriding "need to improve" has not been demonstrated.[24]

Despite Air Force satisfaction with its close air support provision in Vietnam, evidence from Army sources and the Air Force's own Air Liaison Officers and Forward Air Controllers suggests that the Air Force Tactical Air Control System was not always sufficiently responsive, at least as far as the demands of the United States' attritional strategy in Vietnam were concerned. It was in these circumstances that the Army's own tactical air support capability—composed entirely of armed helicopters after the McConnell-Johnson Agreement—came into its own.

Even the Air Force thought its own response times could be improved if certain procedures were adopted, though these would involve trade-offs. One such procedure was airborne alert in which missions would be preplanned to deal with contingencies by loitering over an area until a target of opportunity presented itself. However, the report cautioned that this would not be a perfect solution as there could never be any guarantee that the airborne alert aircraft would be carrying the most appropriate weapon load for any targets encountered. It should be noted, however, that diverted preplans also sometimes resulted in aircraft striking targets with inappropriate ordnance loads.[25] The implementation of an airborne alert system in Northern I Corps, after the introduction of Single Management in April 1968, did produce an average response time from immediate request to bombs on target of 15 minutes for air alert aircraft.[26] However, air alerts remained rare.[27]

A variation on the airborne alert theme was the arming of the FAC aircraft themselves. Since the FAC aircraft were already over the target they could obviously respond much more quickly than either scrambled or diverted fighter-bombers to requests for immediate support from the ground. Air Force FACs and ALOs themselves frequently requested the arming of FAC aircraft in order to improve response times.[28] This, of course, was rather similar to the arming of Army surveillance aircraft like the OV-1 Mohawk to which the Air Force had reacted so strongly.

Certainly ground troops preferred aircraft that remained on station above them for long periods, ready to respond instantly to threats as and when they emerged. Thus, Lieutenant Colonel Frank G. Bell, the ARVN 24th Division ALO, reported that the Australian Canberra and the US Air Force B-57, with their extended loiter capabilities, were the aircraft most appreciated by both United States and ARVN troops.[29]

The ability of supporting aircraft to loiter overhead was particularly valuable for the support of airmobile operations. In the absence of heavy weapons on the ground, airmobile troops were especially dependent on air

128

support to provide suppressive fires in the assault phase. Unlike preplanned air strikes, which did not necessarily arrive at the optimum time to provide timely support of airmobile assaults, loitering aircraft were able to fit in more effectively with the tempo of airmobile operations. Presumably this had been one of the attractions of the AV-1 armed Mohawk in the original Howze plan for airmobile divisions. In the absence of the AV-1, as one ALO wrote of airmobile operations in January 1969, "It is at this point that the helicopter gunship comes into its own."[30]

Most contacts with the enemy involved only a handful of their soldiers and the delay involved in requesting tactical air strikes often facilitated their withdrawal.[31] Given the USA's attritional strategy, speed was of the essence in engaging these fleeting targets and Army helicopter gunships proved a faster method of doing so than requesting Air Force tactical fighters. This was because the Army's organic armed helicopters were at the exclusive disposal of the ground forces and because they tended to remain close to the supported units. In fact, Army commanders tended to find their own armed helicopters more responsive to most of their requirements than Air Force fighters.

The Army was eager to establish its right to operate its own close air support aircraft, but it always accepted the continued importance of Air Force tactical airpower in South Vietnam. In Vietnam, the Army saw helicopter gunships merely as occupying one point in a spectrum of escalation from the infantry's personal arms to Air Force tactical aircraft.[32] Rather than competing, Army officers in Vietnam came to believe that helicopters and tactical aircraft actually complemented each other; or at least that until more sophisticated rotary-wing gunships became available helicopters could only supplant fixed-wing tactical aircraft up to a point.

Westmoreland himself testified before a congressional committee that the projected Air Force A-X fixed-wing ground support aircraft and AH-56 Army attack helicopter would be compatible. Though there would be some overlap between them, Westmoreland thought that this was true for all weapon systems and that in this case he believed the "overlap will be small and desirable . . ."[33]

For its part, the Air Force pronounced itself satisfied with its own close air support performance during the Tet Offensive of 1968. However, the Air Force acknowledged it had experienced difficulty delivering air support to ground troops at night due to a shortage of AC-47 fixed-wing gunships, which illuminated the targets for the service's tactical fighters. This led, during the first week of the Tet Offensive, to ground troops having to wait from an hour to an hour and a half for the fulfillment of their requests for air strikes at night. "It was extremely fortunate," said an Air Force report "that the US Army Light Fire Teams flying UH-1s [helicopters] were able to fill this gap." Controlled by Forward Air Controllers, these helicopters "were usually available in a few minutes . . . In the early days of the offensive, the TACS [Tactical Air Control System] FACs considered the [Army] Light Fire Teams more important to them in this type of situation than tactical fighters, particularly because of their almost immediate response time."[34]

While accepting the usefulness of the Army helicopter gunships at night, the Air Force observed that they did not, however, have the firepower of Air Force fighters. This was true, but in many cases, the Army actually found the lightness of the armament of its gunships useful in that fire could be delivered more closely to friendly troops than the heavier ordinance carried by Air Force aircraft and that should heavier ordinance be required, the Air Force could always be called upon to deliver it:

> Thus, one of the most significant lessons learned during the Tet Offensive was the importance of combining the Army's Light Fire Team capability with the tactical air capability and using the FAC as the catalyst.[35]

An Army 101st Division (Airmobile) policy guide of 1969 reflected the Army's preference for using its organic fire support capability over that of the Air Force by ordering that Air Force close air support should not be requested if organic support were available. Indeed, the policy guide warned that, compared with organic artillery and gunships, requests for immediate air strikes by the Air Force necessarily involved a delay.[36] Nevertheless, the Army was not about to pass up the opportunity of utilizing the considerable firepower of Air Force tactical fighters when the occasion demanded.

Considering the A Shau Valley campaign of December 1968 to May 1969, in which the 101st Division was involved, Air Force sources recognized that "usually artillery and helicopter gunships responded appreciably faster than tactical air."[37] They also accepted that Army organic support was always likely to be faster than that provided by the Air Force, as the use of heavier weapons such as high-performance, multirole aircraft would require approval at higher echelons. Furthermore, according to a survey carried out in the summer of 1969, at the order of the Deputy Commanding General, II Field Force, Army artillery and helicopter gunships killed more enemy troops than Air Force tactical air strikes.[38]

However, while the Air Force had, by 1969, come to accept that Army helicopter gunships provided effective and economical, on-call, direct fire support, it also insisted that the Army could not compete with the firepower of the Air Force's own strike aircraft, nor the sophistication of its Tactical Air

Control and Forward Air Control systems. While the 101st Airborne Division had tended to use its organic fire support for brief, small-unit actions during the A Shau campaign, the Air Force noted that the heaviest ordinance carried by the Army gunships—the 2.75-inch rocket—was not particularly effective in penetrating thick jungle canopy, and the Army made much heavier use of Air Force close air support in static actions such as airmobile assaults, in defense of fire support bases and when assaulting bunker complexes.[39]

Friction between the Air Force and the Army on the issue of armed helicopters in South Vietnam never entirely abated. Air Force opposition to the Army's use of helicopter gunships in Vietnam centered on the failure of the Army to integrate its aircraft into the Air Force's TACS, the high incidence of Army friendly fire incidents and the service's conviction that helicopters were more vulnerable to enemy air defenses than Air Force fighter-bombers.[40] Keeping Army gunships outside the Air Force TACS both guaranteed that the resource remained at the exclusive disposal of the Army and facilitated its responsiveness vis-à-vis Air Force fighter-bombers. The disadvantage was that it probably did also contribute to the number of friendly fire incidents though this was a price the Army leadership seems to have been willing to pay in order to retain an organic close air support capability.[41]

The relative vulnerability of Army attack helicopters when compared with Air Force fighter-bombers remains a matter for debate. They probably were more vulnerable and continued Army acceptance of the need for Air Force tactical air support might be taken as an acceptance of this, suggesting that if the enemy were sufficiently well armed with antiaircraft weapons, the Army might rely entirely on the Air Force for support. However, Army plans for war with the Warsaw Pact on the European Central Front never excluded the helicopter. Instead, the Army developed increasingly sophisticated helicopters and ultra, low-level, "nap-of-the-earth" flying techniques to increase their survivability in severe air defense environments.

Though ostensibly resulting from the controversy surrounding the Army's use of the CV-2 fixed-wing tactical transport, the 1966 McConnell-Johnson Agreement was actually much more far reaching. In abandoning the AV-1 and then signing the 1966 agreement, General Johnson also drew a line under some of the more ambitious projects of the Army's aviation fraternity. Although it referred only to Army fixed-wing tactical transports, the agreement had the effect of exorcising once and for all the specter of high-performance Army jets that had so haunted the Air Force and, it seems, General Johnson himself. After April 1966, helicopters presented the only weapons platforms available to the Army. As such, the McConnell-Johnson

Agreement at last confirmed the fact that, with the establishment of the independent air force in 1947, the Army had lost the right to operate fixed-wing aircraft, both transport and attack.

Although clearly forbidden by existing policy, the Army's operation of helicopters in the close air support role in South Vietnam was an established fact by 1966. The McConnell-Johnson Agreement acknowledged this fait accompli by recognizing the Army's right to operate helicopters in this role.

The 1966 agreement also provoked controversy regarding the Air Force's own use of helicopters. Under the terms of the agreement, the Air Force could use its own helicopters for search and rescue and special warfare operations, but nobody thought to define special warfare operations. Predictably, in a pathetic mirror image of the Air Force complaints about the Army's use of armed helicopters, General Johnson expressed disapproval when a number of helicopters from the Air Force's 20th Helicopter Squadron, based at Nha Trang, fired on the enemy while operating in support of ground troops. The 1966 agreement was, therefore, amended to read that armed Air Force special air warfare helicopters would support Air Force units, other government agencies, and indigenous forces only when operating without Army advisers, or not under Army control.[42]

That the interservice debate over the Army's use of helicopter gunships continued after April 1966 reveals the paradoxical nature of the McConnell-Johnson Agreement. On the one hand, the agreement eliminated one of two air forces competing for the tactical air transport role by eliminating the Army's fixed-wing combat aircraft. On the other hand, the agreement resulted in the official sanction of two air forces competing for the close air support role. In some ways, this intensified the rivalry between the services with regard to the close air support mission. The Army continued to expand its close air support capability with increasingly sophisticated attack helicopters, the existence and development of which now seemed to be guaranteed by the McConnell-Johnson Agreement itself.

Like the armed UH-1 variants before it, the AH-1 Cobra was still only an interim measure while the Army awaited the development of an attack helicopter from the ground up. The Army identified a requirement for such a helicopter in February 1965 when it began the process of defining what it called an Advanced Aerial Fire Support System. Contracts for the resulting AH-56 Cheyenne attack helicopter were issued in July 1966.

The Air Force did not passively accept the Army's attempt to secure this extremely sophisticated combat aircraft. Secretary of the Air Force Harold Brown attacked both the AH-1 and AH-56 programs on the grounds that since they seemed to be intended to fill the close air support role, and this was already an Air Force responsibility, they should be evaluated against equivalent Air Force aircraft to avoid unnecessary duplication. The Air Force also objected to the AH-56 on the grounds that because it had stub-wings, in addition to its rotors, it was actually a compound aircraft and therefore not a helicopter at all! According to this view, the AH-56 contravened the Air Force's monopoly of fixed-wing aircraft agreed by McConnell and Johnson in April 1966.

General Johnson responded that the Air Force's attack on the AH-56 itself contravened his agreement with General McConnell that, he felt, implied an undertaking from the Air Force to drop its opposition to the Army's use of helicopter gunships. While this clearly was the spirit of the agreement to which the Army thought it had subscribed, the Air Force applied to it a strict interpretation with rather different results. The Air Force had promised only to drop its claim to sole responsibility for helicopters performing intratheatre movement, fire support and supply of Army forces. The McConnell-Johnson Agreement said nothing about Air Force opposition to individual Army helicopter programs on the grounds that they duplicated roles already conducted by Air Force fixed-wing aircraft.

This may well have been part of the reason behind the Air Force's abandonment, under the leadership of General McConnell, of its insistence on using multirole aircraft for close air support purposes. Determined to avoid the loss of any further territory to the Army, McConnell resolved to improve the Air Force's own close air support service by procuring a specialized tactical attack aircraft. The Department of Defense approved the resulting A-X project in 1968, and such was the service's haste that it selected an off-the-shelf model: the Navy's A-7 Corsair—the Air Force version of which first flew in October 1972—as an interim aircraft to fill the gap until the A-X could come into service.[43]

Thus, while the Army signed the McConnell-Johnson Agreement in order to secure its own organic close air support provided by helicopters, one of the effects of the agreement may have been to improve the quality of the provision of close air support provided by the Air Force with its fixed-wing aircraft, at least in the short term.

As one of General Johnson's main reasons for surrendering the CV-2s to the Air Force was to put an end to Air Force opposition to the Army's helicopter program, some Army officers felt that continued Air Force criticisms about Army helicopter gunships proved that the agreement was fundamentally flawed.[44] However, while Air Force attacks on the Army helicopter program did not abate, it has to be said that the Office of the Secretary of Defense rejected the Air Force's position, and in 1968, it approved both the purchase of 375 AH-56s for the Army and the development of the Air Force's A-X close support aircraft.

The AH-56 was in fact cancelled in 1969, but this was due to technical problems and the Army immediately announced a replacement program that finally bore fruit as the Army's AH-64 Apache attack helicopter. The parallel AH-64 and A-X programs again came under scrutiny by Deputy Secretary of Defense David Packard who, in January 1970, called upon the secretaries of the Army and Air Force to provide rationales for the two aircraft. While the results implied continued disagreement on roles and missions between the services, the two secretaries were unable to agree that just one of the projected aircraft could conduct every mission under the general heading of combat air support. They, therefore decided that both aircraft should proceed to the prototype stage.[45]

In Vietnam, both the Army and the Air Force criticized each other's provision of close air support, or damned it with faint praise. The Army claimed that Air Force response times were too slow, while the Air Force claimed that Army helicopter gunships were vulnerable, inaccurate weapons platforms and lacked firepower compared to its own tactical fighters.

However, the realities of combat gradually led to an acceptance by both services that each other's close air support capability was there to stay. The services did eventually reach a practical working arrangement for joint operations in South Vietnam with the concept of different but compatible close air support performed by the Army's helicopter gunships and the Air Force's tactical fighters.

By way of roughly contemporaneous examples, a 1971 Army report on air-delivered weapons distinguished between the close air support delivered by the Air Force's fixed-wing aircraft and the close-in support delivered by the Army's own armed helicopters, and an Air Force report of July 1970, on Army aviation in Vietnam, accepted that the acquisition "of organic aviation has increased the combat potential of Army ground units tremendously."[46]

A 1972 congressional subcommittee report on close air support found in Vietnam helicopters were "superior to fixed-wing aircraft for providing light, but sustained suppressive firepower in escort of other helicopters and in support of troop ships during landing operations."[47] As the report put it:

> The battlefield firepower contributed by armed helicopters is distinctly different from the firepower provided by fixed-wing aircraft, so calling both close air support may be in error in that it adds to the controversy . . . It appears that there is a place for both fixed wing aircraft and attack helicopters on the battlefield, and that

interservice rivalry over this issue is counterproductive to the goal of providing the best possible firepower support for the soldier on the battlefield.[48]

However, to many Air Force officers the notion of "different but compatible" close air support seemed little more than a sleight of hand device designed to rationalize the practical fact that both Air Force (fixed-wing) and Army (rotary-wing) close air support capabilities existed in parallel.

# NOTES

1.  Ernie S. Montagliani, *Army Aviation in RVN - A Case Study* (Special Report Contemporary Historical Examination of Current Operations [CHECO] Report 11July 1970), Air Force Historical Research Agency, Maxwell AFB, AL., (hereinafter referred to as AFHRA), K717.0413-82, 49.

2.  Final report of the US Army Tactical Mobility Requirements Board, (hereinafter referred to as the "Howze Report"), (Fort Bragg, NC, 29 August 1962), US Army Centre of Military History, Washington DC, 32.

3.  In a 1972 interview Air Force Chief of Staff General Curtis E. LeMay recounts the Joint Chiefs of Staff debating Army claims to exclusive responsibility for counterinsurgency operations. Curtis E. LeMay, GEN (USAF), (8 June 1972), AFHRA, K239.0512-592, transcript, 10-11 & William W. Momyer, *USAF Southeast Asia Monograph Series*, Vol. III, Monograph 4, *The Vietnamese Air Force, 1951-1975: An Analysis of its Role in Combat* (Washington, DC, Office of Air Force History, 1985), 4.

4.  John J. Tolson, *Vietnam Studies, Airmobility* (Washington, DC: Department of the Army, 1973), 32.

5.  William C. Westmoreland, *A Soldier Reports* (New York, 1976), 86-87.

6.  Robert F. Futrell, *The United States Air Force in Southeast Asia, The Advisory Years To 1965*, (Washington, DC: Office of Air Force History, 1981), 79 & David J. Dean, *The Air Force Role in Low-Intensity Conflict*, (Maxwell AFB, AL: Air University, 1986), 87.

7.  William W. Momyer, *Airpower in Three Wars*, (New York, 1980), 252-253 & Futrell, *op cit.*, 82.

8.  Dean, *op cit.*, 88.

9.  Momyer, *Airpower in Three Wars*, 253 & Futrell, *op cit.*, 80.

10. Under the terms of the agreement the VNAF was permitted to replace its equipment "on the basis of piece-for piece of the same type and with similar characteristics," but it possessed no jet aircraft in 1954. William W. Momyer, *The Vietnamese Air Force*, 2 & Article 17, paragraphs a & b, "Agreement on the Cessation of Hostilities in Vietnam," 20 July 1954, in Marvin E. Gettleman, ed., *Vietnam: History, Documents and Opinions on a Major World Crisis* (Greenwich, Conn., 1965), 143.

11. In fact, the air commandos had already fired on the enemy during some early familiarization flights. Futrell, *op cit.*, 80-82.

12. George P. Seneff, LTG, Interview (1978), 36 & Robert R. Williams, LTG, Interview (1978), tape 1, transcript, 8, Senior Officer Oral History Program, US Army Military History Institute (hereinafter cited as MHI), Carlisle Barracks, PA.

13. Momyer, *Airpower in Three Wars*, 265.

14. Ibid., 81.

15. Tolson, *op cit.*, 31.

16. Momyer, *Airpower in Three Wars*, 256.

17. Association of the US Army (AUSA), "Airmobility Symposium," *Army*, Vol. 14 (December 1963), 67.

18. This according to an Interview with Delbert Bristol, COL (USA), Senior Officer Oral History Program, MHI (1978), tape 1, transcript, 64.

19. MAJ John R. Albright, USAF (Khanh Hoa Sector ALO) to HQ 7th Air Force (31 Jan. 1969) & LTC Frank G. Bell, USAF (ALO, 21st Inf. Div. [ARVN]) to HQ 7th Air Force (28 Jan. 1969), "Air Response to Immediate Air Requests in South Vietnam – Special Report" (CHECO Reports, Vol. 2, Supporting Documents, AFHRA, K717.0413-56.)

20. Momyer, *op cit.*, 250.

21. Melvin F. Porter, "Air Response to Immediate Air Requests in South Vietnam," (CHECO Report, 15 July 1969), AFHRA, K717.0413-56, 1:2.

22. Ibid., 1:4-8 & 14-15.

23. Ibid., 1: xi.

24. Ibid., 1:19.

25. Ibid., 1:22 & Bell to HQ 7th Air Force, (28 Jan. 1969), "Air Response to Immediate Air Requests in South Vietnam," Vol. 2, Supporting Documents.

26. LTC Charles H. Parsons (I Corps ARVN ALO) to 7th Air Force, (2 Feb. 1969), "Air Response to Immediate Air Requests in South Vietnam," Vol. 2, Supporting Docs.

27. Momyer, *Airpower in Three Wars*, 277-279.

28. Bell to 7th Air Force (28 Jan. 1969); Albright to HQ 7th Air Force (31 Jan. 1969) & discussion between MAJ Kracht (FAC, 199th Light Infantry Brigade) & Kenneth Sams (Project CHECO), (6 Feb 1969), "Air Response to Immediate Air Requests in South Vietnam," Vol. 2, Supporting Docs.

29. The B-57 was a developed version of the Canberra.

30. Bell to HQ 7AF (28 Jan 69), "Air Response to Immediate Air Requests in South Vietnam," Vol. 2, Supporting Docs.

31. Bert B. Aton, "A Shau Valley Campaign – Dec. 1968-May 1969 – Special Report," CHECO Report (15 October 1969), AFHRA, K717.0413-75, 30.

32. Montagliani, *op cit.*, 48-51.

33. Westmoreland quoted in Ibid., 50.

34. A.W. Thompson & C. William Thorndale, "Air Response to the Tet Offensive – 30 Jan.-29 Feb. 1968 – Special Report," (CHECO Report 12 Aug. 1968), AFHRA, K717.0413-32, 16.

35. Ibid., 16-17.

36. 101st Airborne Division policy guide quoted in Aton, *op cit.*, 27.

37. Ibid., 27.

38. Ibid., 24-27.

39. Ibid., 28-30 & 40.

40. Montagliani, *op cit.*, 45-46.

41. Aton, *op cit.*, 28-30.

42. John Schlight, *The United States Air Force in Southeast Asia, The War*

*in South Vietnam, The Years of the Offensive: 1965-1968* (Washington, DC: Office of Air Force History, 1988), 238-239 & GEN J.P. McConnell, USAF & Harold K. Johnson, USA, "Addendum to the Agreement of 6 April 1966 ["The McConnell-Johnson Agreement"] Between the Chief of Staff, U.S. Army and the Chief of Staff, U.S. Air Force" (19 May 1967), Richard I. Wolf, *The United States Air Force: Basic Documents on Roles and Missions* (Washington, DC: Office of Air Force History, 1987), 384.

43. The A-X later became the A-10 Thunderbolt. McConnell did have something of a tactical pedigree, having commanded the 3d Tactical Air Force during the Second World War and having served in Tactical Air Command after the war. However, he had also served ten years in Strategic Air Command. Richard G. Davis, *The 31 Initiatives: A Study in Air Force – Army Cooperation* (Washington, DC, Office of Air Force History, 1987), 19 & 21.

44. Williams, *op cit.*, tape 1, transcript, 6 & 7.

45. Davis, *op cit.*, 21-22.

46. Montagliani, *op cit.*, 61. See also USARV Air Delivered Weapons System Study Group, "Air Delivered Weapons Systems in Vietnam" (1 April 1971), National Archives and Records Administration, RG 472, USARV Command Historian, History Source File, Box 1.

47. *Report of The Special Subcommittee on Close Air Support of the Preparedness Investigating Subcommittee of the Committee on Armed Services, United States Senate* (Washington, DC, 1972), 16.

48. Ibid., 18.

# CHAPTER 6

## KHE SANH: INTERSERVICE RIVALRY
## OR INTERSERVICE COOPERATION?

*This [Khe Sanh] was not just a victory for airpower, but also a
victory for interservice airpower cooperation.[1]*

In the early months of 1968, the Marine combat base at Khe Sanh,
in the northernmost, or I Corps military region of South Vietnam, was
besieged by some 15,000 to 20,000 troops from three North Vietnamese
Army (NVA) divisions.[2] Occurring simultaneously with the communist Tet
Offensive throughout South Vietnam, the war in Southeast Asia seemed to
be reaching a crescendo at Khe Sanh.

A superficial resemblance between Khe Sanh and the decisive siege
of Dien Bien Phu during the First Indochina War heightened the sense
of urgency in 1968. Like Dien Bien Phu before it, Khe Sanh seemed a
distant base, cut off from relief by ground forces and entirely dependent
on a tenuous airborne line of communication for reinforcements, food and
ammunition. As they had done at Dien Bien Phu, the Communists subjected
the 6,000 US Marines and ARVN Rangers at Khe Sanh to a continual, and
often intense, bombardment. Most ominously, the communists began to
dig trenches around the base, apparently in preparation for the seemingly
inevitable wave infantry assaults that had, ultimately, spelled defeat for
the elite airborne forces of the French army at Dien Bien Phu and, indeed,
had signaled the collapse of the entire French effort in the First Indochina
War. The scenario seemed complete to the last detail with the appointment
of the Communist victor of Dien Bien Phu, General Vo Nguyen Giap, as
commander of the besieging NVA forces at Khe Sanh.

Regardless of any considerations of the outpost's real strategic value,
the attention of both politicians and the media focused, myopically, on
the fate of the garrison at Khe Sanh. The commander of the Military
Assistance Command Vietnam (COMUSMACV), General William C.
Westmoreland, encouraged this emphasis. While Westmoreland was well
aware that Khe Sanh was, in itself, hardly worth expending any great
effort to defend, he saw the siege as an opportunity to use the enormous
firepower of his own forces to inflict a heavy price on the besieging NVA
units. Here too, Khe Sanh appeared to resemble Dien Bien Phu for the
French also envisaged their base as a "honey pot" against which the Viet

Minh would dash themselves to pieces, mounting futile infantry assaults in the face of overwhelming French firepower.

It was, then, with considerable fanfare, and no little relief, that after two months of bombardment, the siege of Khe Sanh was lifted in early April. The successful defense of the outpost was widely perceived in the United States as a resounding victory, and what was more, a resounding victory for airpower. As such, the siege of Khe Sanh highlighted the increasing importance of air power in the American way of war and demonstrated some of the new military aviation developments that were coming to fruition at the time of the siege. Khe Sanh also throws many of the main interservice aviation issues of the Vietnam era into sharp relief.

The siege illustrates key aspects of the debate over tactical airlift that had arisen between the Air Force and the Army as a result of the development of the latter service's airmobile concept in the early 1960s. However, there were no Army troops at Khe Sanh and the Army bore no responsibility for any aspect of the air supply effort in support of the base. That role fell to a combination of Air Force and Marine aircraft. Khe Sanh also provided a forum for the public exposition of ongoing arguments between the Marines and the Air Force over the centralization of tactical air power. This devolved into an unsightly squabble between the Air Force, the Marines and MACV that eventually demanded the attention of the Joint Chiefs of Staff and the highest reaches of government. As a result of non-operational, interservice political considerations, the Joint Chiefs were unable to agree to a definitive solution to the problem. Consequently, the Office of the Secretary of Defense imposed a short-term compromise solution on the services.

## THE SIEGE OF KHE SANH

The village of Khe Sanh lay in Quang Tri Province, in the northwestern corner of South Vietnam, 16 kilometers from the Laotion border to the west and 25 kilometers from the Demilitarized Zone (DMZ) between South and North Vietnam, to the north. Situated on a plateau in a plain of forest and dense undergrowth, the Khe Sanh combat base was dominated to the north and west by a series of hills, the possession of which was vital for the defense of the base. The base was linked by road to South Vietnamese Highway 9 that, in turn, joined Highway 1, the country's main north-south route, near Dong Ha.

Khe Sanh was originally a Special Forces base established to gather intelligence on communist forces moving into South Vietnam through the DMZ, or from Laos via the Ho Chi Minh Trail. In 1967, the base assumed greater importance against a background of evidence suggesting an impending communist offensive would involve the movement of communist forces through the area. Consequently, units of the 3d Marine Amphibious Force (III MAF) took control of Khe Sanh while special forces moved to the nearby village of Lang Vei. As part of the expansion of the base carried out by the Marines, US Navy Seabee engineers extended and resurfaced the base's runway—originally built by the French—with pierced steel planking to permit its re-supply and reinforcement by large fixed-wing transport aircraft.

Airpower's contribution to the defense of Khe Sanh comprised two main aspects: tactical airlift and close air support. At the beginning of the siege, Khe Sanh was effectively cut off from its main supply base at Da Nang by the loss of several bridges along Route 9 due to flooding and communist demolition. General Westmoreland rejected any early effort to reopen this line of communication by ground forces until weather conditions improved in the spring.[3] However, he decided that sufficient supplies could be airlifted to Khe Sanh for its defense by some five battalions or so of US Marine and ARVN Ranger troops. Denied re-supply by land, the defenders of Khe Sanh were to rely exclusively on their air line of communication.

Dien Bien Phu had also relied exclusively on re-supply by air. The fall of the French garrison suggested that the earlier air supply effort had failed dismally, but the French logistics bases were further away from Dien Bien Phu than Da Nang was from Khe Sanh, and the more primitive French transport aircraft had suffered from much smaller load capacities than their American equivalents in 1968. Early in the French siege, the runway at Dien Bien Phu had become unusable. As the net of Viet Minh trenches around the base tightened, the airdrop technology of the French transport force had proved inadequate for the shrinking drop zone causing ever greater amounts of French supplies to fall into communist hands. While the runway at Khe Sanh also came under fire, and was eventually closed to the largest American tactical transport aircraft, the C-130, it was never closed entirely. Throughout the siege, Air Force and Marine transport aircraft were able to maintain the aerial highway to the base and supply it with the materials essential for its survival. The smaller C-123 and C-7 transport aircraft continued to use the strip while the C-130s, using the latest methods of airborne extraction, continued to make accurate drops of materials to the garrison. It might be said, therefore, that the United States had the airlift technology required to make the defense of Khe Sanh practical in the way that the defense of Dien Bien Phu never was.[4] In the absence of relief on the ground, air supply became vital for the defense of Khe Sanh, as was the close air support effort expended in support of the base.

This took the form of an intensive operation codenamed NIAGARA. During the course of this effort, US air forces expended some 100,000 tons (US) of air-delivered ordnance, providing Khe Sanh with the dubious distinction of being the most "bombed" place in history, to that date. While no serious attempt was ever made by the NVA to assault the base, United States military authorities attribute this to the success of Operation NIAGARA.[5]

In December 1967, Marine patrols, sent out from Khe Sanh detected signs of a build up of communist forces in the vicinity of the base. Convinced that Khe Sanh would soon be under siege, General Westmoreland ordered his deputy for air, General William W. Momyer, to prepare for the coordinated use of all available air assets in defense of the base. The resulting plan for Operation NIAGARA, called for the placing of all the fixed-wing aircraft of the First Marine Air Wing (I MAW), less the command's transport aircraft, under Momyer's "single management," a term lacking official definition, but which both Momyer and the Marines were to interpret as operational control.

Following a number of actions around the base, the siege of Khe Sanh proper opened on 21 January 1968 when the NVA assaulted the Marine outpost on Hill 861 and began a bombardment of the base itself that would continue at varying levels of intensity for the next two months. On that first day of bombardment, communist rounds ignited a conflagration in the base's main ammunition dump causing the loss of most of its contents and highlighting the demands that the siege was likely to place on the base's airborne line of communication. In response to the developing situation at Khe Sanh, Westmoreland ordered the execution of Operation NIAGARA, but was forbidden by the Commander in Chief Pacific (CINCPAC), Admiral Ulysses S. Grant Sharp, to proceed with the implementation of the single-management aspect of the plan.[6]

The following day, representatives of 7th Air Force and III MAF met at Da Nang to establish procedures for the coordination of their air assets in defense of Khe Sanh. With all eyes riveted on the combat base, the Communists launched the Tet Offensive throughout South Vietnam on the night of 30-31 January, but attention reverted to the vicinity of Khe Sanh when, on 7 February, using tanks for the first time, NVA forces overran the nearby Special Forces compound at Lang Vei.

After a month of bombardment during which Operation NIAGARA provided heavy air support to the base, including the use of B-52 heavy bombers, operating in a tactical role, General Westmoreland again requested that he be allowed to appoint General Momyer single manager for air, and this time received Admiral Sharp's approval on 2 March 1968. Due to go into operation on 10 March, full implementation of the initiative was held up until 21 March—after NVA forces had begun to withdraw from the vicinity of Khe Sanh.

General Westmoreland now ordered Operation PEGASUS to relieve the garrison at Khe Sanh. Rather than mount a conventional ground drive, Westmoreland decided to use an airmobile division. While elements of the 3d Marine Division and engineers began to advance from Ca Lu along Route 9 towards the base units of the 1st Cavalry Division (Airmobile) acted as a screening force, operating to the flanks of the Marines in terrain that would have been less accessible to conventional ground forces. The Cavalry were able to use their particular mobility attributes to leapfrog forward from landing zone to landing zone, establishing covering firebases into which artillery was flown by helicopter as the advance proceeded.[7] Beginning their advance on 1 April, these forces linked up with Khe Sanh's defenders on 8 April, declaring Route 9 open some four days later.[8] No doubt the siege could have been lifted by conventional ground drive, but even though many of the Communist forces besieging Khe Sanh had withdrawn, the airmobile division's role at Khe Sanh was significant, not only in lifting the siege, but also as the trigger for the implementation of single management. Having raised the siege of an outpost considered vital to the US national interest between January and March 1968, American forces abandoned the base at the end of June.

**TACTICAL AIRLIFT**

The tactical airlift effort at Khe Sanh highlighted the varying capabilities of the different types of transport aircraft servicing the base. It will be recalled that the C-130, with its large cargo capacity (15 tons), was the Air Force's transport of choice while the C-7s (3 tons) were the old Army dedicated CV-2 Short Takeoff and Landing (STOL) transports that had been transferred to the Air Force as a result of the McConnell-Johnson Agreement of 1966. The C-123 (5 tons) was an older intermediate aircraft, originally designed as an "assault transport" for support of Army airborne forces. At Khe Sanh, of course, the Air Force transports were not supporting the Army, but the Marines, who themselves operated some KC-130s which saw service during the siege.[9] As we know, the Air Force favored the C-130 as the sole solution to its tactical transport requirements. It had never wanted the C-123, but these aircraft made up a large proportion of the transport fleet pending the opportunity to procure more C-130s, or a more advanced follow-on aircraft. We also saw that the Air Force had never wanted the C-7, but had agreed to operate the aircraft in order to retain its unique STOL abilities for the Army.

The Air Force, then, believed that C-130s were the best aircraft for the support of Khe Sanh, but the C-130 fleet would have to be supplemented by the smaller C-123s. Given the Army's concerns about the vulnerability of long-prepared runways under fire, it presumably expected the C-7 to be particularly useful in the circumstances of Khe Sanh, but the aircraft's relatively small payload meant that it could never play more than a minor role in the overall Khe Sanh air supply effort. Nevertheless, Khe Sanh presented an opportunity for the demonstration of what might be described as the Air Force and Army's competing tactical airlift concepts under combat conditions.

The heavy C-130s and C-123s were naturally much tougher on the runway at Khe Sanh—which was especially subject to damage due to the wet weather conditions in the area—than the lighter C-7s. During 1967, C-7s were the only aircraft able to fly into Khe Sanh for a time and the runway had to be repaired for further use by the bigger aircraft.[10] During the siege itself, however, the small C-7s could not possibly hope to haul supplies sufficient for five battalions into Khe Sanh and even the C-123 proved unequal to the task.

As at Dien Bien Phu, the communists sought to close Khe Sanh's runway by positioning antiaircraft weapons around the approaches to the base, with some results. Damage to transports flying into the base in January and February led to MACV concerns that C-130s and C123s might have to be restricted to airdrops of supplies, while the runway could remain open only to the C-7, a smaller target which need remain exposed to enemy fire for less time than the big transports during its short take-off and landing runs. While the C-130 had a landing run of approximately 2,000 feet, the C-123's was only 1,400 feet. This meant that while the C-123s could usually be slowed sufficiently and quickly enough to enable them to swing straight off the runway to the sandbagged unloading point, the C-130 often overshot the turn off forcing it to brave enemy fire as it taxied back down the runway.

Up to 10 February, the Air Force had seven C-130s damaged flying into Khe Sanh. On 10 February, a Marine KC-130F, loaded with fuel was hit coming into land at Khe Sanh and was lost to fire on the ground with eight of those on board dying in, or as a result, of the conflagration. The next day, an Air Force C-130 was immobilized by fragments from a rocket that landed nearby. Hit again the following day, the aircraft was finally flown out on 13 February after temporary repairs had been completed. Consequently, General Momyer decided that the C-130s were too valuable and too vulnerable to continue landing at Khe Sanh and on

12 February 7th Air Force ceased flying C-130s into Khe Sanh, increasing C-123 flights in an unsuccessful effort to compensate. Marine KC-130s continued landing at Khe Sanh for a further 10 days before the commander of III MAF, Lieutenant General Robert E. Cushman Jr., issued a similar order. Momyer's ban on C-130 landings at Khe Sanh continued until 25 February when the Air Force resumed landing the big transports, but the loss of a C-123 while taking off on 1 March led General Momyer to once again discontinue the landings.[11]

In the five days from 12 February, C-123s were able to deliver only a daily average of 48 tons of supplies to Khe Sanh compared with an actual average daily requirement of 235 tons (US).[12] The C-123 simply did not have enough cargo capacity to supply the requirements of the base by itself, while the C-7, of course, had an even smaller cargo capacity. 7th Air Force, therefore, agreed with the Marines to begin supplying the base by airdrop from C-130s supplemented by C-123 and C-7 landings, the latter aircraft being confined to the most critical loads where safety of the cargo was of essence, such as passengers, medical evacuation cases, and other very fragile loads.

C-130s conducted supply airdrops by two main systems: parachute container delivery and low-altitude cargo extraction. The former involved dropping supplies attached to wooden pallets into a drop zone just west of the base. Accuracy was guaranteed by using radar to guide the drops. The latter was really two systems: the first, and most common, Low Altitude Parachute Extraction System (LAPES) involved flying low along the Khe Sanh runway at an altitude of five feet with the cargo pallets being extracted by the opening of a trailing parachute attached to the pallet; the second, less successful, Ground Proximity Extraction System (GPES) involved actually touching down on the runway with the pallet being extracted by arrester hook and wire and the aircraft accelerating back into the air without ever having come to a stop.

Helicopters proved the only possible medium of supply for the vital hill outposts around Khe Sanh. As we have seen, the Air Force only developed its own assault helicopter squadrons during the 1950s with great reluctance and the Army's refusal to use them had come almost as something of a relief to Air Force officers with scant enthusiasm for rotary-wing aircraft. Not surprisingly, therefore, the Air Force raised no objection to the supply of the hill outposts by Marine CH-46 and CH-53 medium-lift helicopters. By the end of February, increasing ground fire here also, obliged the Marines to develop a flak suppression tactic called the "Super Gaggle" which involved the close coordination of Marine fixed-wing jet fighter-bombers and helicopter gunships with the Marine helicopter transports.[13] Given Air Force reservations about the vulnerability of helicopters in the combat zone, it is unlikely that many of the service's officers believed techniques like the "Super Gaggle" would remain a practical propositions in a high-intensity war against the Warsaw Pact in Western Europe.

The Air Force then, supplemented by a number of Marine KC-130s, provided the vast majority of the fixed-wing supply assets for the Khe Sanh combat base. The Army had argued that the big C-130 transports would be unable to use the small, unprepared airstrips from which airmobile forces would operate. Khe Sanh's was a more extensive runway than these, but as the Army had predicted, the Air Force—and soon after the Marines also— proved reluctant to risk the expensive C-130s and their crews in the face of heavy ground fire. The C-130's long take-off and landing roll made it just too vulnerable. Only lighter STOL aircraft of the type favored by the Army for the support of its airmobile forces were able to get in and out of Khe Sanh within tolerable safety limits, but they could not deliver sufficient supplies. While the smaller aircraft performed a vital role, hauling priority and fragile cargo, it was still the C-130s that delivered the vast bulk of supplies to Khe Sanh via airdrops. It should be noted however, that even though these did not require actual landings in the conventional sense, even GPES and LAPES required the luxury of a long runway that was never closed by the communists at Khe Sanh. Though the air supply effort at Khe Sanh was a success and could not have been conducted by aircraft in the C-7 and C-123 classes alone, the siege pointed up the accuracy of some Army reservations about the C-130 and the value of STOL capability for fixed-wing transport aircraft.

### COMMAND AND CONTROL (SINGLE MANAGEMENT)

While there was a reasonably amicable division of responsibilities between the Air Force and the Marines with respect to the air supply effort at Khe Sanh, the same cannot be said for the command relationship between the two services for the control of close air support in I Corps. The main issue of contention was the successive attempts to coordinate Air Force and Marine strike and reconnaissance aircraft that culminated in the introduction of the single manager system over Marine protests.

Prior to 1968, the command arrangements under which United States air power operated in South Vietnam had their origins in the 1963 report of the CINCPAC Tactical Air Support Board chaired by Marine General Keith B. McCutcheon. This suggested that in a multiservice force, under the overall authority of CINCPAC, the force commander should delegate a "coordinating authority for tactical air operations."[14] Such an officer would have the authority to compel subordinate service components to consult over air power matters, but not the authority to force compliance with any advice he might offer beyond this. In general, these arrangements found favor with the Army and the Navy, but not with an Air Force that, as we know, desired the centralization of all air assets, regardless of service of origin, under the operational control of the force's air component commander who would, of course, normally be an Air Force officer. Successive Air Force commanders in Vietnam desired the realization of this doctrinal objective which, in its most extreme form, would involve the bringing under Air Force operational control of both Marine and Army (essentially rotary-wing) air assets, making the [Air Force] air component commander "single manager" for all air operations, though they never achieved this objective in its entirety.[15]

Immediately, the 3d Marine Expeditionary Force—later renamed the 3d Marine Amphibious Force (III MAF)—arrived in South Vietnam in 1965. General Westmoreland attempted to assert his authority over its supporting First Marine Air Wing (I MAW) by bringing Marine jet aircraft under the single management of his air component commander. While neither the then CINCPAC, Admiral Harry D. Felt, or his replacement, Admiral Ulysses S. Grant Sharp, accepted the McCutcheon Board's report in its entirety, they endorsed its "coordinating authority for tactical air operations" formula by ordering Westmoreland to settle for a compromise command arrangement for MACV air assets.[16] Issued as MACV Directive 95-4 in July 1965, this gave the commander of 7th Air Force "coordinating authority" over all air assets in South Vietnam, but retained operational control of all Marine aircraft under the III MAF. While I MAW was to give priority to the support of III MAF, any sorties additional to III MAF needs were to be made available, on a daily basis, to 7th Air Force. In practice, however, by January 1968, the Marines reported few additional sorties available to 7th Air Force.[17] A June 1966 modification of MACV Directive 95-4 provided for all available air assets to be brought, temporarily, under the Air Force Tactical Air Control System in the event of a "major emergency." It was left to COMUSMACV to define what constituted such an emergency.[18] Before 1968, therefore, the MACV air deputy controlled 7th Air Force operations in support of the Army in I Corps, but he had only very limited control of I MAW aircraft. Obviously, this was inconsistent with the Air Force belief in the single management of air power.

Single management of tactical air resources reemerged as an issue in I Corps because of the build up of non-Marine forces in the region. Until late 1967, the vast majority of allied forces in I Corps were US Marines and so Westmoreland placed the region under the control of the Commanding

General of III MAF, but in response to increasing communist activity in the region, Westmoreland began to move additional Army units north. The first such unit was an Army brigade designated Task Force Oregon, under the command of Lieutenant General William J. Rossen which took up position at the southern end of III MAF's area of responsibility in April 1967. Task Force Oregon drew most of its air support from 7th Air Force, but this posed few problems as those aircraft, flying from their bases south of I Corps, did not impinge on the operational areas of Marine units, either in the air or on the ground. Later in the year, Task Force Oregon was expanded to form the Americal Division with a corresponding increase in area of responsibility, but again, this posed few problems as Marine units were drawn further north by increased fighting nearer the DMZ.

In autumn 1967, Army units in I Corps were further increased by the addition of elements of the 1st Air Cavalry Division (Airmobile), initially positioned, again, to the south of the Marines. However, with communist activity increasing to the north, especially around Khe Sanh and Hue, the Army division was assigned to the operational control of III MAF on 21 January 1968 and concentrated between the 3d Marine division to the north and the 1st Marine Division to the south.[19] Third MAF's order of battle was then further supplemented by yet another Army division: the 101st Airborne, the first elements of which arrived in I Corps on 13 February.[20]

With the passing of the Army's Air Cavalry to the operational control of III MAF, the argument for some kind of coordination of Marine and Air Force aircraft began to build. Thus, ironically, the extension of Marine operational responsibility to non-Marine ground units created a demand for the Marines to lose operational control of their own air units because of what appeared to be a reluctance on the part of the Marines to provide air support to these non-Marine ground units and because it created an increasing requirement for 7th Air Force involvement in the area. This led to an inevitable clash between the separate air control systems of the two services.

With the number US divisions in I Corps increasing, Westmoreland now established a MACV forward headquarters subordinate to III MAF, under General Creighton Abrams at Phu Bai, to control the Army Air Cavalry and 101st Airborne Divisions, and the 3d Marine Division. This became Provisional Corps Vietnam under General Rossen, on 10 March.[21]

The Army Air Cavalry Division, as now deployed in I Corps, found itself between two Marine divisions: the 3d Marines of Provisional Corps Vietnam to one flank and the First Marines to another. This provided the Army division's commander, General Tolson, with an ideal vantage point from which to compare Marine close air support with that normally provided by the Air Force to Army divisions. Tolson found that the Marines received more support from their 1st Marine Air Wing than Army divisions did from 7th Air Force and he made this point in situation reports to Westmoreland.[22]

This is unsurprising as a higher level of close air support than that provided by the Air Force to the Army was a Marine doctrinal requirement. As the Marines' primary mission was amphibious warfare, Marine divisions had less supporting artillery than those of their Army cousins. Preferring to expend their resources on fixed-wing aircraft, the Marines had also invested less heavily than the Army in helicopter gunships. Marine air power was, therefore, optimized to compensate for a relative shortfall in other types of firepower and closely integrated with Marine ground forces under the concept of the "air-ground team." Indeed, Marine air had no other mission except the close air support of Marine ground units, whereas the Air Force had a whole series of missions to perform, including air superiority, interdiction, and strategic air warfare, and as we already know, close air support was not the Air Force's first priority. In the Marine view, as ground-support specialists, Marine pilots were more proficient in the art than their Air Force cousins, and they believed their air control system, designed specifically for close air support, more suited to the task than that of the Air Force. Undoubtedly, few in the Air Force would have agreed.

On 5 January 1968, General Westmoreland ordered the beginning of an airborne intelligence gathering campaign in support of Khe Sanh (NIAGARA I). General Momyer was to begin simultaneous planning for Operation NIAGARA proper (NIAGARA II). Operation NIAGARA owed its origins to Operation NEUTRALIZE of 1967. Mounted in defense of Con Thien, NEUTRALIZE had involved the coordination of all available air power assets—both tactical and strategic—with artillery and naval gunfire support. The same techniques, known as SLAM (for Seek, Locate, Annihilate and Monitor) were to be used in defense of Khe Sanh.[23]

By January 1968, pressure was building for a revision of the command arrangements governing the control of air power in I Corps. More Army battalions necessitated increasing 7th Air Force activity to support them and as a result Marine combat sorties were declining as a percentage of the total flown in I Corps. Momyer told Westmoreland that the Marine arrangements for controlling air resources committed to Khe Sanh were inadequate and that centralized control was, therefore, essential.[24]

On 17 January, therefore, Westmoreland informed Cushman that as a result of the increase in Army strength in I Corps, indications of impending enemy offensive action and the concomitant requirement for him to be able to deploy his airpower in a more flexible manner, he was considering placing the operational control of I MAW under his deputy for air, "as a temporary measure to meet the current situation" and that, in order "to meet the threat in the Quang Tri-Thua Thien area" he had ordered Momyer to plan for the concentration of all available air resources, initially, in the defense of Khe Sanh (Operation NIAGARA II).[25] Not surprisingly, General Cushman objected to such a proposal when he met with Westmoreland and Momyer to discuss the issue on the same day.[26]

The Marines interpreted this measure as a repeat of the loss of operational control of their air assets to the Air Force that they had so bitterly opposed during the Korean War, a first step towards the formal centralization of air assets under Air Force control and the beginning of the end of the Marines' air ground team. While the Marines regretted their experience at the hands of 5th Air Force during the Korean War, General Momyer made no secret of his belief that Khe Sanh presented an opportunity to return to the kind of arrangements for the command and control of tactical air resources that had obtained in Korea.[27]

On 18 January 1968, following the ambush of a Marine patrol in the vicinity of Khe Sanh, General Westmoreland sent the following message to Sharp:

> The changing situation places a demand for greater organization and control of air resources and a premium on the need for rapid decision making. It is no longer feasible, nor prudent, to restrict the employment of the total tactical air resources to given areas. I feel the utmost need for a more flexible posture to shift my air effort where it can best be used in the coming battles. Consequently, I am proposing to give my Air Deputy operational control of the 1st Marine Air Wing, less the helicopters.[28]

This was consistent with Westmoreland's authority, under MACV Directive 95-4 of 1966, though Westmoreland argued that he had the authority simply by virtue of his position as commanding general of a unified field command.[29]

Against the background of escalating dispute between MACV, the Marines and the Air Force, Sharp was reluctant to change the command arrangements governing Marine air power in Vietnam. He told Westmoreland that the existing command arrangements seemed to "have worked well for nearly three years of combat," and that his own objective was "to establish procedures which satisfy operational requirements, while minimizing the interservice debate which has much newspaper appeal, but little in the way of constructive suggestions." He refused to make any decision on single management until Westmoreland had re-examined Momyer and Cushman's conflicting views on the matter.[30]

A communist bombardment of Khe Sanh on 21 January prompted Westmoreland to order the implementation of NIAGARA II. Prevented, for the moment, from establishing actual single management, Westmoreland settled for greater coordination between the Air Force and the Marines. On 22 January, representatives of the 7th Air Force and the III Marine Amphibious Force met at Da Nang to discuss the issue and agreed to coordinate the Air Force Tactical Air Control System with the local Marine Direct Air Support Center at Khe Sanh through an Air Force Airborne Battlefield Command and Control Center (ABCCC) callsign HILLSBORO. As before, Marine aircraft would provide close air support to Marine units on the ground with surplus sorties being made available for 7th Air Force's use. At their own insistence, the Marines would bear responsibility for air strikes in the immediate vicinity of the Khe Sanh combat base with the Air Force concentrating on deeper interdiction targets that might affect the tactical situation at Khe Sanh.[31]

In the view of the commander of I MAW, General Norman J. Anderson, the Da Nang agreement constituted an acceptance by the Air Force that close air support of Marine ground forces was a job to be accomplished by the specialized members of the Marine air-ground team, while other air resources took on more distant targets, but although 7th Air Force representatives may have agreed to this arrangement at Khe Sanh, they did not agree with it as a matter of principle.[32] Fundamentally, it placed limitations on the Air Force's ability to shift and concentrate any and all air resources, including those of the Marines, anywhere within South Vietnam. Of course, the agreement reached at Da Nang concerned only the defense of Khe Sanh, not all of South Vietnam, or all of the Southeast Asian war zone, but even in regard to Khe Sanh, the agreement restricted the ability of the Air Force to shift resources throughout what it defined as the wider Khe Sanh battlefield encompassing Quang Tri and Thau Thien provinces, and including the immediate vicinity of the Khe Sanh combat base itself.

While doctrinal considerations drove the Air Force's campaign for single management, Westmoreland grew increasingly frustrated at Marine resistance to his initiatives and an apparent lack of any sense of urgency regarding Khe Sanh. On the same day as the Da Nang meeting, Westmoreland told the Chief of the General Staff General Earle Wheeler:

As you perhaps appreciate, the military professionalism of the Marines falls far short of the standards that should be demanded by our armed forces. Indeed, they are brave and proud, but their standards, tactics and lack of command supervision throughout their ranks requires improvement in the national interest . . . I would be less than frank if I did not say that I feel somewhat insecure with the situation in Quang Tri province . . . [33]

The Marines, however, were inclined to believe, with some justification, that the Air Force was "opportunistically" exploiting Khe Sanh as a mechanism by which to increase its control over Marine air assets as a precedent for the future. Marine suspicions in this respect were heightened by the expansion of the NIAGARA area of operations on 13 and 14 February to encompass most of Quang Tri province and as far south as Hue in Thua Thien province. All tactical aircraft operating within this area had to report to ABCCC HILLSBORO for assignment to forward air controllers.[34]

Marine protests over the expansion of the Operation NIAGARA area led to a further meeting on 17 February at III MAF headquarters in Da Nang between General Anderson and the 7th Air Force Deputy Chief of Staff Major General Gordon F. Blood to try to resolve the differences between the services on the issue. General Anderson assured General Blood of the Marines' intention to cooperate with the Air Force, but stated his case that he could not see how the entire NIAGARA area could be associated with Khe Sanh. Furthermore, he argued that the arrangements would actually limit his ability to provide support for the Marines at the base. General Blood explained that 7th Air Force believed that air reconnaissance intelligence gathered from the entire NIAGARA area was relevant to Khe Sanh and that an interdiction effort throughout the area would also make a positive contribution to the defense of the base. At Da Nang, the two services had agreed that I MAW should be responsible for the defense of the immediate area around the Khe Sanh combat base, but now General Blood suggested that as most of the transport aircraft flying into Khe Sanh were Air Force aircraft, 7th Air Force should assume responsibility for flak-suppression missions in the vicinity of the base. Not surprisingly, Anderson objected, arguing that Khe Sanh was a Marine responsibility and that the Marines were already providing adequate support for the base and the transport aircraft servicing it.[35]

The Air Force continued to press for full, single management on the grounds that the existence of two separate air control systems in I Corps caused serious coordination problems in the air defense of Khe Sanh.

According to one Air Force study, there was an uneven flow of aircraft over the target causing periodic congestion that was both dangerous and that sometimes necessitated the return of aircraft to their bases before they could attack targets. Transport aircraft sometimes flew through air strikes and sometimes B-52 strikes took place without the knowledge of other aircraft operating below their altitude.[36] Sometimes, the Air Force claimed, Marine pilots attacked targets outside their assigned zones without checking in with the ABCCC.[37] General Westmoreland decided to try for single management again and ordered the willing General Momyer to prepare the necessary plans in consultation with the reluctant General Cushman. Not surprisingly, General Momyer's discussions on the issue with Generals Cushman and Anderson provoked further protest, but Westmoreland again proposed single management to Sharp on 26 February.[38]

General Westmoreland's immediate justification for his renewed request for single management did not, however, directly concern the coordination of aircraft at Khe Sanh. Rather, Westmoreland claimed that he was moved to request the system again as a result of the failure of the Marines to provide adequate air support for units of the Army's First Air Cavalry division when it came under the operational control of III MAF at the end of January. During this period, Westmoreland personally instructed Generals Cushman and Anderson, at a meeting between all three, that he expected I MAW to provide the Army division's air support. Yet, on a visit to the Commanding General of the Army division, General John J. Tolson's headquarters, within the first couple of days after it had relocated to its position between the First and Third Marine Divisions, Westmoreland discovered that no contact had been established between the Air Cavalry and the Marines. Blaming the failure on the Marines, Westmoreland insisted that the incident necessitated prompt action to establish a single air control system in I Corps instead of the competing individual service systems which he described as a "dog's breakfast."[39]

However, the Marines argued that while they had agreed to provide air support to the Air Cavalry, they understood it to be the Cavalry's responsibility to establish the required communication nets with the division's own resources. Cushman ordered Anderson to take action to resolve the problem and Marine communications specialists were then sent to the Army division.[40] For what may have been perfectly logical reasons —possibly because of a lack of compatible communication equipment that had to be returned by previously supported Army units before it could be delivered to the Air Cavalry—it seems to have taken a further two or three days to establish the necessary communication nets, increasing Westmoreland's frustration with the Marines.[41]

General Anderson of I MAW has stood this argument on its head by suggesting that single management was brought about not by the Marines' failure, but by the Air Force's failure to adequately support the Army's First Cavalry Division. According to Anderson, once positioned in between two Marine divisions, General Tolson was able to observe that I MAW provided more air support to the Marine divisions than he received from 7th Air Force—a point that he made in situation reports to General Westmoreland. Therefore, Westmoreland took operational control of their aircraft away from the Marines to ensure that under the single management system increased Marine air support for Army units would make up for the inadequacy of Air Force support.[42]

According to Anderson, the Air Force's response to requests for better air support of the 1st Cavalry Division was to establish such a large area for Operation NIAGARA that it would bring not only all those aircraft operating in direct support of the Khe Sanh combat base, but also all those aircraft operating in support of the First Cavalry Division under the control of the Air Force's Airborne Command and Control Center.[43] This was, in Anderson's view then, but a stepping stone towards full-blown single management and since the Army wanted better air support of Army ground units and single management seemed to be a way of achieving this aim, the Army—specifically General Westmoreland—was perfectly happy to press for single management. Equally, Westmoreland and his successor as COMUSMACV, General Creighton W. Abrams, were happy to maintain single management even after the emergency in I Corps had passed because, for them, better air support of Army units was the central issue behind the policy, not Khe Sanh.

Anderson even goes so far as to suggest that it was this desire for improved air support that prompted Westmoreland to place the First Air Cavalry in between Marine divisions in the first place, thus precipitating a requirement for single-managed support for the Army division that would necessarily utilize Marine aircraft. Otherwise, it would have been more logical, says Anderson, to place the Army division on the flank of the Marines. That Westmoreland did not do this, said Anderson, must either be due to Westmoreland's failure to understand the different capabilities and operating procedures of his subordinate forces, or a deliberate attempt to place the Air Force in a position where it would be obliged to introduce systems which would enable Army units to be provided with a similar level of air support to Marine units.

Anderson may well have had a point that the extension of the Operation NIAGARA area was more due to Air Force doctrinal objectives than operational considerations. However, his argument that the Army used Khe

Sanh as an opportunity to improve air support for its units at the expense of the Marines seems to ignore Anderson's own acceptance that the Air Cavalry incident served to crystallize Westmoreland's decision to press ahead with single management, that a system to coordinate aircraft from many services in the immediate vicinity of Khe Sanh was necessary, that General Cushman had himself approved the deployment of the First Air Cavalry Division because the terrain suited light mobile forces, and that the Marines were also given the opportunity to consolidate their divisions in a separate corps from the Army divisions.[44] In fact, the Army does seem to have enjoyed an improvement in the quality of its air support as a result of single management, but there seems little evidence that the Air Force was Westmoreland's target. What does seem clear is that Westmoreland genuinely lost patience with the Marines and this prompted him, once more, to seek single management in February 1968.

Anderson also, by implication, criticized what he saw as the selective unfairness of a single management system that singled out the more vulnerable Marines for treatment that was potentially fatal to their air-ground team while ignoring the Army because of its greater political clout. The point here is that single management did not include the Army's helicopters. The Marine air control system did include both helicopters and fixed-wing aircraft and until the arrival of the Air Cavalry, with its large numbers of helicopters, in I Corp army rotary-wing aircraft in the region had conformed to the Marine system. The Air Cavalry's armada of UH-1s swamped the Marine system, however, so that only the most general control could be maintained over these machines. Anderson argued that these machines were not included in single management because the Army and the Air Force had forged an unholy alliance with the McConnell-Johnson Agreement of 1966.[45] To suggest that the Air Force was in bed with the Army is, of course, rather ironic since we know that the Air Force would have liked, not only to absorb the Army's helicopters into its tactical air control system, but also into the Air Force itself where, presumably, their numbers would have been reduced. The McConnell-Johnson Agreement was, of course, a compromise designed, on the Air Force's part, to preserve Air Force roles and mission, but every compromise involves losses and gains and the development of an Army helicopter force outside the Air Force's air control system was clearly perceived as a loss within the service.

As we have seen, the intensity of the fighting in I Corps sucked increasing numbers of Army units into the region. As the total number of allied units rose, it became necessary to bring in more Air Force (and some Navy) air power to support the increased ground forces. This produced a situation in which two separate tactical air control systems were in operation in I Corps, leaving the way open for clashes between the Marines and the Air Force. Both services understood that the operation of two parallel systems was undesirable. The Air Force, doctrinally opposed to such an arrangement, sought to resolve it by the implementation of the single manager system. The Marines wanted the Air Force in I Corps to conform to their own procedures on the grounds that they had been solely responsible for the tactical zone for some time.

Though doctrinally wedded to a more devolved tactical air control system, some Marines may even have desired the absorption of Air Force aircraft committed to the region into their own tactical air control system leading to a Marine single manager for I Corps who, presumably, would have been General Anderson.[46] In a way, the Marines already had this when they enjoyed a virtual monopoly of air and ground forces in I Corps, but they began to lose it when the increase in Army ground forces led to a concomitant increase in 7th Air Force support for those units. The Marines themselves had sought the augmentation of their forces in I Corps with Army units because there were no more Marine units to be had, and in doing so, General Anderson and his predecessor at I MAW, General Keith B. McCutcheon, had considered simply factoring the Army units into their own air support system. This would have involved accepting responsibility for the air support of Army units—something the Marines never did. The idea was rejected on the grounds that it might suggest the Marines had spare air capacity, which they believed they did not, and that, according to General Anderson, "was likely to look like poaching an Air Force role."[47] Apart from the more obvious doctrinal justification, another Air Force motive in seeking single management may have been the pre-empting of a loss of roles and missions to the Marines themselves, should III MAF try to obtain operational control of all air assets in I Corps, a region which the Marines had come to regard as their own special area of responsibility.[48]

At last, Sharp approved Westmoreland's proposal for a single manager on 2 March, with the modification that Marine requests for immediate air support should go directly to I MAW rather than through the 7th Air Force Tactical Air Control Center and the proviso that General Cushman retain the right of appeal above the level of MACV.[49] Single management would undergo evaluation by CINCPAC over a 30-day period after initial implementation.

Under the original single management directive of 7 March, Westmoreland ordered I MAW to make its strike and reconnaissance aircraft available to the commander of 7th Air Force for what was termed "mission direction."[50] This was a new phrase without official definition, but 7th Air Force and III MAF/I MAW interpreted it as operational control.

Before single management, the senior control agency for Marine air operations was the I MAW Tactical Air Direction Center (TADC) at I MAW headquarters, Camp Horn, Da Nang. Subordinate to the TADC were five Marine Direct Air Support Centers (DASCs) located at division level and below. (These Marine agencies are not to be confused with the USAF/VNAF Tactical Air Control System agencies of the same name that controlled Air Force tactical assets at the corps level.) Requests for preplanned air support missions were prepared by battalion commanders about a day in advance and sent up the chain of command to the division headquarters where a collocated DASC consolidated the requests. From there, the requests went to III MAF headquarters at Da Nang and thence to the collocated TADC where the details of the missions were finalized and orders dispatched to three Marine fixed-wing air groups for execution. The whole process took about 20 hours from request to the aircraft attacking the target.[51] I MAW matched its available fighter-bomber sorties with requests for air support from Marine ground units and informed 7th Air Force, on a daily basis, of any surplus sorties. These excess sorties were then available for use by 7th Air Force for the support of non-Marine ground units or for missions outside South Vietnam.[52]

Requests for immediate support by troops in contact with the enemy were sent from the ground unit concerned to the closest Marine DASC. If the request for support were approved, the Marine DASC could scramble ground alert aircraft of which a number, loaded with a variety of different ordinance configurations, were always on standby. This was the preferred Marine solution to immediate requests, but if necessary, the DASC could divert aircraft already on their way to preplanned targets in the area. The TADC at Da Nang monitored all Marine air operations and could divert aircraft from outside the DASC's immediate region if required.[53] In periods of particularly heavy fighting, the Marines might employ aircraft on airborne alert as a more responsive alternative to ground alert.[54]

The Marine TADC was equivalent to the Air Force's Direct Air Support Center (DASC) of which there was one in each Corps area. Thus, there were, effectively, two DASCs in I Corps: the USAF/VNAF IDASC and the marine TADC. As Air Force tactical air support doctrine called for the establishment of a DASC to support each Army Corps, a further

DASC—DASC VICTOR—subordinate to IDASC, was established at Phu Bai to support Provisional Corps Vietnam. Under single management, this arrangement was to be simplified by the merger of I DASC and the Marine TADC to form HORN DASC. Interestingly, while the Marines fought the centralization of their air power under Air Force control in the single management system, the VNAF also balked at the loss of operational control of its own air assets that it feared would result from the absorption of I DASC into HORN DASC. Consequently, I DASC remained operative for the direction of VNAF aircraft alongside DASC VICTOR and the new HORN DASC.[55]

Under single management, the Marines had to adopt essentially the same system for preplanned air strikes as that operated by the Army. Requests for preplanned support were to proceed from battalion to the local Marine DASC, then to III MAF headquarters (via Provisional Corps Vietnam for the 3d Marine Division) from where they were to be sent to 7th Air Force headquarters at Than Son Nhut, Saigon and then to the 7th Air Force Tactical Air Control Center which allotted the available resources from both Air Force and Marine sources to approved targets. As far as possible, Marine aircraft were to support Marine ground units, but they could also be ordered to support non-Marine ground forces.[56] Under the new system, I MAW no longer informed the 7th Air Force TACC of any sorties it deemed surplus to its immediate requirements, but was obliged to advise the TACC of its total capability on the basis of one sortie per aircraft, per day. The Air Force Tactical Air Control Center would also be able to divert preplanned Marine sorties and launch Marine ground alert aircraft for immediate support of troops in contact in the same way that it could for Air Force aircraft.[57] Immediate requests for support under single management involved two additional stages after the local DASC: a Provisional Corps DASC (DASC VICTOR), followed by a I Corps DASC (IDASC).

Apart from the immediate issue of losing a measure of control to the Air Force, the Marines objected to single management on the grounds that it was less responsive to the needs of the ground forces because the system was composed of a greater number of layers. There, undoubtedly, were more layers to single management and, in contrast with the earlier Marine system, it took much longer to implement, requiring Marine ground commanders to place their requests for air strikes about two days in advance rather than the one day that was previously required.[58] Furthermore, adoption of the Air Force system involved a much greater reliance on preplanned and diverted missions than that of the Marines, thus sometimes depriving the original requestor of his air strikes, and increasing the problem of diverted aircraft arriving over the target with inappropriate weapon loads. If missions were to be preplanned, then one might be forgiven for thinking they were important, but in Vietnam it seems that many missions were preplanned simply to provide an alert pool to fulfill immediate requests for support. According to Marine figures, only 5% of immediate requests for air support were met by diverted aircraft between 1 January and 10 March—before the implementation of single management. In the week of 5-11 April 1968, after the implementation of single management, this figure had risen to 77% with the consequent loss of many preplanned air strikes. By illustration, on what the Marines believed to be the "typical" day of 20 April, of the 172 requests for preplanned air strikes by Marine ground commanders only 64 targets were approved by 7th Air Force and only 31 of these actually struck, as a result of diverting aircraft to fulfill immediate requests for support.[59]

The Marines also feared that single management would result in the expenditure of an increasing number of I MAW sorties in support of the Army, thus reducing the aerial firepower available to the Marines on the ground. In fact, while the number of Marine sorties flown in support of the Army did increase, and the percentage of I MAW air strikes flown in support of III MAF did decrease, the actual number of I MAW sorties flown in support of III MAF did not decline appreciably. According to the Marines' own figures, I MAW support for Army units averaged about 1.1% of the total strike sorties flown prior to the implementation of single management.[60] In March 1968, the month before single management was fully implemented, the number of I MAW sorties flown in support of Army units stood at 153 or 2.25% of the total flown, while I MAW sorties flown in support of Marine ground units stood at 6,030 or 88.9% of the total.[61] In the first month, after the implementation of single management, the number of I MAW sorties flown in support of the Marines had fallen to 5,190 while Army support sorties had risen to 958.[62] By the end of the year, I MAW sorties flown in support of the Army had risen to in excess of 20% of the total flown.[63] However, I MAW had increased its sortie rate, thus maintaining a relatively steady number of sorties in support of Marine ground units despite this figure being a declining percentage of the total sorties flown. For example, while I MAW sorties in support of Marine ground forces declined to 77.6% of the total flown in May 1968, this figure still represented 6,088 sorties, more than I MAW had flown in support of Marine units in either March or April.[64]

Though the number of Marine sorties flown in support of Marine ground forces remained roughly the same, the Marines were not happy with the extra strain the higher sortie rate imposed on planes and pilots.

Despite Marine reservations, this may simply represent a more efficient use of the I MAW resource when applied to all allied services represented in I Corps. Single management involved at least the potential for the release of I MAW aircraft for purposes other than close air support. Interdiction and out-of-country air operations were part of MACV's strategy on which Air Force air component commanders placed a high priority, but the Marines felt they should concentrate their own air assets on close support of III MAF in I Corps. Whatever one thinks of MACV's strategy, this leaves the Marines open to the twin accusations that they concentrated only on their own private war in I Corps at the expense of the bigger picture and that in times of low-combat intensity Marine aviation assets were wasted by the Marine's doctrinal insistence their aircraft be used exclusively for close air support tasks when they could have been employed on interdiction missions.[65]

Despite the association of single management with Khe Sanh, the system was actually implemented too late to have much effect on the battle and continued long after the emergency represented by the siege and the Tet Offensive had passed. On 9 March, the Marines received a directive to implement single management on the following day, but they were able to delay compliance until 21 March, while the Marine and Air Force air control systems were integrated in I Corps.[66] The first preplanned sorties did not begin until 22 March, only nine days before the end of Operation NIAGARA on the 31st.[67] Training of Marine and Air Force personnel for joint operation of HORN DASC and DASC VICTOR was not finally completed until 1 April, the day after NIAGARA ended.[68] Only one week later, the siege of Khe Sanh was lifted. Of course, implementation of single management back in January would probably have established the system by the time of Operation NIAGARA, but the evidence suggests that Khe Sanh was not Westmoreland's only justification in establishing the system. We know General Westmoreland had requested something like single management as far back as 1965 and, once established, single management continued even into the post-Tet, US withdrawal period where a general decline in combat activity might be said to have reduced the requirement for the system still further.[69]

On the assumption that if the system were shown to be faulty then it would be abandoned, the Marines were, if anything, even more critical of single management after it had been implemented than they had been before.[70] Marine hopes that the departure of Westmoreland from South Vietnam might have this effect were dashed when his successor, General Abrams decided to continue with the system. However, while the Marines were unsuccessful in their ultimate objective of abolishing single management, they did succeed in forcing extensive modifications to the system.

Largely, as a result of Marine pressure, Westmoreland ordered a modification of single management as it affected preplanned close air support missions to go into effect on 30 May. This involved the division of Marine preplanned sorties into two groups. 30% of these Marine sorties were to continue to be handled on a daily basis under the existing single management procedures, but the other 70% were to be included in a new weekly fragmentary order. While, in theory, this involved 7th Air Force allotting mission information to Marine aircraft as much as a week in advance of the actual sorties, in practice, it amounted to handing back 70% of Marine sorties for use in any way that the ground commanders to be supported saw fit.[71] This was roughly the same percentage of 1st Marine Aircraft Wing sorties as were directly allotted Marine ground units before the introduction of single management.[72] The remaining 30% of preplanned sorties would continue be allocated by 7th Air Force on a daily basis.

Marine resistance to single management was probably reinforced by the fact that while heavy bomber operations were coordinated with the single management effort by Strategic Air Command (SAC), officers serving at 7th Air Force Headquarters, the B-52s, remained formally outside the system. There were a number of reasons for this seeming anomaly. As we have seen, the Air Force's emphasis on strategic air warfare had led it to prioritize SAC over the Tactical Air Command. As the US government's official position on the war in Vietnam placed the source of the South Vietnamese insurgency north of the DMZ, many Air Force officers believed that the best air strategy for the War would involve an intensive strategic air campaign against North Vietnam. In the Air Force's view, the ROLLING THUNDER campaign against the North was not the realization of this strategy because it involved only a gradual increase in the application of air power on the assumption that there would come a point at which the North would withdraw from the war. In addition to the target limitations of ROLLING THUNDER, SAC's B-52s were not employed over North Vietnam, though paradoxically, they were used in a tactical role over South Vietnam while Air Force and Navy tactical fighter-bombers carried the war to the North. Air Force commanders preferred to hold SAC's aircraft apart from the rest of the Air Force's operations in South Vietnam in readiness for their reversion to their primary strategic role in the event of a national emergency, or their employment in a campaign against the North which coincided more closely with the Air Force ideal—as finally happened in the LINEBACKER I and II campaigns of 1972. Some Air Force officers appreciated that this intraservice division was hardly a positive example to those other services whose own air power assets the Air Force wished to include in single management. Admiral Sharp also subscribed to the Air Force view that an intensive strategic campaign against North Vietnam was likely to be decisive and he reinforced the exclusion of the B-52s from the single management system by insisting on retaining control of the air war over the North rather than placing it under the operational control of COMUSMACV.

Shortly before the implementation of single management, Commandant of the Marine Corps, General Leonard Chapman, took III MAF's case to the Joint Chiefs of Staff. The Marines argued that single management would result in increasing the response time of air support for Marine ground forces because of the additional levels of authority through which requests for air support would have to be processed. In the Marines' view, this made single management wrong, but they also argued that in invoking the single management directive, Westmoreland had exceeded his authority by placing I MAW aircraft under Momyer's control as this contravened the establishment of III MAF as an autonomous command. As the JCS itself had approved this arrangement in 1966, the Marines argued that only the JCS had the authority to change it.[73]

The Chiefs found themselves divided on the issue of single management with the fracture conforming to perhaps predictable service lines—with one notable exception. Given the Air Force doctrine of the centralization of air assets under Air Force control and the fact that he had himself commanded 7th Air Force's precursor in South Vietnam, the 2d Air Division, Air Force Chief of Staff General John P. McConnell could be relied upon to support Westmoreland's appointment of his Air Force component commander as single manager. In fact, McConnell wanted to go further, telling the Chairman of the Joint Chiefs of Staff Army General Earle Wheeler:

> Westy has now done something he should have done
> a long time ago. He should also, in my opinion, place
> Navy air into the same structure. Also, I consider that
> Westy has the authority to do what he has done.[74]

Wheeler too, as an Army officer, predictably, supported the Army COMUSMACV. As part of the Navy, the Marines might also have expected to receive the support of the Chief of Naval Operations, Admiral Thomas C. Moorer, and were not disappointed in this respect. After all, the next step might be, as McConnell had suggested, for Westmoreland to extend single management to include Navy aircraft as well.[75]

The Marines also received support from an unexpected quarter; Army Chief of Staff General Harold K. Johnson who cut across service lines to endorse the Marine case. At first sight, this might appear a rejection of the narrow parochialism of which the chiefs have sometimes been accused, but it seems reasonably clear that Johnson's decision not to support Westmoreland was less motivated by the immediate operational concerns of the war in South Vietnam than by longer-term considerations. A public dispute with the Air Force over single management might prompt the latter service to demand a more extensive version of the system, which might include the Army's helicopters that were so conspicuously absent from Westmoreland's directives. Johnson's sensitivity to this issue is suggested by his reaction to a proposal that the Army establish an aviation command in US Army Vietnam (MACV's Army component): ". . . we should all recognize that the dispute over who flies and owns rotary-wing resources is far from dead. Continuing compartmentalization of [Army] aviation simply establishes a target for opponents of Army aviation to snipe at or to seize."[76] For his part, Westmoreland objected to what he saw as "parochial considerations' impinging on his right as the commander to make on-the-spot decisions and use resources on the basis of operational responsibilities, and he even considered resigning over the issue.[77]

This is not to say, as General Anderson did, that the Army was in bed with the Air Force over single management. There seems little or no evidence of collusion between the two services on this issue, but General Johnson was being cautious lest Army opposition to single management cause the revisiting of the 1966 McConnell-Johnson Agreement, and the Air Force seems to have taken the view that as a result of that agreement, a line had been clearly drawn between fixed-wing aircraft, which were an Air Force responsibility, and rotary-wing aircraft, which were an Army responsibility. Thus, the very decision by the Army Chief of Staff not to challenge single management was itself rooted in another area of dispute between the services over airpower issues.

Unable to reach a decision amongst the Chiefs, General Wheeler was obliged to pass the issue on to Secretary of Defense Clark Clifford, but he did so with the advice that Westmoreland's justification of single management in the context of the emergency at Khe Sanh meant that the proposal must be regarded as a temporary arrangement designed to meet local circumstances, likely to be modified as those circumstances changed. Single management could not, therefore, be taken as a precedent for the formal centralization of air power across all services in the future. It was, as such, a temporary expedient that Deputy Secretary of Defense Paul Nitze approved single management on 15 May 1968. However, he ordered that the system be subject to monthly evaluation and was quite specific that single management in this case should not be taken as a precedent for the centralized control of air operations in the future. General Westmoreland should "revert to normal command arrangements for III MAF when the tactical situation permits."[78] The debate on single management does not seem to have stopped with the office of the Secretary of Defense. General Cushman tried to take the issue to the very top and General Westmoreland reported that he did receive a telephone call from President Johnson asking him if he was "screwing the Marines."[79]

Despite the conclusion of NIAGARA, single management continued to receive the endorsement of the Office of the Secretary of Defense even after the end of the emergency at Khe Sanh that had, supposedly, formed its primary justification. Monthly evaluations of the single management system continued until September 1968 when General Wheeler reported to the Secretary of Defense that the system was working well and should be continued for as long as Westmoreland saw fit. Secretary Nitze agreed though General Chapman did not concur with Wheeler's analysis. Indeed the Marines never ceased to criticize single management until the system finally became inoperative by default with the withdrawal of the Marines from South Vietnam by June 1971.

However, the stridency of this criticism abated somewhat as the modifications to single management—the retention of exclusive arrangements for immediate requests for support by Marine ground troops in contact with the enemy, the return to Marine control of aircraft to meet specific requirements such as helicopter escort, the return of 70% of their available sorties for weekly allocation by the Marines themselves, plus the fact that the Marines were allowed to calculate their available aircraft on the basis of one sortie per aircraft when they could in fact produce more sorties than this—increasingly indicated that the Marines had not, in practice, lost operational control of their airpower to the single manager. In early 1970, General McCutcheon—a former commander of I MAW and Deputy Chief of Staff for Air at Marine Corps Headquarters—returned to South Vietnam as the new commander of III MAF. Though opposed to single management in principle, McCutcheon believed that the system, as it had evolved in South Vietnam, was not significantly less responsive to Marine requests for support than that of the Marines themselves, and it was actually more responsive to the needs of the Army. McCutcheon, therefore, seems to have adopted a cooler, more philosophical approach to single management than some of his predecessors at III MAF and I MAW, preferring to work within the system to ameliorate what the Marines saw as its worst features rather than rage against the system from without.

However, while McCutcheon believed that single management, as it developed in South Vietnam, did not take operational control of Marine aircraft away from the commander of III MAF, even he worried that it might be only the beginning of a process by which the Marines would lose such operational control in the future. If so, this would be a threat to the Marine air-ground team.[80] In McCutcheon's view, this threat was allayed, however, by a revision of MACV Directive 95-4 on air support in 1970. This defined the terms "mission direction" and "operational direction" used in the original single management directive as the authority of one commander to assign specific tasks to another commander, reaffirming, at least in McCutcheon's mind, "that operational control of Marine air would still be under the commanding general of III MAF who in turn would be under the operational control of MACV." As a consequence, McCutcheon came to believe that perhaps the Marines "reacted a little too strongly, fearing that they [the Air Force] were going to grab operational control and we didn't have as much to fear as we thought we did."[81]

If Khe Sanh was to be held, it had to be supplied, and General Westmoreland believed he had the capability to do so by air. While the Marines were eager to retain their responsibility for the close air support of Khe Sanh, they were perfectly willing for the Air Force to provide most of the tactical air transport aircraft to supply the combat base itself, and the Air Force was equally happy that the Marines provide the transport helicopters to supply the surrounding hill outposts.

Khe Sanh provided an opportunity to test the competing views of the Army and the Air Force with regard to the use of fixed-wing transport aircraft operating into forward bases under fire. Though the lighter C-7s and C-123s favored by the Army did fulfill a vital role hauling the most fragile loads into and out of Khe Sanh, they alone could not supply the base. The Air Force's preferred C-130s were vital to the survival of Khe Sanh though the siege proved the value of a greater STOL capability than that possessed by the heavier Air Force transports.

Ultimately, single management was implemented in South Vietnam. In a holistic sense, this was probably a better system for MACV than the arrangements for I Corps that had preceded it. Single management permitted COMUSMACV greater control over the use of his air assets than he had before the system was implemented. Whereas the Air Force had dictated the proportion of sorties flown inside and outside Vietnam, and within each Corps area, under single management, Westmoreland was able to do this.[82] The system provided slightly more potential for the use of the excellent Marine aviation assets in pursuit of MACV's overall strategy for the war in South Vietnam rather than exclusively in pursuit of a limited Marine strategy for I Corps. The system also led to some improvement in air support for Army units without dramatically affecting the quality of air support received by Marine ground units.

The Marines did suffer as a result of the introduction of single management. It certainly introduced more layers into the tactical air control system, making it somewhat less responsive to the needs of Marine ground units, and single management did rely more heavily on diverted aircraft to fulfill immediate requests for air support than the exclusive Marine system. While the Marines never ceased to criticize single management, compromise agreements with the Air Force did dramatically decrease the severity of its effects on I MAW. If one of the objectives of single management was to remove operational control of Marine aircraft from the Marines and give it to an air component single manager, the system fell far short of this ideal in practice. As we have seen, 70% of Marine sorties were reallocated back to I MAW on a weekly basis and the Wing continued to make its own decisions regarding the availability of air assets, releasing only sorties—not aircraft—to the single management system. In fact, the weekly apportionment of 70% of strikes to major ground commanders might be said to have constituted a decentralized system of the type favored by the Army and the Marines. In practice, then, the Marines never entirely lost operational control of their aircraft and the best the Air Force got was a combination of the Air Force and Marine systems rather than the system it really desired.[83] While this may not have been the Air Force ideal, it may have been consistent with Westmoreland's objectives.[84] In fact, single management fell so far short of the Air Force ideal that on 22 June 1968, General McCutcheon was able to write to Major Charles J. Quilter who replaced General Anderson as commanding general of I MAW:

> . . . it is only us Marines who have noticed the diminution in effectiveness' caused by single management and, in any case, this 'diminution in effectiveness' 'isn't very much now since they [the Air Force] incorporated all our suggested changes.[85]

In fact, in the view of some Marines, the Air Force was too accommodating on the issue of single management. They believed that the Air Force was so willing to compromise with the Marines that the net effect was to defuse Marine arguments for the abandonment of the system.[86] Writing of the 2 May 1968 review of single management, General Anderson noted:

The tenor of this discussion leads me to believe that the Air Force knows it is in some trouble on single management and is willing to modify the system in major respects to keep the system in force... I feel 7th Air Force will go to any length to maintain the air control and scheduling authority single management gives them, in such an atmosphere of accommodation we will be hard pressed to obtain a reversal of the decision to implement single management.[87]

Both services applied doctrinally proscribed views to the circumstances of Khe Sanh, but doctrine is a device for application to operational circumstances. The Air Force consciously exploited the opportunity presented by the siege as a way of achieving its desired goal of single management—where this meant seizing operational control of Marine aircraft—but its officers sincerely believed that this would provide the best air support for MACV as a whole. The Marines believed that their own concept would provide the best support for the immediate defenders of Khe Sanh who were, of course, mostly Marines. General Westmoreland came to side with the Air Force view, not because he subscribed to Air Force doctrine per se, but because he became convinced that it would resolve what he saw as the MACV dilemmas of poor Marine air support for Army formations and poor coordination between Air Force and Marine aircraft in I Corps.

Admiral Sharp's inhibition of Westmoreland's attempts to establish single management were, according to Sharp, due to the belief that there were not sufficient Army units in I Corps to justify the initiative and to minimize interservice dispute between the Air Force, Marines and MACV, but it may also have been due to other factors. As a Navy officer, Sharp might be expected to take the Marines' part and he was, perhaps, also reluctant to allow Westmoreland to accrue too much power at CINCPAC's expense. Sharp, whose tour as CINCPAC was up in July 1968, may not have wished to hand over to his successor, Admiral John C. McCain, an authority which was in any way diminished by Westmoreland's assumption of greater control of 7th Air Force and Marine air power. Certainly the fact that Sharp could inhibit Westmoreland's initiatives was due to the peculiar command arrangements which split the war into two halves, denying COMUSMACV the status of a full theater commander and retaining exclusive responsibility for the war over North Vietnam with CINCPAC. Ultimately, Sharp agreed to single management on the grounds that the number of Army units in I Corps now exceeded those of the Marines, but from his headquarters in distant Honolulu, he may also have become conscious of the political risks of continued dispute with

Westmoreland as the commander on the ground in Saigon. Once the single management directive was finally issued, it was not fully implemented until after the emergency at Khe Sanh had passed. There seems little doubt that the Marines dragged their feet over this, but the system would clearly have been in place in time for the beginning of the siege proper had Sharp acceded to Westmoreland's earlier requests.

Not only did the Marines drag their feet over the actual installation of the single management system, but they also took their criticisms to the Joint Chiefs of Staff and the Department of Defense. In doing so, the Marines largely restricted themselves to channels of protest deliberately opened for them by Admiral Sharp. In the JCS, they found an unlikely ally in the shape of General Johnson who worried less about the immediate operational issues in South Vietnam than he did about the possibility that a public dispute with the Air Force might lead to a reassessment of the Army's control of helicopters as secured under his 1966 agreement with Air Force Chief of Staff, General McConnell. This made it impossible for the Joint Chiefs to give a clear line on single management until Westmoreland himself became Army Chief of Staff, and involved the office of the Secretary of Defense, with its tendency towards bureaucratic compromise, in the issue.

Westmoreland complained that the Marines made single management a doctrinal issue with the Joint Chiefs.[88] Given that, ultimately, the system was so diluted that the Marines retained a good measure of operational control of their own aviation assets, their initial protests do appear to have had a hysterical quality, but in truth, single management was a doctrinal issue because its full implementation threatened the Marine air-ground team and the loss of the air-ground team threatened the amphibious warfare specialty that had formed the very raison d'etre of the Corps since the Second World War. That the Marines should oppose single management so vociferously was, therefore, inherent in the very existence of the Corps as a separate combined arms sub-service with its own air force.

In South Vietnam, the Marines were engaged in a sustained land campaign rather than the limited duration amphibious operations envisaged in their primary mission. At the time of Khe Sanh, the Marines had been in South Vietnam for three years and they were able to benefit from Army firebase support in addition to their own limited artillery assets.[89] Thus, single management could be justified, as it indeed was, as a temporary expedient in the immediate circumstances of Vietnam with the implication that it need not set a precedent for the dismantling of the Marine air-ground team in future, a point that Deputy Secretary Nitze made when he approved single management in 1968. However, the Marines worried that single management in Vietnam might still establish a precedent by which the Marine air-ground team would be lost in perpetuity—whatever the peculiarities of the immediate context—and there seems little doubt that this is what the Air Force hoped to achieve. The Marines countered the single management initiative with the argument that this was in itself an operational issue should the Marines be called upon to perform their primary amphibious mission in the Vietnamese context.[90] The Marines had, in fact, launched no less than 43 minor amphibious operations in South Vietnam between 1965 and 1967 and expected to participate in any amphibious operations north of the DMZ under consideration by General Westmoreland, should these ever materialize.[91] Thus, in the Marine view, the Marine air-ground team must be preserved, not only for the fulfillment of the Marine primary mission in the future, but also in the immediate context of Vietnam.

Single management was also a doctrinal issue in the sense that, while it was technically a temporary expedient designed to meet immediate operational requirements, if fully implemented, it represented a temporary realization of Air Force doctrine regarding the centralization of air power assets. Regardless of its officially temporary status, single management was, as we have seen, actually a very open-ended arrangement, but despite its title, with its implication that there was now one tactical air control system, single management was not in fact the full realization of the Air Force concept as the Marines retained de facto operational control of much of their air power assets. This left the way clear for continued dispute after the Vietnam War.[92]

# NOTES

1. Dr Harold Brown, Sec of AF, Remarks before the Phoenix Chamber of Commerce (16 May 1968), Selected Statements on Vietnam by DoD and Other Administration Officials, 1 Jan-30 June 1968, Air Force Historical Research Agency (hereinafter referred to as AFHRA), Maxwell AFB., AL., K168.04-47.

2. William W. Momyer, *Airpower in Three Wars* (New York, 1980), 306-308.

3. Roy L. Bowers, *The United States Air Force in Southeast Asia, Tactical Airlift* (Washington, DC: Office of Air Force History, 1983), 295-296.

4. However, as the author of the USAF official history has pointed out, it was not really the failure of the French re-supply effort at Dien Bien Phu that caused the base to fall. In fact the weight of supplies delivered by air to the defenders of Dien Bien Phu was about the same as that brought overland by their more numerous attackers. Consequently, even if the French, in 1952, had possessed the airlift capability the United States enjoyed in 1968, they would still have suffered defeat at Dien Bien Phu. Ibid., 20.

5. I MAW Command Chronology, March 1968, Marine Corps Historical Center (hereinafter referred to as MCHC), p. 2-2. American commentators have tended to place remarkable faith in largely anecdotal evidence that the survival of Khe Sanh was due to the success of US air power in spoiling Communist assault preparations and inflicting heavy casualties on a largely unseen enemy. In any case, the Air Force official historian John Schlight has pointed out that the air support of Khe Sanh may not have been without cost as it absorbed some 50% of the US air effort in South Vietnam for about two months. While there were sufficient air assets to service the requirements of both Khe Sanh and the Tet Offensive this left the communists "with a permissive environment in which to prepare for a second offensive in May." John Schlight, *The United States Air Force in Southeast Asia, The War in South Vietnam, The Years of the Offensive, 1965-1968* (Washington, DC: Office of Air Force History, 1988), 285. Contemporary commentators and historians, subsequently, have even questioned the seriousness of Communist intentions towards the base, suggesting that the siege was merely a ruse designed to lure allied forces away from the targets of the Tet offensive. It does, however, at least seem reasonably clear that the communists would have assaulted the base had they felt they could do so at little cost.

6. Warren A Trest, "Khe Sanh (Operation NIAGARA), 22 January-31 March 1968, Special Report" (13 September 1968), Contemporary Historical Examination of Current Operations (CHECO) Report, AFHRA, K717.0413-35, 13 September 1968, 1:46.

7. Bernard C. Nalty, *Air Power and the Fight for Khe Sanh* (Washington, DC: Office of Air Force History, 1986), 99.

8. III MAF Command Chronology, April 1968, MCHC, 9.

9.    The KC-130 was an in-flight refuelling tanker variant of the C-130 that could be rapidly reconfigured for conventional cargo haulage.

10.   Nalty, *op cit*, 8-9.

11.   *Ibid*, pp. 35-36 & 43-45; & Jack Shulimson et al, *U.S. Marines in Vietnam, The Defining Year, 1968* (Washington, DC: History and Museums Division, Headquarters, U.S. Marine Corps, 1997), 480-481.

12.   Bowers, *op cit*, 302-303.

13.   Nalty, *op cit*, 56.

14.   Report of CINCPAC Tactical Air Support Procedures Board (December 1963), McCutcheon Papers, MCHC, 6:2.

15.   In a 1969 interview the commander of the 2d Air Division General Rollen H. Anthis said that he had desired the implementation of a single management system that would include not only Air Force and Marine assets, but also the Army's helicopters. Rollen H. Anthis, Interview (17 November 1969), U.S. Air Force Oral History Program, AFHRA, K239.0512-240, 46-47.

16.   Keith B. McCutcheon, "Marine Aviation in Vietnam, 1962-1970," *U.S. Naval Institute Proceedings*, 1971, 135-136.

17.   Shulimson, *op cit*, 466.

18.   Schlight, *op cit*, 162 & *The Pentagon Papers*, Senator Gravel Edition, Boston: Beacon, 1971, Vol. 3, 2,200-2,201.

19.   III MAF Command Chronology (January 1968), MCHC, 8.

20.   Ibid. (February 1968), 8.

21.   Donald J. Mrozek, *Air Power and the Ground War in Vietnam, Ideas and Actions* (Maxwell A.F.B., AL, 1988), 42 & III MAF Command Chronology (March 1968), MCHC, 8.

22.   Norman J. Anderson, Draft Memo: "Single Management of Marine Fixed-Wing Air Assets in Southeast Asia" (12 March 1969), Anderson Papers, MCHC, 6-7.

23.   William C. Westmoreland, *A Soldier Reports* (New York, 1980), 266.

24.   Momyer, *op cit*, 109.

25.   Westmoreland to Sharp (21 January 1968) Westmoreland Papers, Message File, COMUSMACV (1-31 January 1968), Box 15, Folder 376, RG 319, US National Archives, College Park, MD. (hereinafter referred to as USNA).

26.   Willard J. Webb, "The Single Manager for Air in Vietnam," *Joint Force Quarterly* (Winter 1993-94), 91.

27.   Robert M. Burch, "Single Manager for Air in South Vietnam, May-December 1968" (18 March 1969) CHECO Report, AFHRA, K717.0413-39, Vol. 1, p. 5 & Anderson to Simmons (8 September 1983), Anderson Papers, MCHC, 4.

28.   Quoted in Momyer, *op cit.*, 309.

29.   Ibid., 81-82 & 88-106.

30.   Sharp to Westmoreland (22 January 1968), Westmoreland Papers, Box 15, Folder 376, Message File, COMUSMACV (1-31 January 1968).

31.   Schlight, *op cit.*, 277-278.

32. Quoted in Nalty, *op cit.*, 73.

33. Westmoreland to Wheeler (22 January 1968), Westmoreland Papers, Box 15, Folder 376, Message File, COMUSMACV (1-31 January 1968).

34. In a 1983 interview General Anderson was quite specific that he did not believe, "that the enlargement of the area for Operation NIAGARA was justified. It could have been enlarged in the direction of the enemy, but to enlarge it in reverse, in the direction of the base of the 1st Cavalry Division (Airmobile) in order to encompass their base and therefore to have 7th Air Force responsible for the coordination of all air operations that related to the Cavalry Division's work - seemed to me to be opportunistically jumping on a situation in order to develop a rationale for its continuance, for continuing its control" [sic]. Norman J. Anderson, MG. (USMC), Interview (1983), USMC Oral History Collection, MCHC, 227.

35. Anderson's summation of the conference with Blood was that: "In all the…areas the divergence of opinion was clear. In none other than time-sharing was there any meeting of minds." Norman J. Anderson, Memo for the Record, Subj.: "Control of Air in the Defence of Khe Sanh" (17 February 1968), Anderson Papers, 4.

36. John J. Sbrega, "Southeast Asia," Benjamin F. Cooling, ed., *Case Studies in the Development of Close Air Support* (Washington, DC: Office of Air Force History, 1990), 457.

37. Schlight, *op cit.*, 286.

38. Shulimson, *op cit.*, 491.

39. Westmoreland, *A Soldier Reports*, 450.

40. Anderson to Simmons (8 September 1983), Anderson Papers, 4.

41. Stephen J. McNamara, *Air Power's Gordian Knot: Centralized Versus Organic Control* (Maxwell A.F.B., AL., 1994), 117, n.51.

42. Anderson may have simply been producing a "counter rationale" with which to combat Air Force pressure for the continuance of single management. Anderson, "Single Management of Marine Corps Fixed-Wing Air Assets in Southeast Asia," 1-2.

43. Ibid., 6-7 & Anderson, Interview, 193.

44. Anderson, "Single Management of Marine Corps Fixed-Wing Air Assets in Southeast Asia," 13-14.

45. Anderson, Interview, 197-198 & Anderson, Memo for the Record, Subj.: "Control of Air Defence of Khe Sanh," (17 February 1968), Anderson Papers, 3.

46. Anderson, Interview, 195.

47. Anderson, "Single Management of Marine Fixed-Wing Air Assets in Southeast Asia," 10.

48. According to General McCutcheon, as the fighting at Khe Sanh escalated, message traffic between 7th Air Force and Pacific Air Force headquarters, read by the Marines, suggests this. McCutcheon, Keith B., Interview (1971), AFHRA, K239.0512-1164, 8-9.

49. Nalty, *op cit.*, 77 & Sbrega, op cit., 457.

50. I MAW Command Chronology (March 1968), 2-2.

51. Shulimson, *op cit.*, 467-469.

52. McCutcheon, "Marine Aviation in Vietnam," 137.

53. Sbrega, *op cit.*, 460.

54. Shulimson, *op cit.*, 469-470.

55. John J. Lane Jr., *The Air War in Indochina*, Vol.1, Monograph 1, *Command and Control and Communications Structures in Southeast Asia* (Maxwell A.F.B., AL: Air War College, 1981), 83-85.

56. Webb, *op cit.*, 93.

57. Nalty, *op cit.*, 78-79.

58. Shulimson, *op cit.*, 498.

59. Sbrega, op cit., pp. 460-461. In a memo on the 2 May 1968 review of single management, General Anderson noted that: "It seemed agreed by all, including General Momyer, that preplanning merely results in placing a certain amount of air effort airborne and available for any use a specific ground commander may wish." Norman J Anderson, Memo for the Record, Subj.: "Single Management of Strike and Reconnaissance Assets" (n.d.), Anderson Papers, 3.

60. I MAW Command Chronology (October 1968), 8.

61. Ibid. (March 1968), 2-3.

62. Ibid. (April 1968), 2-2.

63. The figure stood at 26.4% in November 1968. Ibid. (November 1968), p. 8 & (December 1968), 9.

64. Ibid, (May 1968), 2-2.

65. William W. Momyer, Memo for Frank M. Batha, Subj. "Airpower in the Vietnam War" (27 October 1981), MCHC.

66. Anderson, Interview, 216.

67. Cushman to Westmoreland, Memo: "Single Management of Strike and Reconnaissance Assets, Summary of the Situation as of 31 March," Anderson Papers.

68. Robert F. Futrell, *Ideas, Concepts, Doctrine: Basic Thinking in the United States Air Force, 1961-1984* (Maxwell A.F.B., AL., 1989), 285.

69. Sbrega, *op cit.*, 463.

70. Anderson, Interview, 201. On 2 May 1968, at a meeting at the headquarters of Provisional Corps Vietnam to review single management after one month's operation, General Momyer said that the purpose of the meeting was to correct any flaws in single management. General Anderson subsequently noted that he saw the purpose of the meeting as to decide whether single management should continue. Anderson, "Single Management of Strike and Reconnaissance Assets," 1-3.

71. Shulimson, *op cit.*, p. 507.

72. Anderson, "Single Management of Marine Corps Fixed-Wing Air Assets in Southeast Asia," 8-9.

73. Web, *op cit.*, 94.

74. McConnell to Wheeler (4 March 1968), quoted in ibid, 93.

75. Shulimson, op cit., 495.

76. Johnson to Beach (CINCUSARPAC), Subj.: "Activation of an Aviation command in USARV," (062130Z Jun.), Westmoreland Papers, Box 13, Folder 364, Message File, COMUSMACV, 1 April-30 June 1967.

77. Westmoreland, *A Soldier Reports*, 451-452.

78. Nitze quoted in Futrell, *op cit.*, 284.

79. Sbrega, *op cit.*, 462; Shulimson, *op cit.* 495 & Westmoreland, *A Soldier Reports*, 452-453.

80. McCutcheon, op cit., 137-138.

81. McCutcheon, Interview, 6-7.

82. Ibid., 9-10.

83. Stephen J. McNamara, *op cit*, 112.

84. Westmoreland said that he wanted a system for MACV that would combine the best features of the Air Force and Marine house systems. Orr Kelly, "Dispute Over Khe Sanh Lingers On," *Washington Star* (11 January 1972).

85. Shulimson, *op cit.*, 512.

86. Anderson, Interview, 201 & Anderson, "Single Management of Strike and Reconnaissance Assets," 1-3.

87. Anderson, "Single Management of Strike and Reconnaissance Assets," 4.

88. Westmoreland, *A Soldier Reports*, 451.

89. At Khe Sanh the Marines received artillery support from sixteen Army 175mm guns situated fourteen miles away at Camp Carrol.

90. Anderson, Interview, 196-197.

91. Sbrega, *op cit.*, 459.

92. Joseph H. Moore, Interview (22 November 1969), AFHRA, K239.0512-241, 20.

# CONCLUSION

This study has shown that there was rivalry and dispute between the armed services of the United States over various facets of the military application of airpower during the Vietnam period. The consequences of interservice rivalry over airpower issues in Vietnam are difficult to gauge with certainty, but these disputes did have significant strategic, operational and tactical consequences for the pursuit of United States national policy in Southeast Asia.

At the most fundamental level, the services disagreed about the theater-level command arrangements by which the United States conducted the Vietnam War. As a result of unresolved doctrinal differences between the Army and the Air Force, the United States developed complex theater-level command arrangements for the war in Southeast Asia where command authority was fragmented between the Commander in Chief Pacific (CINCPAC) and the commanding general of Military Assistance Command Vietnam (COMUSMACV). Unchecked by a unified theater command on the supreme headquarters model, this fragmentation of command authority was reflected in a similar dispersal of responsibility for air power resources committed to the Vietnam War. The result was that General Westmoreland did not have overall control of all the air assets committed to Southeast Asia, or even to South Vietnam itself. Westmoreland could not, therefore, use all these air assets exactly as he saw fit.

Westmoreland complained about his lack of authority for those 7th Air Force aircraft based in Thailand and, even though the Marines in I Corps did operate under his official command authority, the Khe Sanh record illustrates Westmoreland's mounting frustration with the absence of their aircraft from the Air Force Tactical Air Control System (TACS) under the control of his air deputy General Momyer.[1] The problem of fragmented control of air assets in Southeast Asia, with its detrimental effect on Westmoreland's ability to deploy those assets with maximum flexibility in South Vietnam, was insurmountable because it stemmed from the lack of unity of command. It would likely have been greatly alleviated had General Westmoreland been appointed a Southeast Asia theater commander, but this was impossible under the political circumstances of the time and place.

At the theater command level, the services proved resistant to learning the lessons of Vietnam; they did not confront the fragmented theater command issue that had so dogged them in Southeast Asia until forced to do so by Congressional criticism of their parochialism in the mid-1980s. The resulting Goldwater-Nichols Department of Defense Reorganization Act of 1986 provided the authority for theater commanders to organize their commands as they saw fit and order subordinate commands to execute assigned tasks without interference from the individual services.[2] Thus, the United States appointed Army General H. Norman Shwartzkopf as a unified theater commander for the country's next major conflict against Iraq in the Gulf War of 1991.

Prior to Vietnam, the Air Force believed strongly in the centralized control of all air assets under an Air Force officer who would report directly to the theater commander. The fragmented command arrangements established for Southeast Asia, with their concomitant division of responsibility for airpower assets, served only to reinforce the Air Force's view in this respect and the service got its way in the Gulf where the Air Force component commander General Charles A. Horner was made Joint Force Air Component Commander (JFACC) with the theoretical authority to direct US Air Force, US Navy, US Marine Corps, and allied air assets—but not Army aircraft—in the Gulf theater.

As might be expected, there is a close relationship between the command arrangements adopted by the United States for the prosecution of its war in Southeast Asia and the strategic direction of the war. The US government and the Department of Defense's strategy was dictated not only by operational circumstances on the ground, but also by political considerations and interservice rivalry in which airpower played a key role. Concomitant with the decision to fragment command authority between CINCPAC and Military Assistance Command Vietnam (MACV) was the decision not to give priority either to the Army strategy of a land war supported by tactical airpower or the Air Force strategy of a strategic air campaign against North Vietnam with a holding land campaign in South Vietnam. This may have been a wise course, but it left successive US administrations open to the accusation that instead of pursuing one strategy decisively they pursued both halfheartedly. Certainly, the Air Force continually argued that although there was an air war over North Vietnam, the Air Force was not allowed to pursue that war with the vigor required to defeat North Vietnam and thus, win the Vietnam War overall. Army criticisms were perhaps slightly more muted, but the view of many Army officers that it was forced to fight the war "with one hand tied behind its back" is well known.

In fact, the preferred Air Force strategy of a strategic air campaign against North Vietnam was almost certainly folly in the context of time, place and national objectives. In the mid-60s, despite some improvements in accuracy, the manned bomber remained a relatively imprecise instrument largely dependent on unguided munitions and, despite claims to the contrary, there was little evidence in the historical record to suggest that strategic air operations might be decisive. For example, the deep interdiction STRANGLE II bombing campaign in Korea had not yielded the hoped for, decisive results.[3] Although strategic bombing clearly had significant effects in terms of tying up scarce enemy resources in the Second World War, North Vietnam's undeveloped nature made it particularly impervious to strategic air warfare.[4] Even if US airpower had forced North Vietnam to withdraw its support for the National Liberation Front in the south, it would still have retained the option to reengage at a later date once the United States had withdrawn.

Since the Vietnam War, the United States has tended to use its airpower in lieu of ground forces, but as the decisions to commit US forces to both a ground war in South Vietnam and an air war over North Vietnam were taken virtually simultaneously, the air campaign could not fulfill this proxy role in Vietnam, casting further doubt on the necessity for a strategic air campaign in the first place. It might be argued that the air war against North Vietnam, as it actually developed, was really more of a deep interdiction campaign than the strategic knock-out blow envisaged by early Air Force targeting plans. And although it and subsidiary operations against the Ho Chi Minh trail in Laos were unsuccessful in the sense that they never actually reduced North Vietnamese infiltration into South Vietnam, they must have at least limited the increases in North Vietnamese infiltration. While there may be some truth in this, the guerrilla war in South Vietnam was largely self-supporting and did not place great demands on the North for supplies and troops during much of the course of ROLLING THUNDER.[5]

In Vietnam, the sensitivity among the services regarding ultimate responsibility for roles and missions that had emerged as a result of the service unification dispute of the late 1940s manifested itself in a series of demarcation disputes. This was particularly true regarding those between the Army and the Air Force over responsibility for close air support (CAS) and tactical airlift. In the absence of political approval for a strategic air campaign against North Vietnam, the Air Force was not about to pass up any other opportunities for participation in the war. It therefore settled for a tactical campaign in South Vietnam. While some sort of strategic campaign against the North did eventually emerge, the tactical air war continued in the South. Though not philosophically inclined towards tactical air operations, the Air Force set about them with a will in the hope of monopolizing the tactical air war, or at least securing overall control of all air support assets through the Air Force Tactical Air Control System (TACS).

The Korean War had revealed a continuing requirement for tactical air operations and thus showed the Air Force's excessive emphasis on Strategic Air Command (SAC) at the expense of Tactical Air Command (TAC) to have been in error. However, as a result of its inherent bias toward strategic air warfare, the Air Force chose to ignore the tactical airpower lessons of Korea and once again abandoned the tactical air doctrine it had first developed during the Second World War. Thus, the Air Force had to relearn tactical air techniques for a third time in Southeast Asia. This clearly had a detrimental effect on the combat efficiency of tactical airpower in South Vietnam during the learning process and contributed to the very long delay between requests for CAS and the arrival of aircraft over the target in the early days of US Air Force involvement in the war.

While it may have been back in the tactical airpower business in South Vietnam, the Air Force remained disinclined to provide close air support in the manner desired by the Army. The Air Force wanted a centralized system while the Army wanted a decentralized one and the Army argued that the centralized system that emerged (TACS) was insufficiently responsive to its battlefield needs, particularly in the context of South Vietnam where contacts between opposing ground forces were usually so short that requests for immediate support were likely to arrive over the target after the resulting combat had concluded. However, the war in South Vietnam represented the first opportunity for the Army to fill the perceived gap between the demands of its ground forces and the close air support provided by the Air Force—through the TACS—with its own combat aircraft and so the two competing tactical air support systems clashed. Again, this dispute had detrimental consequences for the combat efficiency of tactical airpower in Vietnam. As the Air Force was not prepared to fill the kind of close air support role offered by Army aircraft, its efforts to deny this capability to the Army were simply obstructive and cost the Army some of the enhanced combat efficiency likely to accrue from its organic air assets.

With the withdrawal of the AV-1 Mohawk from the Army's airmobile division and the compromise ushered in by the McConnell-Johnson Agreement, the Air Force succeeded in destroying the Army's fixed-wing combat aircraft programs in Vietnam. It did so, not as a result of operational concerns on the South Vietnamese battlefield, but because it did not want the Army to have its own close air support aircraft in contravention of existing formal roles and missions agreements, and because it simply was fundamentally opposed to organic Army aircraft. This was a policy driven by political and doctrinal considerations, but it was not entirely devoid of an operational dimension. Air Force officers genuinely believed that the centralization of air assets under Air Force control constituted the most efficient basis for the provision of support to the Army's ground forces under any circumstances and saw no reason to believe that Vietnam constituted a special case in this respect.

The Air Force was successful in preventing the dispatch of Army AV-1 attack aircraft to Vietnam and in curtailing the use of its OV-1 sister aircraft in its subsidiary close support role. However, the Air Force lost the argument with the Army over helicopters. While the Army expressed broad satisfaction with the close air support it received from the Air Force in Vietnam, it still sought alternative organic air support, mainly through the medium of helicopter gunships. Army supplementation and even substitution of Air Force close air support by its own helicopters was bitterly opposed by the Air Force until the Air Force appeared to concede the debate in the 1966 McConnell-Johnson Agreement. While both services declared the agreement a compromise, the fact is that it confirmed the Air Force's loss of formal exclusive responsibility for the close air support mission and its weary acceptance that the Army's gunship helicopters were there to stay.

Though the Air Force still opposed individual Army attack helicopter programs, these continued to receive approval from the Secretary of Defense, and in Vietnam, the Air Force increasingly came to accept the Army's own justification of its helicopter gunships as performing a different and supplemental role to that of Air Force attack aircraft. Although the Air Force as an institution refused to accept it, in the context of the Vietnam period this ad hoc arrangement actually represented a natural division of tactical airpower responsibilities between the services with the Army concentrating on immediate close air support and the Air Force concentrating on preplanned sorties, particularly interdiction. This suggests that centralization was desirable up to a point, or rather down to a point, beyond which the Army would have best provided its own immediate close air support requirements probably with helicopters, but also with specialist intermediate performance close air support aircraft in the AV-1 or A-1 Skyraider class and, ultimately, with the projected A-X jet aircraft. If such an arrangement had been implemented, it would have been necessary for the Department of Defense to police it in order to avoid either service impinging on the different, but complimentary tactical capabilities of the other. The Howze Report shows that the Air Force had a point when suggesting that the Army's adoption of its own fixed-wing tactical air capability might be the thin end of a wedge that would lead to the development of another air force in direct competition with the USAF and that post-Vietnam developments up to and including the 1991 Gulf War against Iraq have tended to bear this out.

The particular manner by which the US armed services came to control their tactical airpower in Vietnam had important consequences for its actual application. The Army successfully carved out a form of organic air support—provided by helicopter gunships. This was clearly more responsive to the Army's immediate needs than the close air support provided by Air Force tactical fighters through the TACS, but it did not fulfill the Army's need for heavier aerial fire support. The Air Force had damaged the Army's capabilities in this respect by denying it the use of fixed-wing aircraft—which would have been more survivable and packed a heavier punch—while at the same time making it clear that it would not provide this kind of support in a dedicated and sufficiently timely manner for the Army's purposes. The Air Force's attitude to dedicated close air support encouraged Army reluctance to call for air support through the TACS until after organic sources had been tried. This meant that the Army sometimes used its helicopter gunships where heavier Air Force firepower was a more appropriate first course, with a consequent cost in combat efficiency. Also, Air Force officers rationalized their own objections to Army airpower by arguing that retention of an organic Army close air support capability outside the TACS meant that it was not then available for deployment by the TACS for missions beyond the remit of the Army corps commanders to whom the Army gunships were allotted. However, there is no evidence that this was ever a significant disadvantage in Vietnam, where the short range and relatively low speed of Army aircraft would probably have limited their usefulness in this respect, both in the eyes of Air Force officers coordinating the TACS, and in fact.

Even before the Vietnam War ended, the Army sought to fill this organic firepower gap with more capable attack helicopters; first, with the AH-56 Cheyenne and then, following the cancellation of that program, with the AH-64 Apache. The latter aircraft proved itself a formidable machine in the Gulf War, again raising the issue of the presence of Army attack helicopters outside the Air Force tactical air control system. This suggests that, by the Gulf War, increasingly capable Army attack helicopters were becoming the equivalent of Army fixed-wing combat aircraft, thus reopening the dispute between the Army and the Air Force over organic airpower. If the Army's aircraft were to be placed under the control of the JFACC, as the Air Force wished, this again would raise the question: why have an Army air arm at all? In addition, why have helicopters at all when the Air Force continues to believe multirole fixed-wing jets both more capable and more flexible?[6]

One of the factors driving the explosion in the Army's employment of helicopters in Vietnam was the introduction of airmobile formations and techniques. The model of airmobility used by the Army in Vietnam was a unilateral one developed from the deliberations of the 1962 Howze Board and the subsequent 11th Air Assault division tests. Naturally, Secretary of Defense Robert S. McNamara bore the ultimate responsibility for the commissioning of the Howze Board's report, but he did so at the urging of a few Army aviation enthusiasts who had obtained positions of significant influence in the Office of the Secretary of Defense. There, Army Colonels Robert R. Williams and Edwin L. Powell were able to realize their own minority views through the medium of the Secretary of Defense.

Both McNamara and the army aviation proponents embarked upon the airmobility project out of the sincere expectation that this would improve Army mobility and thus lead to an increase in the operational efficiency of the US armed forces in general. It never occurred to McNamara that there was any need for an official competition between Army and Air Force concepts for increasing Army mobility. Presumably, the secretary expected— if he thought about it at all, and the chances are that he did not—the Army Board to make the best use of all aviation resources for improving Army mobility regardless of their service of origin. However, given the origins of the Howze Board with Colonels Williams and Powell, their selection of its key members, including the chairman, and the Army's recent air support experience at the hands of the Air Force, which seemed to suggest that the latter service could not, or would not, provide adequate support for the new airmobile formations unless somehow forced to by the Department of Defense, the Army concept was always likely to be very parochial.

The Air Force claimed that the Howze concept involved the Army straying into roles and missions formally reserved for the Air Force. This, it certainly did in the areas of tactical airlift and close air support. Such objections were, however, based on dogma rather than real operational considerations as the very nature of these roles was undergoing a revolutionary transformation under the impact of airmobility, with which the Air Force was out of step. Under the influence of airmobility doctrine, a real requirement had emerged for aircraft in the AV-1 and CV-2 class. As the service primarily responsible for airpower, it was the Air Force's responsibility to respond to the new requirements and operate these new types of aircraft in a manner satisfactory to the Army, or move over and let the Army do it. Of course, the Army had developed these aircraft without reference to the Air Force, but it was perfectly clear that even if it had been consulted, the Air Force would have been entirely opposed to both of them, and the missions they were designed to accomplish.

Air Force protests against Army airmobility did pay off to some extent, however, with the Army's loss of its fixed-wing aircraft—first with the AV-1, and then with the CV-2—in the McConnell-Johnson Agreement. The Air Force had never approved of the concept of the light tactical 'assault transport,' or dedicated use by the Army of such aircraft. Having gained control of the Army's light tactical transport fleet, it allowed both ideas to wither on the vine.

The wisdom, or lack thereof, of the Air Force's neglect of CV-2/C-7 class aircraft is indicated by events at Khe Sanh in 1968. The siege of the Marine combat base represented an opportunity for a demonstration of what might be described as both the Army's and the Air Force's competing tactical airlift concepts under combat conditions. As the Army had predicted, the Air Force, and soon after the Marines, proved reluctant to risk their heavy C-130 Hercules tactical transports in the face of heavy ground fire at Khe Sanh because their long take off runs made them too vulnerable. Only lighter short takeoff and landing (STOL) aircraft of the type favored by the Army for the support of its airmobile forces were able to get in and out of Khe Sanh with tolerable safety, but they could not deliver sufficient supplies. Instead, C-130s delivered the bulk of supplies by airdrop, but even this required the luxury of a long runway that the communists never closed at Khe Sanh. Though the air supply effort at Khe Sanh was a success, and could not have been conducted by aircraft in the C-7 and C-123 classes alone, the siege pointed to the accuracy of some Army reservations about the C-130 and the value of STOL capabilities for fixed-wing transport aircraft.

Khe Sanh, therefore, proved the value of *both* the Air Force's favored tactical transport aircraft class, represented by the C-130, *and* the Army's favored tactical transport aircraft class, represented by the C-7. However, the Air Force was not interested in the latter class of aircraft. The Air Force wanted to run a scheduled freight haulage service, and against this criterion, the small C-7 could never be as efficient as the C-130. The C-7 did, however, possess some very important attributes for airmobile warfare. It could get in and out of very small strips which were inaccessible to the C-130, thus providing accurate delivery of priority loads to ground forces and the potential for wounded and other personnel extraction from the combat zone.

Thus, the technical inefficiency of small C-7 loads was a price worth paying for its greater flexibility—and therefore, greater combat efficiency—in airmobile operations. Since, as it turns out, the Air Force proved it could not be trusted to retain aircraft in the C-7 class in its inventory, it would have been better had the Army been able to hang on to these aircraft. Once again, this was rivalry pure and simple. The Air Force did not want to operate aircraft in the C-7 class, but at the same time, it was intent on denying them to the Army. The transfer of the CV-2s, to the Air Force, may have increased the technical efficiency of the Air Force transport system, but it reduced the combat efficiency of the aircraft with respect to Army airmobility in the context of Vietnam, and cost the Army any prospect of this kind of tactical airlift in the years after Vietnam, when the Air Force had abandoned the type.

At the level of the operational control of US airpower resources in Vietnam, the interservice debate centered on Air Force efforts to bring the airpower assets of the other services under the TACS. The Army and the Marine Corps fought back in an effort to retain the responsiveness of their organic airpower and increase the tactical flexibility of their own formations. This response was, however, at the expense of the bigger picture in which tactical air resources might be redeployed out of their immediate area by the Air Force single manager. It seems clear here that more than abstract theoretical doctrine was at stake. Realization of Air Force objectives would have had serious consequences for Army and Marine Corps organic aviation. Absorption of Army aircraft into the Air Force TACS would have called into question the point of having Army aircraft at all, and absolute single management of Marine aircraft by COMUSMACV, exercised through his air deputy, would have spelled the end of the Marine air-ground team in Vietnam, setting a dangerous precedent for the survival of this concept beyond the war. However, the Army was successful in keeping its air resources outside the TACS, and while a form of single management was applied to the Marines, this was so attenuated that it probably never had long-term effect on either the Corps or the Air Force.

Incompatible doctrine drove the dispute between the Air Force and the Marines over the use of their airpower resources in I Corps. This involved operational considerations in the sense that both services believed that their own doctrine offered the most efficient use of their respective airpower resources. This might have been partially justifiable in the case of the Marines while the First Marine Air Wing (I MAW) supported only Marine ground forces, but by late 1967 there were many non-Marine formations in I Corps. Marine air doctrine prescribed Marine air support for Army formations that was inferior to that for Marine ground forces, and there was poor coordination of Marine and Air Force air power in I Corps. This encouraged Westmoreland to accept the Air Force argument that single management was necessary, and the system did go some way towards improving the air support service provided by the Marines for Army units.

Single management could have been in place at the beginning of the siege of Khe Sanh had Westmoreland's early representations to this effect been heeded, but for reasons of interservice rivalry, the Marines deliberately dragged their feet over this issue. Implementation of the system was also obstructed as a consequence of the fragmented command arrangements at the theater level, which were themselves, at least partly, the result of interservice rivalry. The existence of continued interservice rivalry over the issue of single management led to the dilution of the concept in practice, limiting the ability of the Air Force single manager for air to deploy his forces with maximum flexibility.

In fact, the imposition of single management at the time of the siege of Khe Sanh had negligible impact on the Air Force-Marine relationship regarding the command and control of Marine tactical air assets and, therefore, negligible operational consequences in Vietnam. Adoption of a single management directive with real teeth would have resulted in a considerable improvement in the flexibility with which the Air Force single manager could have tailored the employment of Marine airpower to the needs of the ground forces through the TACS, but it would also have meant some further decline in the responsiveness of Marine airpower to the demands of Marine ground units. In fact, while they did suffer some diminution of responsiveness, the Marines admitted that this was minimal because they did not actually lose *de facto* operational control of their aircraft.

If it had been applied rigorously, single management would have meant a greater diminution of the combat efficiency of Marine tactical airpower in support of the Corps' ground forces in Vietnam, but Marine high-performance aircraft could have made a much greater contribution to the TACS under genuine single management. As single management of Marine aircraft operating through the TACS would have enhanced the combat efficiency of tactical airpower operating in support of all US units in I Corps—not just the Marine ground forces—then Air Force aircraft might just as well have done the job. This represents an argument for the disbandment of the Corps' air arm, perhaps with the exception of intermediate performance specialist tactical aircraft along the lines of those already suggested for the Army. This would solve some of the problems inherent in the Marine Corps' anomalous position as a kind of all-arms 'imperial guard,' which serves only to complicate the command and control picture and compound the problems of interservice rivalry, but such a solution was politically impossible in 1968 and remains so.

The Gulf War revealed that despite the Goldwater-Nichols Act, the fundamental disagreement between the Air Force and the Marines over single management had still not been resolved. The Marines continued to believe that single management by the Air Force could not be sufficiently responsive to their requirements on the battlefield, and they never accepted the authority of the JFACC, who they referred to only as 'joint force air coordinator' in message traffic.[7] Both the Marines and the Army found the JFACC system unwieldy and complained about the length of time required to generate the daily Air Tasking Order, which included all preplanned missions. This meant that requests for preplanned air strikes could not be fulfilled until 48 hours after the original request. Consequently, while at the beginning of the war, the Marines released some 50% of their air sorties to the JFACC, from the second day of the campaign they began the steady reduction of this percentage until, by the end, they were running an independent air war, concentrating almost exclusively on their preferred air tasks of CAS and battlefield air interdiction (BAI). Although General Horner could have tried to overrule the Marines, he chose to avoid a Vietnam-type clash with them over the issue.[8]

Army-Air Force-Marine arguments over the relative short-field performances of their respective tactical transport aircraft and the responsiveness of their respective close air support aircraft in South Vietnam were manifestations of more fundamental doctrinal differences between the services regarding centralized versus organic control of airpower. The interservice disputes between the services over roles and missions were sometimes so bitter and so visible in Vietnam that the service chiefs sought compromise lest they spiral out of control, with consequent serious damage for the various service aviation programs, and even—in at least one case—for the survival of one of the services. Early attempts to reach such compromises achieved only limited success because of the extent of the doctrinal gulf between the services. Indeed, the services never resolved their basic doctrinal differences during the Vietnam period.

Clearly, the interservice rivalry and resulting operational difficulties that occurred in Vietnam might have been alleviated by shared doctrine between the services, but this was never a realistic option during the Vietnam period and, despite the fact that the United States was eventually defeated, the communist enemy never seemed to provide a sufficiently pressing emergency to alter the fundamental political considerations that underlay interservice rivalry at the level of the service chiefs. Instead they wrestled, as best they could, with a series of technological and doctrinal developments that did not permit of any neat solution beyond the mediocrity of bureaucratic compromise. Ultimately, pressing practical concerns obliged the services to hammer out ad hoc compromise arrangements by which they established discrete service aviation fiefdoms, supported the parallel development of each other's aviation programs (whether they overlapped or not), and developed practical working relationships for joint operations in the field. The fundamental problems, however, remained unresolved.

While the enemy in Vietnam never seemed to provide sufficient justification for joint doctrinal development while the war was in progress, there were some indications that actual defeat in Southeast Asia might have done so. Army and Air Force post-Vietnam public pronouncements suggested an acknowledgement of the detrimental effects on the combat efficiency of tactical airpower brought about by interservice dispute. Whether or not the Army had sought to usurp Air Force roles in Vietnam, the development of post-Vietnam Army doctrine asserted the vital importance of Air Force support for the ground forces. The Army's 1976 'Active Defense' doctrine declared that it could not 'win the land battle without the Air Force.' The importance of the Air Force in Army doctrine was sustained in the move to the Army's new 'AirLand Battle' doctrine in 1982.[9]

In return, in a 1981 joint position paper, the Air Force expressed a willingness to adopt NATO-style tactical air support doctrine, as favored by the Army. This involved a combination of CAS and a British-inspired version of Battlefield Air Interdiction (BAI) where the Air Force would fly interdiction missions closer to the front lines than it would otherwise have preferred. The Air Force also accepted that its allocation of sorties between CAS and BAI would be dependent on the development of intelligence at the Army corps.[10]

In May 1984, the Army and Air Force chiefs of staff appeared to usher in a new era of interservice cooperation when they signed a memorandum of agreement on 'US Army-US Air Force Joint Force Development Process.' Attached to the memorandum were 31 initiatives for action and so the document soon became known as 'The 31 Initiatives.' The agreement was drafted with a view to increasing the cost efficiency of combined air and land forces. Amongst the initiatives, number 21 called for the Army and the Air Force to develop procedures for the coordination of BAI with the ground forces and number 24 reaffirmed 'the Air Force mission of providing fixed-wing air CAS to the Army.' 'The 31 Initiatives' also called for the Army and the Air Force to 'establish specific service responsibilities for manned aircraft systems' (initiative 26a) and 'procedures for developing coordinated joint positions on new aircraft starts prior to program initiation' (Initiative 26b).[11]

While the above suggests Army recognition of tactical air support as an Air Force role and Air Force acceptance of the responsibility, including CAS and 'shallow' BAI, the Air Force never actually renounced its fundamental commitment to a strategic nuclear doctrine, as represented in post-Vietnam versions of its basic doctrine manual AFM1-1.[12] In the late 1980s, and in the planning for the DESERT STORM air campaign against Iraq in the Gulf War, the Air Force began to formulate new techniques and procedures by which a decisive conventional air campaign might be conducted independently of a ground campaign, and although a ground offensive remained essential in the Gulf, the Air Force largely achieved this objective against Iraq. Subsequently, it may possibly be said to have achieved similar successes in Kosovo, and most recently in Afghanistan.

The air campaign in the Gulf was a strategic campaign aimed at destroying Iraq's war making and war running potential, proceeding in a series of phases only the fourth and final one of which was designed to support the ground forces once the ground war began. Thus, while the post-Vietnam Air Force claimed to have accepted the importance of CAS, this suggests that the support of ground forces really remained quite low on its list of priorities.

An indication of just how low support of ground forces might come in the Air Force scheme is indicated by the fate of the specialist ground support aircraft. The A-X ground attack aircraft project, under discussion during the last years of the Vietnam War, did result in an operational aircraft: the A-10 Thunderbolt II. While this might be interpreted as a declaration of Air Force intent to support the Army in the manner to which it aspired, and despite a successful combat record in the Persian Gulf, the Air Force has, at the time of writing, never implemented a program to replace the A-10 and has now transferred its surviving A-10s to the Air National Guard and Air Force Reserve.[13]

Similarly, while post-Vietnam Army doctrine accepted, as indeed the Army always had, that close air support was an Air Force mission, one should remember that the Army retained its tactical air support capability with its gunship helicopters and continued to develop the attack helicopter. The Army AirLand Battle doctrine emphasized 'deep' operations including the interdiction of enemy second echelon formations before they actually came into contact with friendly troops. It therefore required the Army's AH-64s not only to provide 'close-in' air support, but also to operate up to 70 kilometres behind enemy lines. Such operations would have to be coordinated with Air Force fixed-wing aircraft flying BAI missions which themselves had now taken on greater importance in Army minds.

While the Army and the Air Force did work on the development of tactical procedures for cooperation between their various forces in the deep operations called for by AirLand Battle doctrine, they continued to disagree over command authority for BAI missions. The Air Force wanted to control these missions at theater level with the Army having a say only in the allocation of close air support, whereas AirLand Battle Doctrine suggested that the Army should have a say in interdiction at sub-theater command levels.[14]

The two services were also unable to find a definitive solution to the problem of establishing the Fire Support Coordination Line (FSCL) behind which the Air Force is required to coordinate its operations with the ground forces. Traditionally, this had been set at the extreme range limit of conventional artillery—about 30 kilometers. The AirLand Battle Doctrine and the increased range of Army weapon systems, including missiles and helicopters, rendered a 30-kilometer FSCL illogical from the Army point of view, but extension beyond this limit suggested Army targeting interference in what had previously been an exclusive Air Force zone of responsibility. The establishment of the FSCL was to prove controversial during the ground campaign of the Gulf War.[15]

As it had in Vietnam, the Army pronounced itself generally satisfied with the support it received from the Air Force in the Gulf. Certainly, relations between the two services were much better during DESERT STORM than they had been in Southeast Asia. Much of this can be put down to the fact that the Army had no fixed-wing aircraft in the Gulf over which to clash with the Air Force. However, the "100-hour war" also demonstrated the persistence of serious differences between the services over airpower issues. The Army and the Air Force disagreed over the control of Army attack helicopters in their deep strike role, the Army complained at the Air Force's failure to strike many of its proposed interdiction targets, the Air Force questioned the deep penetration of Army airmobile forces behind enemy lines into a part of the battlefield that the Air Force had previously presumed to be its exclusive responsibility and without what it saw as appropriate coordination, and we have already seen how the Marines continued to oppose single management of its air resources by the Air Force in the Gulf.[16] Given the persistence of these differences between the services over airpower issues at the time of the Gulf War, a longer land campaign and a more powerful enemy could easily have tested the seemingly harmonious relations between them to destruction.

Interservice rivalry over airpower issues during the Vietnam period occurred largely because each service genuinely believed that the independent development of doctrine and equipment that suited its own immediate concerns was the best way to serve the interests of the United States—though it has to be said that the services were also motivated by the simple desire to accumulate or retain resources and authority. In the case of the Army and the Air Force, and perhaps also the Navy, this attitude was motivated by an absolute certainty that they should have a preeminent role in any future conflict. Taken in isolation, one can appreciate the merit of individual service doctrines, but they were often mutually incompatible on the South Vietnamese battlefield. They were also largely inapplicable to the actual circumstances of Vietnam because they were tailored primarily for high-intensity conflict with the Soviet Union and its satellites. The services found it hard to resolve these doctrinal differences in Vietnam for fear that to do so would involve the sacrifice of individual service precepts thought vital for war with the Soviet Union. Thus, the services found Vietnam insufficiently important to justify fundamental change.[17]

The Gulf War showed that many of the interservice airpower disputes of the Vietnam period still lingered at least some 15 years later, and that they were potentially more serious than ever as a result of the Army's deep battle doctrine and the increased range of Army weapon systems, including its attack helicopters. The persistence of the doctrinal differences between the services over airpower issues at the time of the Gulf War is rooted in the fact that both during and after Vietnam the services tended to see the war as an anomaly with no lessons for the future—or at least they found it psychologically attractive to regard it as such. They returned, therefore, to their pre-Vietnam emphasis on war with the Soviet Union. The 'Evil Empire' has now been removed from the military equation, but there is no reason to believe that each service has discarded the sense of its own preeminence that contributed so much to interservice dispute over airpower issues during the Vietnam period. Only in the absence of this certainty can the services make a genuine attempt at formulating joint doctrine.

# NOTES

1.  John Schlight, *The United States Air Force in Southeast Asia, The War in South Vietnam, The Years of the Offensive: 1965-1968* (Washington, D.C., Office of Air Force History, 1988), p. 29.

2.  Stephen J. McNamara, *Air Power's Gordian Knot: Centralized Versus Organic Control* (Maxwell AFB, AL, Air University, 1994), p. 122.

3.  Richard P. Hallion, 'Battlefield Air Support: A Retrospective Assessment,' *Airpower Journal* (Spring 1990), www.airpower.maxwell.af.mil/airchronicles/apj/2spr90.html, 27 November 2001, p.4.

4.  Robert A. Pape, Jr., 'Coercive Air Power in the Vietnam War,' *International Security* (Fall 1990), pp. 124-125.

5.  Ibid., pp. 126-128.

6.  McNamara, *op cit.,* pp. 129-130.

7.  Quoted in *Ibid.*, p. 124.

8.  *Ibid.*, pp. 127-128.

9.  Quoted in Harold R. Winton, 'Partnership and Tension: The Army and the Air Force between Vietnam and Desert Shield,' *Parameters* (Spring 1996), www.army.mil/usawc/parameters/96spring/winton.html, 27 November 2001, pp. 3 & 7.

10. Ibid., p. 10.

11. Gen John A. Wickham, Jr. (Army Chief of Staff) & Gen Charles A. Gabriel (US Air Force Chief of Staff), Memorandum of Agreement on US Army-US Air Force Joint Force Development Process ['The 31 Initiatives'], 22 May 1984, Richard G. Davies, *The 31 Initiatives: A Study in Air Force-Army Cooperation* (Washington, DC, Office of Air Force History, 1987), pp. 105-115.

12. Kurt A. Chichowski, *Doctrine Matures Through A Storm: An Analysis of the New Air Force Manual 1-1* (Maxwell AFB, AL, Thesis, School of Advanced Airpower Studies, Air University, June 1993), pp. 11-12.

13. Hallion, op cit., p. 8; Winton op cit., p. 13 & McNamara, *op cit*, p. 144.

14. Winton, op cit, p. 9.

15. Ibid., p. 12.

16. We have already seen the difficulties between the services engendered by the development of Army airmobile forces, but to some extent the issue of the actual use of these forces on the ground in Vietnam was hidden by the fact that there were no front lines behind which the airmobile forces could penetrate in that conflict. In the Gulf, Army airmobile forces of divisional size performed deep penetration operations up to 150 miles in the enemy's rear and thus trespassed, without any real coordination, on Air Force territory. McNanara, *op. cit.,* p. 129.

17. For example, see Andrew F. Krepinevich, Jr., *The Army and Vietnam* (Baltimore, 1986) for an exposition of the view that the US Army in Vietnam remained fixated on fighting a high intensity war in Europe.

# BIBLIOGRAPHY

## MANUSCRIPT SOURCES

### UNITED STATES AIR FORCE HISTORICAL RESEARCH AGENCY, MAXWELL AFB., AL.

Contemporary Historical Examination Of Current Operations (Checo) Reports Of Southeast Asia (1961-1975)

Aton, Bert B. *A Shau Valley Campaign – Dec. 1968-May 1969 – Special Report, Vol. 1*, 15 Oct. 1969, K717.0413-75.

Burch, Robert M. *Single Manager for Air in South Vietnam, May-December 1968*, 18 March 1969, K717.0413-39.

Hickey, Lawrence J. *Operation HICKORY – Special Report*, 24 Jul. 1967, K717.0413-18.

Montagliani, Ernie S. *Army Aviation in RVN – A Case Study – Special Report*, 11 Jul. 1970, K717.0413-82.

Porter, Melvin F. *Air Response to Immediate Air Requests in South Vietnam – Special Report, Vol. 1*, 15 July 1969, K717.0413-56.

**Vol. 2, Supporting Documents**

Sams, Kenneth. *Operation HARVEST MOON – 8-18 Dec. 1965 – Special Report*, 3 Mar. 1966, K717.0413-3.

Thompson, A.W. & Thorndale, C. William. *Air Response to the Tet Offensive – 30 Jan.-29 Feb. 1968 – Special Report, Vol. 1*, 12 Aug. 1968, K717.0413-32.

Trest, Warren A. *Khe Sanh (Operation NIGARA) – 22 Jan.-31 Mar. 1968 – Special Report, Vol. 1*, 13 Sep. 1968, K717.0413-35.

Whitaker, Bernell A. & Paterson, *L.E. Assault Airlift Operations – Jan. 1961-Jun. 1966*, 23 Feb. 1967, K717.0414-2.

Headquarters Pacific Air Force, *Summary Air Operations Southeast Asia*, K717.3063.

Project Corona Harvest, *Command and Control of Southeast Asia Air Operations, 1 January 1965-31 March 1968*, Air University, January 1973, K239.034-4.

*Ryan, John D. Collection*

Simmons, W.E. *Fundamental Considerations of Strategy for the War in Southeast Asia* (RAND Corp., 16 November, 1966), K146.003-21.

2d Air Division, Records originating with. K526.

Disosway Board Report, *Tactical Air Support Requirements*, 14 August 1962, K177.

*Tactical Air Support in Southeast Asia*, 10 March 1967, K143.042-33.

## UNITED STATES AIR FORCE ORAL HISTORY COLLECTION

Anthis, MG. Rollen H. (USAF), Interview August 1963, K239.0512-154.

-----. Interview 17 November 1969, K239.0512-240.

Armistead, Capt. Joseph D. (USA), Interview 22 January 1969, K239.0512-114.

Armstrong, Gen. Alan J. (USMC), Interview September-October 1973, K239.0512-1155.

Belli, LC. Robert E. (USAF), Interview 29 January 1973, K239.0512-645.

Brown, Gen. George S. (USAF), Interview 19-20 October 1970, K239.0512-365.

Disosway, Gen. Gabriel P. (USAF), Interview 4-7 October 1977, K239.0512-974

Harris, Gen. Hunter. (USAF), Interview 8 February 1967, K239.0512-377.

LeMay, Gen. Curtis E. (USAF), Interview 8 June 1972, K239.0512-592.

-----. Interview (29 March 1972), K239.0512-593.

McConnell, Gen. John P. (USAF), Interview 28 August 1969, K239.0512-1190.

McCutcheon, LG. Keith B. (USMC), Interview 22 April 1971, K239.0512-1164.

Moore, LG. Joseph H. (USAF), Interview 22 November 1969, K239.0512-241.

Sharp, Dudley C. Interview 29 May 1961, K239.0512-790.

Sharp, Adm. US Grant, (USN), Interview 19 Feb 1971, K239.0512-409.

White, Gen. Thomas D. (USAF), Interview 27 June 1961, K239.0512-606

## UNITED STATES ARMY MILITARY HISTORY INSTITUTE, CARLISLE BARRACKS, PA.

Army Aviation Center Papers.

Osmanski, Frank A. Papers.

Seneff, Gen. George P. Papers.

## SENIOR OFFICER ORAL HISTORY PROGRAM

Bristol, Col. Delbert. Interview (1978).

Goodhand, BG. O. Glenn. Interview (1978).

Howze, Gen. Hamilton H. Interview (1977).

Johnson, Gen. Harold K. Interview (1972-1973).

Kinnard, LTG. Harry W.O. Interview (1977).

Oden, MG. Delk M. Interview (1977).

Powell, BG. Edwin L. Interview (1978).

Seneff, LTG. George P. Interview (1978).

Tolson, LTG. John J. Interview (1977).

Williams, Gen. Robert R. Interview (1978).

## UNITED STATES ARMY CENTER OF MILITARY HISTORY, WASHINGTON DC

JCS Memo for the Secretary of Defense, *The Army's Proposal to Reorganize the 1ˢᵗ Cavalry as an Airmobile Division*, 20 March 1965.

Sorrill, Barbara A. & Suwalsky, Constance J. *The Origins, Deliberations, and Recommendations of the US Army Tactical Mobility Requirements Board (Howze Board)*, Fort Leavenworth, KS., US Army Combat Developments Command, Combat Arms Group, April 1969.

United States Strike Command, *Command History*, 1964.

US Army Tactical Mobility Requirements, *Howze Board Final Report,* Fort Bragg, NC., 20 August 1962.

## UNITED STATES MARINE CORPS HISTORICAL CENTER, WASHINGTON NAVY YARD, WASHINGTON, DC

Anderson, Norman J. Papers.

Background Files on Khe Sanh, Single Management, Close Air Support etc.

Command Chronologies.

McCutcheon, Keith B. Papers

## US MARINE CORPS ORAL HISTORY COLLECTION

Anderson, Norman J. MG. (USMC), Interview 1983.

Chaison, John R. MG. (USMC), Interview 1969.

McCutcheon, Keith B. LG. (USMC), Interview 1971.

Stubbe, Ray W. Papers.

## UNITED STATES NATIONAL ARCHIVES, COLLEGE PARK, MD.

MACV After Action Reports, RG 472.

Records of the Army Staff, Center of Military History – *Vietnam Monographs*, RG319.

USARV Command Historian, History Source File, RG 472.

USARV Command Historian, Operational Reports – Lessons Learned, RG 472.

USARV Command Historian, Senior Officer Debrief Reports, RG 472.

Westmoreland, William C. Gen. (USA) Papers, RG 319.

Westmoreland, William C. Gen. (USA) v CBS Litigation Collection, RG 407.

# PRINTED ORIGINAL SOURCES

BDM Corporation, *A Study of Strategic Lessons Learned in Vietnam* (McLean, VA., 1979).

Broughton, Jack. *Thud Ridge* (New York, 1985).

Commander, French Forces in Indochina, *Lessons of the War in Indochina, Vol. 2*, transl. V.J. Croizat, RAND Corp. Memo RM-5271-PR (May 1967).

Douhet, Giulio. Trans. Ferrari, Dino. *The Command of the Air* Washington, DC, Office of Air Force History, 1983.

Emme, Eugene M. ed., *The Impact of Air Power, National Security and World Politics* (Princeton, 1959).

Enthoven, Alain C. & Smith, Wayne K. *How Much is Enough? Shaping the Defense Program, 1961-1969*, (New York, 1972).

Gavin, James M. *War and Peace in the Space Age*, (New York, 1958).

Gettleman, Marvin E. ed., *Vietnam: History, Documents, and Opinions on a Major World Crisis* (Greenwich, Conn., 1965).

Howze, Hamilton, H. 'Airmobility Becomes More Than a Theory,' *Army*, Vol. 24 (March 1974), 18-24.

-----. *A Cavalryman's Story: Memoirs of a Twentieth Century General* (Washington, DC, 1996).

-----. 'The Howze Board,' *Army*, Vol. 24 (February 1974), 8-14.

-----. 'Winding Up a "Great Show,"' *Army*, Vol. 24 (April, 1974), 18-24.

Johnson, Lyndon B. *The Vantage Point: Perspectives on the Presidency, 1963-1969* (New York, 1971).

Kelly, Orr. 'Dispute Over Khe Sanh Lingers On,' *Washington Star* (11 Jan. 1972).

McNamara, Robert S. *In Retrospect: The Tragedy and Lessons of Vietnam* (New York, 1995).

Kinnard, Douglas. ed., *The War Managers* (Hanover, NH., 1977).

Reinburg, J. Hunter. 'Close Air Support,' *Congressional Record*, (17 May 1962), pp. A3712-A3714.

Rowny, Edward L. *It Takes One to Tango*, (Washington DC, 1992).

Sharp, U.S.G. & Westmoreland, William C. *Report on the War in Vietnam* (Washington, DC, 1968).

Sharp, U.S.G. *Strategy for Defeat: Vietnam in Retrospect* (Novato, CA., 1998).

Special Subcommittee on Close Air Support of the Preparedness Investigating Subcommittee of the Committee on Armed Services, United States Senate, 'Report on Close Air Support' (Washington DC, 1972).

*United States Air Force Basic Doctrine* [AFM1-2], (Washington, DC, 1959).

*United States Air Force Basic Doctrine* [AFM1-1], (Washington, DC, 1964).

United States Department of Defense, *The Pentagon Papers* (Boston, Senator Gravel Edition, 1971).

Westmoreland, William C. *A Soldier Reports* (New York, 1980).

Wolf, Richard I. *The United States Air Force, Basic Documents on Roles and Missions*, (Washington DC, Office of Air Force History, 1987).

## UNPUBLISHED THESES

Dembosky, Andrew D. "Meeting the Enduring Challenge: United States Air Force Basic Doctrine Through 1992." M.A., North Carolina State University, 1993.

Elzy, Martin I. "The origins of American Military Policy, 1945-1950." PhD., Miami University, 1975.

Gallucci, Robert L. "United States Military Policy in Vietnam: A View from the Bureaucratic Perspective." PhD., Brandeis University, 1974

Handel, David P. "The Evolution of United States Air Force Basic Doctrine." Research Study Maxwell AFB., AL., Air University, May 1978.

Horwood, Ian A. "The United States and Indochina During the Truman Years." MA., University of Missouri, 1993.

Morgan, Forrest E. "Big Eagle, Little Dragon: Propaganda and the Coercive Use of Airpower against North Vietnam." Research Study, Maxwell AFB., AL., Air University, 1994.

Weed, Sylvia Lee. "Low Intensity Conflict: An American Dilemma," PhD., University of Alabama, 1988

Ziemke, Caroline F. "In the Shadow of the Giant: USAF Tactical Air Command in the Era of Strategic Bombing, 1945-1955." PhD., The Ohio University, 1989.

## BOOKS

Ballard, Jack S., *The United States Air Force in Southeast Asia, Development and Employment of Fixed-Wing Gunships, 1962-1972* Washington, DC, Office of Air Force History, 1982.

Berger, Carl. Ed., *The United States Air Force in Southeast Asia, 1961-1973* Washington, DC, Office of Air Force History, 1977.

Bergerson, Frederic A., *The Army Gets an Air Force: Tactics of Insurgent Bureaucratic Politics,* Baltimore, 1980.

Bowers, Ray L., *The United States Air Force in Southeast Asia, Tactical Airlift* Washington, DC: Office of Air Force History, 1983.

Cable, Larry. *Unholy Grail: The US and the Wars in Vietnam, 1965-8* London, 1991.

Cheng, Christopher C.S. *Air Mobility: The Development of a Doctrine* Westport, CT., 1994.

Chichowski, Kurt A. *Doctrine Matures Through a Storm; An Analysis of the New Air Force Manual 1-1.* Maxwell A.F.B., AL: Thesis, School of Advanced Airpower Studies, Air University, June 1993.

Clarke, Jeffrey J. *United States Army in Vietnam, Advice and Support: The Final Years, 1965-1973.* Washington, DC: US Army Center of Military History, 1988.

Clifford, Kenneth J. *Progress and Purpose: A Developmental History of the United States Marine Corps, 1900-1970.* Washington, DC: History and Museums Division, Headquarters, US Marine Corps, 1973.

Clodfelter, Mark. *The Limits of Air Power: The American Bombing of North Vietnam.* New York, 1989.

Coleman, J.D. *Pleiku: The Dawn of Helicopter Warfare in Vietnam.* New York, 1988.

Colloquium – Naval Historical Center. *Command and Control of Air Operations in the Vietnam War.* Washington, DC, Department of the Navy, 1991.

Cooling, Benjamin F. (ed.), *Case Studies in the Development of Close Air Support.* Washington, DC: Office of Air Force History, 1990.

Davis, Richard G. *The 31 Initiatives: A Study in Air Force – Army Cooperation* (Washington DC: Office of Air Force History, 1987).

Davis, Vincent. *The Admirals' Lobby* (Chapel Hill, NC., 1967).

Dean, David J. *The Air Force in Low Intensity Conflict* (Maxwell AFB., AL., Air University, 1986.

Eckhardt, George S. *Vietnam Studies, Command and Control.* Washington, DC: Department of the Army, 1974.

Fails, William R. *Marines and Helicopters, 1962-1973.* Washington, DC: History and Museums Division, Headquarters, US Marine Corps, 1978.

Fall, Bernard B. *Hell in a Very Small Place: The Siege of Dien Bien Phu.* New York, 1967.

Futrell, Robert F. *Ideas, Concepts, Doctrine: A History of Basic Thinking in the United States Air Force, 1907-1964.* Maxwell AFB., AL: Air University, 1980.

-----. *Ideas, Concepts, Doctrine: Basic Thinking in the United States Air Force, 1961-1984.* Maxwell AFB., AL, 1989.

-----. *The United States Air Force in Korea, 1950-1953.* Washington, DC: Office of Air Force History, 1961.

-----. *The United States Air Force in Southeast Asia, The Advisory Years to 1965.* Washington, DC, 1981.

Gropman, Alan L. *USAF Southeast Asia Monograph Series*, Vol. V, Monograph 7, *Airpower and the Airlift Evacuation of Kham Duc*. Washington, DC: Office of Air Force History, 1985.

Harvey, Frank. *Air War – Vietnam*. New York, 1967.

Hay, John H. *Vietnam Studies, Tactical and Material Innovations*. Washington, DC: Department of the Army, 1974.

Herring, George C. *America's Longest War: The United States and Vietnam*. 1950-1975 New York, 1986.

Hoopes, Townsend. *The Limits of Intervention: An Inside Account of How the Johnson Policy of Escalation in Vietnam was Reversed*. New York, 1987.

Howard, Michael. *History of the Second World War, Grand Strategy*, Vol. IV, *August 1942-September 1943*. London, 1972.

Kolko, Gabriel. *Anatomy of a War*. New York, 1985.

Krepinevich, Andrew F. Jr. *The Army and Vietnam*. Baltimore, 1986.

Lane, John J. *The Air War in Indochina*, Vol. 1, Monograph 1, *Command and Control and Communication Structures in Southeast Asia*. Maxwell AFB., AL: Air University, 1981.

Lewy, Guenter. *America in Vietnam*. Oxford, 1980.

Littauer, Raphael & Uphoff, Norman. Eds. *The Air War in Indochina*. Boston, 1972.

Luttwak, Edward. *The Pentagon and the Art of War*. New York, 1985.

-----. *Strategy: The Logic of War and Peace*. Cambridge, Mass., 1987.

McNamara, Stephen J. *Air Power's Gordian Knot: Centralized Versus Organic Control*. Maxwell AFB., AL: Air University, 1994.

Mathews, Lloyd J. & Brown, Dale E. eds. *Assessing the Vietnam War*. Washington, DC, 1987.

Momyer, William W. *Airpower in Three Wars*. New York, 1980.

-----. *USAF Southeast Asia Monograph Series*, Vol. III, Monograph 4, *The Vietnamese Air Force, 1951-1975: An Analysis of its Role in Combat*. Washington, DC, 1985.

Mrozek, Donald J. *Air Power and the Ground War in Vietnam: Ideas and Actions*. Maxwell AFB., AL: Air University, 1988.

Nalty, Bernard C. *Air Power and the Fight for Khe Sanh*. Washington, DC: Office of Air Force History, 1986.

Palmer, Dave R. *The Summons of the Trumpet*. New York, 1984.

Playfair, I.S.O. & Molony, C.J.C. *History of the Second World War, The Mediterranean and Middle East*, Vol. IV, *The Destruction of the Axis Forces in*

*Africa.* London, 1966.

Pogue, Forest C. *The Supreme Command, United States Army in World War II, The European Theatre of Operations.* Washington DC: Office of the Chief of Military History, 1954.

Rawlins, Eugene W. *Marines and Helicopters, 1946-1962.* Washington, DC: History and Museums Division, Headquarters, US Marine Corps, 1976.

Roy, Jules. Trans. Baldick, Robert. *The Battle of Dienbienphu.* New York, 1966.

Schnabel, James F. & Watson, Robert J. *The History of the Joint Chiefs of Staff, The Joint Chiefs of Staff and National Policy,* Vol. III, *The Korean War.* Wilmington, Delaware, 1979.

Schlight, John. *The United States Air Force in Southeast Asia, The War in South Vietnam: The Years of the Offensive, 1965-1968.* Washington, DC: Office of Air Force History, 1988.

Sheehan, Neil. *A Bright Shining Lie: John Paul Vann and America in Vietnam.* New York, 1988.

Shulimson, Jack et al., *US Marines in Vietnam: The Defining Year, 1968.* Washington, DC, History and Museums Division, Headquarters US Marine Corps, 1997.

Sink, J. Taylor. *Rethinking the Air Operation Center: Air Force Command and Control in Conventional War.* Maxwell AFB., AL: Air University, 1994.

Smith, Perry M. *The Air Force Plans for Peace,* 1943-1945: Baltimore, 1970.

Spector, Ronald H. *United States Army in Vietnam, Advice and Support: the Early Years, 1941-1960.* Washington, DC: US Army Center of Military History, 1983.

Summers, Harry G. *On Strategy: A Critical Analysis of the Vietnam War.* New York, 1984.

Taylor, John W.R. ed., *Janes' All the World's Aircraft, 1967-68.* New York, 1967.

Thompson, James Clay. *Rolling Thunder: Understanding Policy and Program Failure.* Chapel Hill, NC., 1980.

Thompson, W. Scott & Frizzell, Donaldson D. *The Lessons of Vietnam.* London, 1977.

Tilford, Earl H. Setup: *What the Air Force Did in Vietnam and Why.* Maxwell AFB., AL: Air University, 1991.

Tolson, John J. *Vietnam Studies, Airmobility.* Washington, DC, 1973.

Turley, William S. *The Second Indochina War: A Short Political and Military History, 1954-1975.* New York, 1986.

Watts, Barry D. *The Foundations of US Air Doctrine: The Problem of Friction in War.* Maxwell AFB., AL: Air University, 1984.

Weinert, Richard P. *A History of Army Aviation, 1950-1962.* Fort Monroe, VA: Office of the Command Historian, US Army Training and Doctrine Command, 1991.

## ARTICLES

Association of the US Army. "Air Mobility Symposium." *Army,* Vol. 14 (1963).

Blumenson, Martin. "Can Official History Be Honest History?" *Military Affairs,* Vol. XXVI (1962-63).

Bowers, Ray L. "USAF Airlift and the Airmobility Idea in Vietnam," *Air University Review,* (1974).

Butz, J.S. "Tactical Airpower in 1965...The Trial by Fire," *Air Force/Space Digest* (1966).

Clodfelter, Mark. "Of Demons, Storms, and Thunder: A Preliminary Look at Vietnam's Impact on the Persian Gulf Air Campaign," *Airpower Journal* (1991) : 17-32. www.airpower.maxwell.af.mil/airchronicles/apj/clod.html, 27 November 2001.

Demma, Vincent. "The 11th Air Assault Division Tests." Information Paper, US Army Center of Military History, 11 June 1993.

-----. "War Gaming and Simulation in the Development of the 11th Air Assault Division," Information Paper, US Army Center of Military History, 10 April 1992.

Gavin, James M. "Cavalry and I Don't Mean Horses," *Harpers,* April 1954.

Hallion, Richard P. "Battlefield Air Support: A Retrospective Assessment," *Air Power Journal,* Spring 1990, 8-28. www.airpower.maxwell.af.mil/airchronicles/apj/2spr90.html, 27 November 2001.

Lackey, Scott W. ed. "Four Divisional Test Beds." from "Initial Impressions Report: Changing the Army." Fort Leavenworth, KS, CAC History Office, Center for Army Lessons Learned, US Army Combined Arms Command, 1994. http://call.army.mil:1100/call/exfor/specrpt/chp5.htm, 7 October 1997.

McCutcheon, Keith B. "Marine Aviation in Vietnam." *US Naval Institute Proceedings." Naval Review, 1971,* 124-155.

Millett, Alan R., Murray, Williamson & Watman, Kenneth H. "The Effectiveness of Military Organizations," Millet, Alan R. & Murray, Williamson. Eds. *Military Effectiveness,* Vol. 1, *The First World War.* Boston, 1988.

Pape, Robert A. "Coercive Air Power in the Vietnam War." *International Security,* Vol. 15 (1990) : 103-146.

Romjue, John L. "The Evolution of American Army Doctrine." Fort Monroe, VA: Military History Office, US Army Training and Doctrine Command, March 1996.

Schriever, Bernard A. "AF Documents Views on Close Air Support." *Journal of the Armed Forces*, CIII (1966) : 15 & 25.

Summers, Harry G. "The Bitter Triumph of Ia Drang." *American Heritage*, Vol. 35 (1984).

Trueman, H.P. "The Helicopter and Land Warfare: Applying the Vietnam Experience." Moulton, J.L. ed., *Brassey's Annual, The Armed Forces Yearbook, 1971* (1971).

Webb, Willard J. "The Single Manager for Air in Vietnam." *Joint Forces Quarterly* (1993-94) : 88-98.

Winton, Harold R. "Partnership and Tension: The Army and Air Force between Vietnam and Desert Shield, *Parameters,* 1996, 100-119. www.army.mil/usawc/parameters/96spring/winton.html, 27 November 2001.

Wismer, Ralph M. "What is the Helicopter." *Marine Corps Gazette,* February 1952, 47-48.